COMING HOME TO GERMANY?

Dear Christine
and Dave!
The final product seems to have
both worth all our efforts, not
least thanks to you both as editor
and wonderful colleagues. We'll be
where most of the work was done in
an enjoyable atmosphere.
All the best!

Rafa
2-12-02

Culture and Society in Germany
General Editors: Eva Kolinsky and David Horrocks

Turkish Culture and German Society Today
Edited by David Horrocks and Eva Kolinsky

Sinti and Roma: Gypsies in German-Speaking Society and Literature
Edited by Susan Tebbutt

Voices in Times of Change: The Role of Writers, Opposition Movements and the Churches in the Transformation of East Germany
Edited by David Rock

Coming Home to Germany?: The Integration of Ethnic Germans from Central and Eastern Europe in the Federal Republic
Edited by David Rock and Stefan Wolff

The Culture of German Environmentalism: Anxieties, Visions, Realities.
Edited by Axel Goodbody

COMING HOME TO GERMANY?

The Integration of Ethnic Germans from Central and Eastern Europe in the Federal Republic

Edited by David Rock and Stefan Wolff

Berghahn Books
New York • Oxford

First published in 2002 by

Berghahn Books

www.BerghahnBooks.com

©2002 David Rock and Stefan Wolff

All rights reserved.

Library of Congress Cataloging-in-Publication Data

Coming home to Germany? : the integration of ethnic Germans from Central and Eastern
Europe in the Federal Republic / edited by David Rock and Stefan Wolff.
　　p. cm. -- (Culture and society in Germany ; v. 4.)
　Based on a one-day symposium conducted by the Centre for the Study of German
　Culture (Keele University) and Centre for East German Studies (University of Read-
　ing) and held at the University of Reading.
　Includes bibliographical references and index.
　ISBN 1-57181-718-2 (alk. paper) -- ISBN 1-57181-729-8 (pbk. : alk. paper)
　　1. Return migration--Germany--History--Congresses. 2. Germans--Europe, Cen-
　tral--History--Congresses. 3. Germans--Europe, Eastern--History--Congresses. 4.
　Germany--Ethnic relations--Congresses. I. Rock, David. II. Wolff, Stefan. III.
　Series.

IIV640.4.G3 C66 2002
304.8—dc21   2002018271

British Library Cataloguing in Publication Data

A catalogue record for this book is available from the British Library

Printed in the USA on acid-free paper.

ISBN 1–57181–718–2 hardback
ISBN 1–57181–729–8 paperback

Walter Grill: Spaltung (Split), bronze, 1993.

Table of Contents

List of Tables

Preface

For more than two centuries now, there has been a 'German question' in European politics. No matter how the question is phrased, as one of security, integration or division, its roots are always in the unresolved issues of nation and territory, of the geographical mismatch between the German *Kulturnation,* as the German Romantic movement understood the concept, and the German *Staatsnation.* Never since the foundation of the German Reich in 1871 have all Germans lived in one state. This in itself need not be a problem, but in the case of Germany it has, in combination with various other internal and external factors, led to two World Wars that have brought tremendous suffering upon the peoples on the European continent and elsewhere. Since the end of the Second World War, the 'German question' has manifested itself primarily on three levels – as the question of how to overcome the division of Germany into two states since 1949, as the question of how to relate to territories formerly belonging to Germany and/or inhabited by members of German minorities (especially in Central and Eastern Europe), and as the question of how to integrate millions of refugees, expellees and *Aussiedler* (i.e., ethnic Germans from Central and Eastern Europe migrating to Germany after 1950) into German society.

Naturally, East and West Germany, throughout their existence as separate states, treated the first two of these questions very differently. The communist regime in the East always considered them as permanently solved. This assumption proved false inasmuch as German reunification happened in 1990, but it proved correct when West Germany formally recognised the Oder–Neisse line in the border treaty with Poland of 1990 (a step that had been taken by the Eastern government as early as 1950) and when it placed its external minority policy on legal ground by concluding bilateral treaties with all the host-states of German minorities in Central and Eastern Europe in the years following the collapse of Communism.

The third level on which the 'German question' occurred was that of the integration of millions of refugees and expellees who arrived in the immediate postwar years and of *Aussiedler,* especially after 1989/90. The focus of all the chapters in this book will be on the various aspects of this integration process in the Federal Republic, that is West Germany before the fall of the Berlin Wall and unified Germany after 1990.

In the first chapter, Stefan Wolff examines the historical origins and contemporary developments pertaining to the German question. He argues that the phenomenon is multidimensional and politically complex, and that many of the dark chapters of European history – especially in the twentieth century – are best understood as arising from the failure to comprehend this complexity. Even now, with many of its aspects resolved, Germany and Europe still have to confront belated consequences of earlier strategies to address the German question adequately and comprehensively.

Daniel Levy takes a close look at the early stages of the integration of the refugees and expellees in the three Western zones of occupation and the young Federal Republic. His argument is that the integration of ethnic Germans as privileged immigrants into the West German body politic can be viewed as a particular model for immigration, one that is at the same time an example of a state assisting in the (social, economic and political) integration process while failing to address the difficulties the immigrants were confronted with when they had to adjust to a new environment.

The next two chapters by Rainer Schulze and Philipp Ther provide case-studies of the difficult, yet eventually successful integration of those ethnic Germans expelled from various parts of Eastern Europe. Schulze's study of the *Landkreis* Celle in Lower Saxony illustrates the various contributions refugees and expellees have made to (West) German postwar society, and how this society is one shared by 'natives' and refugees and expellees. Both their heritage and traditions, experiences and memories are a legitimate part of this society. Yet ideological prejudice and political considerations on both sides, Schulze demonstrates, have thus far prevented the history of the refugees and expellees from becoming an integral part of the foundations and character of the German state.

Ther focuses on the integration policies pursued in the Soviet zone of occupation and in the later GDR. He considers both the goals and policies of integration and their actual effectiveness. Despite the significant political and economic resources employed, the outcome of the integration policies was rather modest, especially when one considers the declared aim of achieving parity with the indigenous population for the expellees.

The specificity of the German situation after the Second World War meant that, contrary to the intentions of the Allies and many countries in Central and Eastern Europe, the 'German question' was not resolved permanently. The beginning of the Cold War facilitated the creation of two German states integrated into two opposing military blocs, but it also influenced developments outside Germany with direct repercussions for Germans. Millions of ethnic Germans who remained in their original host-countries, were deported to forced labour camps in the Soviet Union. Upon their return to their former home towns and villages, they found their properties looted or confiscated, and for decades to come, many were deprived of basic minority rights. Cold War confrontation severely limited the options of successive West German governments to rectify this situation, except to arrange for their migration to Germany. In different ways from country to country, ethnic Germans were allowed to leave for the Federal Republic in modest numbers even before 1989. With the collapse of Communism in Central and Eastern Europe this situation changed rapidly and Germany, once again, faced a flood of ethnic Germans entering the country.

This migration process of *Aussiedler*, and the difficulties resulting from it for both ethnic German migrants and German society, is the topic of the four chapters concluding Part I of this book. In Chapter 4, Andreas Heinrich provides a case-study on ethnic Germans from Russia in which he explains the particular difficulties experienced by this group of migrants as a result of the conditions in the former Soviet Union and the situation in present-day Germany. Lack of language skills, especially among the younger people, different values and norms of the older generation, and the lack of opportunities to participate in the economic, social and political process in Germany are just some of the difficulties Heinrich analyses.

In Chapters 5 and 6, Stefan Senders and Amanda Klekowski von Koppenfels examine the legal aspects of the migration and integration process of ethnic Germans. Senders contends that the specific conditions under which members of German minorities lived in their host-states in Central and Eastern Europe after 1945 led to a shift in the German practice of *jus sanguinis*, transforming it into what he calls *jus mimesis*. As part of a more complex and longer-lasting process of revising citizenship and repatriation law, *jus mimesis* recognises that a German identity is not and cannot exclusively be defined in terms of descent.

Klekowski von Koppenfels traces the evolution of German legislation governing the immigration of ethnic Germans from Central and Eastern Europe through the history of the Federal Republic and shows how, with the changing conditions in their host-countries and the growing number of *Aussiedler* after 1989/90, the law has become more and more restrictive and benefits have diminished. From that she concludes that legislation passed before the end of the Cold War was never wholly ethnonational in character, but rather determined by political and ideological considerations unsuitable as both foreign and domestic policy guidelines after the end of the East–West conflict.

Thus, the book examines the integration process of ethnic German refugees, expellees, and *Aussiedler* from 1945 to the end of the twentieth century. The analysis at the macro level establishes the multiple dimensions within the wider framework of the integration process as a whole. The successes and difficulties of the integration process mapped out in this first part of the book are then illustrated by individual accounts and interviews on the topic of expulsion and return-migration (*Aussiedlung*), and by reflections on the works of novelists and poets of contemporary Germany, including Nobel laureate Günter Grass, Herta Müller, Richard Wagner, Gudrun Pausewang and the sculptor Walter Grill. These chapters explore cultural manifestations of the identity of people who left their *Heimat* (native land, place of origin) to 'return' to a country their ancestors called home, and they reflect, in more personal ways, the difficulties of this migration process as a whole.

The chapters on Richard Wagner focus on one such individual, shedding further light on the central issues of the book from his personal perspective. In Chapter 7, David Rock provides an introduction to the life and work of Wagner as a German writer with a unique voice reflecting a unique set of experiences. A member of the literary/political Banat Action Group in the 1970s until its destruction by the Securitate, Wagner became disillusioned with the dismal prospects for any reform of Socialism in *Ceauçescu's* Romania, where the future for the German minority looked particularly bleak. The chapter examines the reasons why he left for West Germany in March 1987 together with his then wife, the writer Herta Müller. Rock considers changes in Wagner's artistic position since coming to the West, but also continuity in terms of his sense of Banat identity, which is a main theme in Wagner's original contribution to this volume, the story 'Millennium' (Chapter 9). Rock sees the diversity of forms employed by Wagner since coming to West Berlin as testimony to the range of experiences distilled into his works. His roots, though, are always inherent in his prose writing: usually set in Berlin, the only German city where unification can be experienced directly, it draws its black humour and unique insights from his critical awareness of the often curious ways in which the past (for him invariably associated with his earlier life in Eastern Europe) lives on in the present in this cosmopolitan meeting-point of East and West. In the interview conducted by David Rock and Stefan Wolff, Wagner explains the role of literature in Communist Romania and discusses the fate of the German minority in the Banat, the influence of ethnic identity on his writing, and the impact which his migration to Germany has had on his work.

The uniqueness of the experience of the German *Aussiedler* from Romania is the main concern of Chapter 10, in which Graham Jackman discusses this and three other related themes in key prose works by Wagner: the difficulty of integration, loneliness and the fluidity of identity. The works chosen provide a convincing and illuminating portrayal of the process of migration to Germany, above all in its psychological effects upon the *Aussiedler* whose very identity is at stake. Using Bakhtin's terminology, Jackman explains how language itself is depicted as being at the heart of the *Aussiedler* experiences, which in turn reflect Bakhtin's insights in an unexpected and disturbing way. Focusing on the questions of place and the crisis and duality of identity, the notions of women and 'Kneipen' (pubs) are also explored as expressions of a sense of non-fixity and fluidity, which is experienced as painful and negative by the immigrant and incomer in a city like Berlin, despite the seemingly untroubled *flâneur* pose. Though at times he appears to embrace what Braidotti calls the 'postmodern condition' of a 'nomadic subject', relinquishing all desire for fixity, his ultimately unstable sense of identity belies the decided resemblance to Walter Benjamin's figure of the 'stroller'. The prose work of Richard Wagner is thus shown to provide an understanding both of the difficulties which *Aussiedler* face in a new and frequently hostile environment and of the consequences of this experience for their identity.

John White examines the question of ethnic identity in the literary work of Herta Müller, arguably the most important Romanian–German writer since Paul Celan. Noting her numerous criticisms of the largely hostile treatment meted out to foreigners in West Germany, the chapter focuses on her particularly disturbing accounts (both fictional and real) of the inexcusably unfeeling reception of Romanian–Germans at the hands of the West German immigration authorities specifically responsible for processing ethnic German migrants from Eastern Europe. White also explains Müller's antipathy to the large Swabian German community of the Banat where she grew up, a factor compounding the problems of cultural and psychological integration in West Germany, with important implications for Müller's own complex self-image as an ex-Romanian, ethnic German, literary dissident, anti-Nazi, anti-Ceauçescu, would-be West German. White examines her treatment of the equally complex question of whether she was applying for admission to the Federal Republic on the grounds of ethnic German status or for political reasons, showing that for her, the ultimate question was not a bureaucratic issue, but an ethical one. The chapter provides another improvisation on the themes of identity and integration treated elsewhere; in Müller's case, the *Aussiedler* in Germany feels just as much a foreigner in a foreign country as she did previously in her native Romania, but for different reasons from the other authors featured in this volume – as someone deeply damaged by the past, for whom Nazi (and even present-day) Germany and Ceauçescu's Romania have become impossible to keep separate. Analysing novels and stories written both before and after her emigration to Germany, this chapter thus argues that ethnic identity, as it is reflected in literature, is a continuum in time and space. The literary revisiting of the places of origin and the actual living in a socially, politically and culturally different environment create a dynamic and productive tension that can partly be resolved in literary discourse and partly continues to exist through it.

In Chapter 12, Julian Preece examines the main prose works, political essays and speeches of perhaps the most prominent of all post-war West German writers, Günter Grass, who was born in 1927 to mixed German-Slavic, Protestant–Catholic parentage in the independent city-state of Danzig, whose hinterland contained a wide mixture of racial, religious and linguistic communities in the inter-war years. Interpreting Grass's works in the context of the author's background as an expellee from Poland and his commitment to minority rights, Preece shows how much of his writing is a confrontation with the past and what it entails: the enormity of the crimes committed by Germans in the name of National Socialism; the personal feelings of loss and detachment experienced by Grass himself as *Heimatvertriebener* (expellee), but also recognition of the moral justice of this consequence in the shadow of the Holocaust; and the way his view of his own past and his understanding of his own identity are fractured as a result, with emotional attachment to his home jostling with and ultimately losing out to rational appreciation of the justice of what has happened. One way in which the expellee rationalises the loss of his homeland, and at the same time one of the lessons which Grass the moralist puts across, is that ethnic identity, whether for an individual or a whole nation, is an artificial construct. Preece also focuses on Grass's repeatedly expressed argument for a multicultural Germany: a centuries-old reality, despite various official pronouncements to the contrary.

Kati Tonkin's contribution on Gudrun Pausewang examines the Sudeten Germans. Tracing their origin as an initially heterogeneous group that was forged into a political unit by the historical events following the First World War, namely their integration into the newly established Czechoslovak Republic, Tonkin argues that the process of identity formation reached its (tragic) climax after the collective expulsion of almost the entire Sudeten German population from Czechoslovakia after 1945. Yet the political identity of the group has undergone gradual, but nevertheless significant changes since then: from an identity openly irredentist to one firmly rooted in Germany. Exemplifying the success of the integration process, Tonkin presents a study of the literary works of Gudrun Pausewang, a novelist who grew up in the Sudetenland.

Chapter 14 is an interview with the Bavarian sculptor Walter Grill conducted by David Rock. Expelled as a child from the Sudetenland after the Second World War, Grill spent his entire artistic career in West Germany and went back to his former home only in 1990 when he was one of the first Sudeten German artists to exhibit his works in the Czech Republic. He reflects on how his ethnic and territorial identities have influenced his work before and after 1990.

In the final chapter, Wolff brings together the findings of each of the individual studies and asks whether the integration of refugees, expellees and *Aussiedler* has been successful overall and which aspects of it are still incomplete. In generalising the analyses of the macro and micro levels of integration, he points out that this integration process has become more and more difficult over the years with the growing distance between German minority cultures and the culture of the Federal Republic. Yet, for all ethnic German migrants, integration will only be complete if a more comprehensive process of reconciliation is concluded that includes refugees and expellees and natives in Germany and the populations and governments in their former host-states. They all need to accept that the expulsions have been as unjust as the conditions under which ethnic Germans had to live in Central and Eastern Europe after 1945, and which led to continued migration. Yet, equally, there needs to be recognition of the fact that these are matters of the past that, while having their legitimate, although not yet fully accepted, place in the collective memory of German society, must not prevent the peoples of Central and Eastern Europe from building a bright future together.

David Rock and Stefan Wolff

Acknowledgements

In November 1997, the German Section of the Modern Languages Department at Keele University welcomed Richard Wagner as Visiting Writer. During his stay, he discussed his life and his work, talked to students about his unique problems as a German writer in Ceauçescu's Romania and about his life since coming to Germany, and generally inspired everyone with his wide knowledge and insights, his friendly manner, his sharp wit and his infectious humour. To conclude his stay, the Centre for the Study of German Culture and Society (Keele University) and the Centre for East German Studies (University of Reading) jointly conducted a one-day symposium entitled 'East and Central European Immigrant Writers in Contemporary Germany', held at the University of Reading and organised by David Rock and Graham Jackman. Chaired by David Horrocks, the symposium began with an introductory paper by Stefan Wolff, giving an overview of the problems of ethnic Germans in Central and Eastern Europe and their return-migration to the Federal Republic. Margaret Littler and Brigid Haines then discussed aspects of the works of Herta Müller and Libuse Monikova; Graham Jackman spoke on Wagner's novel *In der Hand der Frauen*; David Rock gave a general introduction to Wagner's works and his life in the Banat; and finally Richard Wagner read from several of his works and discussed some of the problems raised by the previous papers. At this symposium, the idea was born to produce a volume of essays focusing on this particular aspect of German post-war history – both from the perspective of its social and political dynamics and from the viewpoint of individuals about how they experienced and came to terms with their migration (voluntary or forced) to the Federal Republic.

Special thanks are due to the Deutscher Akademischer Austauschdienst for their generous support of the Visiting Writer programme; to Eva Kolinsky and David Horrocks for their painstaking reading of the manuscript and their many helpful suggestions; to the sculptor Walter Grill for discussing his life and work with David Rock in Munich in 1999 and for allowing us to use the photograph of his sculpture, 'Spaltung'; and last but by no means least, to Richard Wagner himself for his support in this undertaking and his contribution of an original short story to this volume.

David Rock and Stefan Wolff

List of Abbreviations

AAG	*Aussiedleraufnahmegesetz – Aussiedler* Acceptance Act
AFG	*Arbeitsförderungsgesetz* – Work Promotion Act
BHE	*Bund der Heimatvertriebenen und Entrechteten* – Union of Expellees and Disenfranchised
BMV	*Bundesministerium für Vertriebene, Flüchtlinge und Kriegs – geschädigte* – Federal Ministry for Expellees, Refugees, and War Victims
BVFG	*Bundesvertriebenen- und Flüchtlingsgesetz* – Federal Expellee and Refugee Law
CDU	*Christlich-Demokratische Union* – Christian Democratic Union
DP	*Deutsche Partei* – German Party
DVdI	*Deutsche Verwaltung des Inneren* – German Administration for Internal Affairs
FDP	*Freie Demokratische Partei* – Free Democratic Party
FRG	*Fremdrentengesetz* – Foreign Pensions Act
GDP	*Gesamtdeutsche Partei* – All-German Party
KfbG	*Kriegsfolgenbereinigungsgesetz* – War Consequences Conciliation Act
KPD	*Kommunistische Partei Deutschlands* – Communist Party of Germany
LAG	*Lastenausgleichsgesetz* – Burden Sharing Law
RuStaG	*Reichs- und Staatsangehörigkeitsgesetz* – Imperial Nationality and Citizenship Law
SED	*Sozialistische Einheitspartei Deutschlands* – Socialist Unity Party of Germany
SMAD	*Sowjetische Militäradministration in Deutschland* – Soviet Military Administration in Germany
SPD	*Sozialdemokratische Partei Deutschlands* – Social Democratic Party of Germany
StaReG	*Gesetz zur Regelung von Fragen der Staatsangehörigkeit* – Citizenship Regulation Act
WoZuG	*Wohnortzuweisungsgesetz* – Residence Assignment Act
ZVU	Central Administrative Authority for *Umsiedler*
ZvD	*Zentralverband vertriebener Deutscher*

Glossary

Ausländer	foreigner
Aussiedler	ethnic German migrating to the Federal Republic after 1950, literally: resettler
Deutschtum	Germanness
Eingliederungsgeld	integration benefit
Flüchtlinge	refugees
Grundgesetz	Basic Law
Heimat	native land, place of origin
Landsmannschaft	regional-cultural organisation (of ethnic German expellees)
Lastenausgleich	burden sharing
Ostgebiete	collective term for those territories of the German Reich ceded to Poland and the Soviet Union after 1945 (i.e., East Prussia and the territories east of the Oder-Neisse line)
Reichsdeutsche	German citizens as of 1937
Staatsangehörigkeit	citizenship
Übersiedler	collective term for refugees from East Germany
Umsiedler	collective term used in East Germany for all ethnic German expellees and refugees resettled there after 1945
Vertriebene	expellees
Volksdeutsche	ethnic Germans, primarily in Central and Eastern Europe, but not German citizens
Volkszugehörigkeit	nationality, ethnic group membership

Introduction

From Colonists to Emigrants: Explaining the 'Return-Migration' of Ethnic Germans from Central and Eastern Europe

Stefan Wolff

To understand the complex social and political dynamics involved in the 'home-coming', or return-migration, of ethnic Germans from Central and Eastern Europe and their integration in the Federal Republic after 1945, a more thorough examination is required of the phenomenon that was, and still is, referred to in European and world politics as the 'German question'. Yet a single German question as such has never existed; rather, a multitude of issues have arisen from a fundamental problem in European history, namely the fact that the German territorial or state-nation and the German cultural nation were hardly ever geographically compatible. A unified German state only came into existence in the second half of the nineteenth century, and even then it did not incorporate all ethnic Germans in Europe. Quite clearly, Germany is no exception in this respect. The demarcation of borders in Europe, and particularly in Central and Eastern Europe, happened according to the interests of the Great Powers rather than according to the distribution of ethnic groups. The gradual withdrawal from Europe of the Ottoman Empire since the late nineteenth century and the dissolution of the Austro-Hungarian Empire in the early twentieth century created a series of new states, hardly any of which was either homogenous or contained all members of the titular ethnic group within its boundaries. The settlement patterns of diverse ethnic groups that had grown over centuries of imperial hegemony in Central and Eastern Europe would, at best, have made it extremely difficult to create states in which political and ethnic boundaries coincided. The fact that borders were established in accordance with the interests of the Great Powers rendered any such attempt impossible. In addition, even though a romantic version of nationalism had become a powerful ideology in the region, not all ethnic groups had a well-established national identity in the sense of expressing a preference for their own or any specific state at all, but instead some of them had developed strong regional identities that were, in the first instance, not focused on ethnicity. Nevertheless, nationalism had made a tremendous impact on interethnic relations in the region, and the three waves of state 'creation' – at the Congress of Berlin in 1878, after the first and second Balkan wars in 1912/13, and after the First World War – left their mark in Central and Eastern Europe by establishing ethnically plural states whose constituent ethnic groups were ill at ease with each other. Thus, if one can just as easily speak, for example, of an Albanian question or a Hungarian question, what makes the German question so unique? An answer to this can only be outlined in very brief terms within the limits of this introductory chapter, but even such an abridged treatment will place many of the issues subsequently raised by other contributors to this volume in their proper historical and political context.

Where and What is Germany?

This is one common way to paraphrase the German question. It is primarily a question about the nature and content of a German national identity, and thus a question that is primarily directed at the Germans themselves. Yet, at the same time, it also gives rise to broader considerations about Germany's place and role in European and world politics – considerations that have been raised by Germany's neighbours, and that have, more often than not in the past century, amounted to serious concerns for the security and stability of the European and international order. From that perspective, the German question is also about how Germany can fit into any system of states without threatening, or being perceived as threatening by, its neighbours. Many answers have been given to this particular dimension of the German question – a loose confederation of states was the answer of the Congress of Vienna in 1815, a German nation-state excluding Austria that of 1871, a state truncated territorially and burdened by reparations that of the Versailles Peace Treaty, an enlarged Germany that of the Munich Agreement of 1938, an occupied and subsequently divided state that of the Potsdam Agreement of 1945, and a unified Germany firmly integrated in NATO and the EU was the answer of 1990. With the exception of the latter (hopefully), none of these proposed solutions to the German question was stable, or even viable, in the long term, although the reasons for the eventual collapse of each such settlement varied considerably over time. What they all had in common was that they only partially addressed the complexity of the German question.

This complexity arises from the fact that the German question is a multidimensional phenomenon. It has been, and to some extent still is, foremost a political problem. As such, the German question has been about whether there should be one German nation-state or more, what the borders and internal political structures of such a state (or states) should be, with what methods it should be achieved, and what consequences this would have for Europe and the world (Geiss 1990: 22). At the same time, the German question is also a cultural problem, or, more precisely, a problem of defining German culture and, related to this, of defining a German identity and thus determining who is German. Obviously, the cultural and the political dimensions of the German question are inextricably linked, although in different ways through time. For example, while Austrians today have a distinctly Austrian (national) identity, i.e., one that is at least politically not a German identity, this was not the case at the time when the German Empire was founded in 1871, and even less so before when a German national identity as such hardly existed. For several hundred years, 'Germanness' had, if at all, been defined primarily in cultural terms. A German identity, in as much as it existed, had been one of an ethnocultural nature relying on language, custom and traditions to set itself apart from other identities. Ironically, Germanness only became politically significant after the collapse of the Holy Roman Empire of the German Nation in 1806, when it proved a powerful tool for mobilising 'Germans' in the Napoleonic Wars. This 'political nationalisation' of Germans was one manifestation of a wider European development. While for hundreds of years ethnocultural differences between people(s) had neither been a problem nor a source of mobilisation, it was with the arrival of nationalism as a political ideology and the emergence of the nation-state as the primary principle of organising people into political units and regulating the relations between these units that ethnicity began to matter as a factor in domestic and international politics. Naturally, nationalist ideologies clashed with each other as demands for the creation of nation-states resulted in the same territories, or parts thereof, being claimed by different aspiring nations. This is where many of the roots of the various national questions in Central and Eastern Europe lie, and consequently that of the German question, too; in particular the roots of those dimensions linked to the topic of this volume – the return-migration of ethnic Germans from Central and Eastern Europe.

As already indicated, the question 'What and where is Germany?' is also a question about who is German. For most of the twentieth century, German citizenship was determined according to descent. The 1913 *Reichs- und Staatsangehörigkeitsgesetz* (Citizenship Act) determined that only descendents of Germans could be German citizens. This was a deliberately chosen adoption of the principle of *jus sanguinis* in order to promote and preserve the ethnic tradition of the German nation-state and to maintain links with ethnic Germans outside the political boundaries of the German nation-state. The complexity of this issue is reflected in the difficulty one faces in finding proper English terms for the three key concepts of German legal and political thought in this respect: *Staatsangehörigkeit* (defined as the formal legal relationship between citizen and state), Staatsbürgerschaft (defined as the participatory membership in a polity or commonwealth) and *Volkszugehörigkeit* (defined in terms of ethnocultural identity) (Brubaker 1992: 50f.). Until the recent changes in German citizenship law, this meant that a German ethnocultural identity was an essential condition for full political participation. In turn, the link established between *Volkszugehörigkeit* on the one hand, and *Staatsbürgerschaft* and *Staatsangehörigkeit* on the other, was problematic inasmuch as it gave rise to issues of potentially conflicting loyalties. The interwar period is probably the best documented example of how such conflicting loyalties were instrumentalised and eventually became self-fulfilling prophecies. The rise of the Nazis in Germany and the way in, and purpose for, which they established links with ethnic Germans across Europe was perceived as a threat by many other European governments. The response of the latter was to curtail the rights of German minorities. This, in turn, encouraged ever larger sections within the minorities to put their hopes in Hitler, as was most obviously the case with the Sudeten Germans, but to a lesser extent also with German minorities elsewhere in Central and Eastern Europe. Prior to the expulsions of 1945–50, the policy of curtailing minority rights had the worst consequences for the German minority in Russia whose members were collectively deported to forced labour camps in Siberia and Central Asia. Even though the ethnonational foundations of *Staatsangehörigkeit* and *Staatsbürgerschaft* had indirectly had such disastrous consequences, it was precisely some of these consequences (namely the expulsions and the discrimination against the remaining members of German minorities in Central and Eastern Europe) that made it apparently impossible and politically undesirable to change German law in this respect, as it would have deprived *Aussiedler* of their entitlement to German citizenship.

Thus, any discussion of the complexity and multidimensionality of the German question also involves acknowledging the (long-term) link between domestic and international dimensions and between political and cultural aspects. In different ways, this link has persisted throughout the existence of the German question, particularly (apart from the interwar period) since the end of the Second World War. Yet, post-1945 developments can only be understood properly on the basis of the historical developments that 'created' ethnic Germans outside Germany. Thus, before turning to an examination of the German question in the second half of the twentieth century, I will explore the origins of ethnic German minorities in Central and Eastern Europe.

The Origins of Ethnic Germans in Central and Eastern Europe

The fact that a large number of ethnic Germans lived, and still live, in many countries in Central and Eastern Europe has its reasons in three distinct, but often interrelated, processes, namely conquest and colonisation, migration, and border changes. The latter are primarily a phenomenon of the twentieth century, connected most obviously with the peace settlements of Versailles and St Germain in 1919 and with the territorial and political reordering of Europe after 1945. The former two processes, in contrast, reach back as far as the twelfth century. In the Carpathian Mountains of today's Slovak Republic, for example, the first German settlers arrived in the middle of the twelfth century, invited by the Hungarian King Bela IV and local aristocrats because of their expertise as miners and vintners. Similarly to the Banat region and Transylvania in today's Romania, where the first ethnic Germans arrived around the middle of the thirteenth century, the colonists enjoyed significant tax and other privileges, such as being elected local officers and councillors, having market rights, and the right to property transactions (Marcus 2000: 99). Similar processes took place in the twelfth and thirteenth centuries in Pomerania, East Brandenburg, Bohemia and Moravia, and Silesia where local aristocrats were keen to have their vast lands colonised and developed. In the thirteenth century, too, the Teutonic Order (*Deutscher Ritterorden*) conquered most of today's Baltic states, i.e., Lithuania, Estonia and Latvia, and East and West Prussia. Similar to the German colonists in other parts of Central and Eastern Europe, the Teutonic knights had been invited by the Polish Prince Konrad of Masovia in 1225. They were charged with the task of subduing the non-Christian Baltic tribes, converting them and colonising their lands, and were promised sovereignty in return for their services. Thus, parallel to the process of conquest between 1231 and 1283, the colonisation of the conquered territories began with the settlement of German farmers, craftsmen and merchants.

After this first stage of colonisation and conquest had come to an end in Central and Eastern Europe in the fifteenth century, relatively little happened for the next several hundred years. In southeastern Europe, this was mostly due to the fact that large parts of Hungary and almost all of the Balkans had been conquered by the Ottoman Empire by the middle of the sixteenth century. However, with the withdrawal of the Ottomans from Hungary and some parts of the Balkans from the late seventeenth century, new opportunities for colonisation arose, leading to the recruitment of German settlers to the Banat, Slavonia and Hungary. The three so-called Swabian Tracks of 1722–6, 1763–73, and 1782–7 brought tens of thousands of Germans to areas that belong to today's Romania, Hungary, and to the successor states of the former Yugoslavia. Towards the end of the eighteenth century, German settlements also emerged in the Bukovina, and in the early nineteenth century in Bessarabia and in the Dobrudja. As all these areas were part of the Habsburg Empire (after 1867 the Austro-Hungarian dual monarchy), German settlers were, and were perceived as, acting on behalf of the emperor; as well as colonising undeveloped regions of the empire, they were also expected to represent the central power and ensure the preservation of the (multiethnic) empire.

The final stage of German settlements in Central and Eastern Europe began in the middle of the eighteenth century in Russia. In 1762 and 1763, the Russian Empress Catherine the Great issued two decrees that granted significant privileges to German settlers willing to colonise areas around the lower Volga River. By the end of the 1760s, more than 20,000 colonists had settled in these areas as free farmers. They were exempted from tax for several years, were not drafted for military service, could use German as the administrative language, were allowed to establish German schools, and enjoyed religious freedom (Stricker 2000: 165f.). A second wave of settlers arrived in the first half of the nineteenth century, settling on the coast of the Black Sea and in the Caucasus.

Thus, by the end of the nineteenth century, ethnic Germans could be found in settlements across the German and Austro-Hungarian Empires as well as in Russia; but in all the areas where they had arrived as colonists and were numerically in a minority position, their privileged status began to decline and relations between them and other ethnic groups and nations began to become more tense. The reasons for these increasing tensions were many, and they differed across Central and Eastern Europe. Among the most prominent ones were the rise of competing doctrines of nationalism among different ethnic groups, which resulted, among other things, in demands for an end to political privileges based on membership in particular ethnic groups (Hungarians, Germans, Russians, etc.) and in the increasing appeal of the concept of popular sovereignty. To some extent, there was also growing competition for scarce economic resources.

With the exception of Russia, where ethnic Germans had always been in a minority position, their status as members of the dominant ethnic group in the German and Austro-Hungarian Empires was only revoked at the end of the First World War. The peace settlements of Versailles and St Germain resulted in significant changes in the political geography of Central and Eastern Europe. The break-up of the Austro-Hungarian Empire was confirmed and with it the creation of several new states, each of which became a host-state of a number of ethnic minorities, including Germans. The size and political significance of these minorities differed vastly and so did the treatment that they received at the hands of their new rulers. In post-Trianon Hungary and in the newly established Kingdom of Serbs, Croats and Slovenes, there were only a few hundred thousand ethnic Germans, but in Romania they numbered almost a million. In Czechoslovakia there were more than three million ethnic Germans in 1919, a figure that made them the second largest ethnic group in the country. The German Empire, too, lost territories in Central and Eastern Europe. The so-called Polish Corridor, which gave Poland access to the Baltic Sea, separated East Prussia from the rest of the territory of the Weimar Republic and contained large numbers of Germans who had been nationals of the Second Empire before 1919. Upper Silesia was divided between Poland and Germany, leaving another significant ethnic German minority in Poland. In all, the territorial changes in Central and Eastern Europe after the end of the First World War left approximately five million ethnic Germans in countries outside Germany and Austria, while almost two million more lived in various parts of the emerging Soviet empire.[1]

Thus, the settlement at the end of the First World War had, in a typical fashion, addressed some aspects of the German question, ignored others, and created new ones. In the West the emphasis had been on securing territorial changes that would increase the defence capabilities of France and Italy. Subjecting Germany to unprecedented reparation payments and curtailing its industrial and military capacities was meant to prevent it from re-emerging as *a*, if not *the*, major economic, political and military power in Europe. In Central and Eastern Europe, the intentions were somewhat different. Here, the peace conference sought to establish a new order that would satisfy the demands of the multiple national movements for the creation of independent nation-states, while establishing a regime under the auspices of the League of Nations that could ensure that those ethnic groups which were either not granted their own nation-state or would not live on its territory would be sufficiently protected. In addition, considerations about the 'economic viability' of Poland and Czechoslovakia led to the territories of these new states being rather ill-defined in terms of their ethnic composition. Thus, not only was a situation created in which any stable political and economic development in Germany was precluded almost from the outset, but revisionist politicians in Germany were also given plenty of ammunition with which to rouse domestic (and, for example, in 1938 even international) political support for their goals, while the increasingly dissatisfied German minorities in many of the states in Central and Eastern Europe served as willing agents of destabilisation in the region. The rise of Nazism in the Weimar Republic was one of the first signs that the settlement of 1919 had, if anything, exacerbated the German question as a problem of European and international security. From this perspective, the Second World War was nothing but the culmination of a development that had arisen from a badly conceived strategy to deal with a problem that, by then, had obviously not been understood in its entirety.

Lessons Learned? Post-1945 Approaches to the German Question and the Fate of the Ethnic Germans in Central and Eastern Europe

The failure of the peace settlement after the First World War, and the (partial) recognition of this failure, heavily influenced the approach to the German question during and after the 1940s. Equally important, however, were individual aspirations of the Allied Powers, their conception of what precisely the German question was, and the relationship that they had with each other and with Germany.

Thus, the lessons learned from the interwar period were only one among many factors. Most crucially, the learning process had been highly selective. The occupation of Germany and the strict control of its political and economic processes by the Allies were two components of this learning process. Over the course of a few years, their consequence was the division of Germany into two states, the development of very different political regimes in each of them, and their integration in the two opposing world systems during the ensuing Cold War. This revived an aspect of the German question in the twentieth century that politicians in Germany and Europe had not had to confront since the second half of the nineteenth – German unification. The geopolitical reality of superpower dominance during the Cold War made the German question as a whole to some extent more easily manageable, if only by marginalising it in the struggle for global dominance and the defence of spheres of interest.

However, the most dramatic way in which lessons had been drawn from the failure to solve the German question in 1919 was the expulsion of more than ten million Germans from Central and Eastern Europe. This included more than three million from Czechoslovakia, approximately seven million from territories that were annexed to Poland and the Soviet Union, and almost two million from other countries in Central and Eastern Europe, primarily from Yugoslavia, Hungary and Romania. It was the most dramatic episode of the learning process because of the sheer magnitude of the migration it involved and because of the brutality with which it was carried out, particularly in the early months after the end of the war before the Allies reached a formal agreement on the 'orderly and humane' transfer of ethnic Germans in the Potsdam Agreement of August 1945.[2] Obviously, the expulsions have to be seen in the context of the Second World War. German warfare and occupation policy in Central and Eastern Europe had been excessively brutal, and many members of ethnic German minorities in the countries affected had played an active role in it. In addition, the forced migration of ethnic Germans had begun much earlier than 1945, although under a different pretext. From the late 1930s onwards the Nazis had initiated a massive resettlement programme aimed at consolidating ethnic Germans in a German core territory consisting of Germany as it had existed since the Munich Agreement of 1938 (thus already including Austria and the Sudetenland) plus parts of occupied western Poland that were systematically cleansed of any non-German population. This so-called *Heim-ins-Reich* policy affected approximately one million ethnic Germans who were resettled in western Poland before the end of the war on the basis of bilateral agreements with some states in Central and Eastern Europe and on the basis of unilateral decisions taken by Germany in occupied countries.[3] A third aspect worth mentioning is that the expulsion of ethnic Germans from Central and Eastern Europe did not just take place in a westward direction, i.e., towards occupied Germany, but many ethnic Germans were also deported to forced labour camps either within their host-states or the Soviet Union. Finally, forced migration also had an internal dimension to it. In the Soviet Union, ethnic Germans had been deported from the European territories of the country to Siberia and Central Asia at the beginning of the War in 1941, and they were not allowed to return to their traditional settlements after the end of the war. To a lesser degree, this also affected ethnic Germans who were allowed to remain in Czechoslovakia.

The forced migration of more than ten million Germans to occupied Germany at the end of the Second World War added an entirely new dimension to the German question. The integration of ethnic Germans who, no matter what their individual level of guilt, had experienced a traumatic uprooting into the economic, social and political process(es) of a collapsed country occupied by powers whose relationship towards one another evolved very quickly into a Cold War, was by no means an easy task, let alone one for which any comparable historical precedent existed.[4] As some of the following contributions (particularly those of Schulze, Ther and Levy) will illustrate, this task was accomplished relatively successfully within the course of less than two decades. What it did not, and probably could not, accomplish was coming to terms with the expulsion as part of German and European history. Despite the politicised rhetoric of the expellee organisations and their opponents inside and outside Germany, German society as a whole has never fully acknowledged the suffering of the expellees, nor has it been able to embrace the history and cultural traditions of former and still existing German minorities as part of a German cultural identity. This failure to acknowledge history for what it is – something that cannot be reversed, but needs to be appreciated in order to prevent its repetition – has extended beyond Germany into Central and Eastern Europe where the issue of the expulsions at the end of the Second World War could now threaten, or at least delay, the enlargement of the European Union.[5] The inability of German postwar and postunification society to deal with the expulsions from the perspective of their impact (or lack thereof) on German identity has also meant that some of the expellees and their descendants persist in their own selective view of history which almost completely shuts out any events predating the expulsions. As such the expulsions and their aftermath are an almost classic example of the multidimensionality of the German question. Equally, they did not solve the German question, perhaps did not even contribute to this process. On the one hand, the expulsions created a small, and perhaps decreasing, but nevertheless vocal political group in Germany letting no opportunity pass to call for a return to the Federal Republic of the former German *Ostgebiete,* i.e., those German territories that were annexed by Poland and the Soviet Union in 1945. The official representatives of the German expellees have since 1990 denounced these demands on various occasions, and support for this extreme position is very small. A larger segment, but again by no means a majority even among the expellees, has always insisted on the right to their homelands, that is, the right to return to the areas from which they were expelled after the Second World War. The problem here is not so much how serious these demands are or how many people support them, but the perception that they created, and still create, particularly in Poland and the Czech Republic, that they can be used as welcome 'proof' of German revisionism by nationalists and Euro-sceptics alike. From that perspective, too, the German question has not lost anything of its European and international relevance.

It is quite important to note that the expulsions, although occurring in unprecedented magnitude, were in fact selective. First, there were exceptions for those who had actively fought against the Nazis. These were very few, and not all of them were, or could be, protected from expulsion, nor were all of those who could have claimed exemption keen on staying behind. Second, some of those ethnic Germans who had intermarried were allowed to remain in their homeland, but again many of them chose to emigrate either during the period of actual expulsions or in later years. Third, in Poland, a distinction was made between those ethnic Germans that had held the citizenship of Germany before the war, i.e., those who had lived in the territories placed under Polish control by the Soviet Union in 1945 (and confirmed in the Potsdam Agreement) and so-called autochthonous 'Germans', that is, those who had had Polish citizenship before the war. Ironically, together with some other distinctions, the decision about who was to be expelled from Poland was thus based on a Polish equivalent to the so-called *Volksliste* of the Nazis, which had determined the degree of Germanness of ethnic Germans in Central and Eastern Europe. The fourth exception made was in many cases only a temporary one and explains why the expulsions were not completed before the end of the 1940s. Particularly for Poland and Czechoslovakia it was essential to guarantee the continued functioning of their economies. Germans had not only owned a number of factories, mines etc., but they were also needed as specialists to oversee the proper running of these enterprises. While farmers could be replaced relatively easily, although again not without causing disruptions, this was less the case with skilled workers, foremen and engineers. Apart from such specialists, a number of ethnic Germans were also prevented from leaving and sent to forced labour camps in their host-countries as well as in the Soviet Union. Many of them spent up to five years in these camps and were only released and expelled in 1949.

The failure of the expulsions to solve the German question is also illustrated by the fact that the 'problem' of German minorities in Central and Eastern Europe persisted after 1950 and became an integral part of German foreign policy towards this region. Post-1950 emigration of ethnic Germans from Central and Eastern Europe had primarily to do with the continued discrimination that ethnic Germans were facing because of their ethnic identity, but partly also because of the general political and economic conditions in the former Eastern Bloc. Consequently, over the course of half a century, German policy priorities in this respect have changed – from consistent attempts throughout the Cold War to arrange for as many ethnic Germans as possible to be allowed to emigrate to Germany, to more recent policies that aim at securing minority rights and decent living conditions for those members of German minorities who still live in Central and Eastern Europe. Neither policy approach has been without difficulties. Until 1993, when changes in German legislation occurred (illustrated by Klekowski von Koppenfels), approximately 3.5 million ethnic Germans had resettled in the Federal Republic. About half of them arrived between 1950 and 1987, mostly from Poland and Romania (62 percent and 15 percent, respectively). Their integration was just as successful as that of the expellees. The other half arrived in the six-year period after 1987; and since the changes in German law in 1993, over half a million more ethnic Germans have emigrated to the Federal Republic. Of them, almost two-thirds came from the successor states of the former Soviet Union. For the period since 1995, their share is a staggering 97 percent. As Heinrich illustrates in his contribution, their integration has been far less successful – because of their lack of knowledge of German, increasingly unwanted occupational profiles, (self-)ghettoisation, the worsening economic situation in Germany, and the increasing xenophobia in German society. As with the expellees, this dimension of the German question is both a domestic and an international one, and, as Senders makes clear, it raises political as well as cultural questions about what and where Germany is.

A Resolution of the German Question?

A glance at the annual immigration figures of ethnic Germans over recent years reveals that their numbers have constantly declined from a peak of almost 400,000 in 1989 and 1990 to just above 100,000 ten years later. It is equally important to note that in their overwhelming majority these ethnic Germans come from the successor states of the former Soviet Union. There are two implications of this. One is that the German policy approach of restricting ethnic German immigration by means of changing the law and simultaneously making financial aid available to the still existing settlement areas of ethnic Germans in Central and Eastern Europe has worked. The other is that the situation in the host-countries has improved sufficiently to make staying an acceptable alternative to emigration. This suggests that the German question as a problem of ethnic German minorities in Central and Eastern Europe seems near to resolution. Other dimensions of the German question, too, have been resolved. In 1990 the unification of the Federal Republic with the German Democratic Republic was achieved by peaceful means, and a treaty was signed between the unified Germany and Poland guaranteeing the border between the two countries as it had been de facto established in 1945. Relations between Germany and Poland, between the German expellees and Poland, and between the German minority in Poland and Poles and the Polish government have significantly improved. The German question as a territorial and bilateral problem between Germany and Poland thus also seems largely to be resolved. Germany's relationship with the Czech Republic has significantly improved, too, although quite a number of problems remain. The German–Czech Declaration of 1997, and various initiatives following from it, have had a positive impact on German–Czech relations. However, they have not been able to resolve all outstanding issues. Many expellees remain disappointed at the refusal of the Czech government to rescind those of the so-called Beneš Decrees of 1945 and 1946 that legalised the collective victimisation of the Sudeten Germans and gave amnesty to anyone who committed a crime in the course of their expulsion (on the decrees in detail, see Blumenwitz 1993: 7–9). More recently, initiatives have been taken in the Czech Republic to address many of these unresolved issues at local level, i.e., in the towns and villages where the expulsions actually happened (Holdsworth 2000). This has been welcomed, but the situation has not yet fundamentally improved, and it is unlikely that this will occur as long as hardliners on both sides give each other the pretext to sabotage a comprehensive process of reconciliation. With other countries, such as Romania, Hungary, or the successor states of the former Yugoslavia, relations have, for a long time, been conducted without any significant influence of the German question. This, too, is the case for the countries of the former Soviet Union, from where emigration of ethnic Germans still continues but no longer to the same extent as it did in the early 1990s. In all of these countries, Germany is no longer seen as a political, economic or military threat but as a valuable partner that can pave the way towards closer integration and cooperation with the West. And in this process, German minorities are seen as an asset rather than as a liability.

In Germany itself, the integration of ethnic Germans into political, social and economic life remains a complicated process. As such it is part of the continued quest for a German national identity. The arrival of more than sixteen million ethnic Germans in the country since the end of the Second World War has been a major contributory factor to this process that has, so far, not been completed satisfactorily. Thus, while the international dimensions of the century-old German question may finally be nearing resolution at the beginning of the twenty-first century, the German question as a question about German national identity still awaits an answer. However, the traditional interconnectedness of political and cultural, and of domestic and international, dimensions of the German question persists. This means that an answer to the question about German national identity can only be given if the Federal Republic and the states and nations of Central and Eastern Europe come to terms with the legacy of the expulsions and emigration of ethnic Germans since the Second World War.

Notes

1. Border changes in Western Europe affected Germany and Austria as well. Alsace–Lorraine became part of France again, after it had been annexed by Bismarck in the Franco-German war of 1870/71, and with it approximately 1.5 million Alsatian-speakers (an Alemanic dialect). Belgium received German territories in compensation for war damage, the inhabitants of these territories numbering tens of thousands. A border referendum in Holstein determined the Danish–German border in such a way that minorities were created on either side, the German minority being approximately 30,000 strong. Finally, Italy was awarded South Tyrol in 1919 with some 350,000 German-speakers.

2. The introductory paragraph to section 'XII. Orderly Transfer of German Populations' of the Potsdam Agreement reads as follows: 'The Three Governments, having considered the question in all its aspects, recognize that the transfer to Germany of German populations, or elements thereof, remaining in Poland, Czechoslovakia and Hungary, will have to be undertaken. They agree that any transfers that take place should be effected in an orderly and humane manner.'

3. Agreements were concluded with Estonia and Latvia in 1939, with the Soviet Union on the evacuation of Germans from Soviet-annexed territories in eastern Poland, the Baltic States, and Romanian Bessarabia and Northern Bukovina in 1939, 1940 and 1941, with Romania in 1940, and with Croatia, Serbia and Bulgaria in 1942. In addition, the Nazis unilaterally decided on the resettlement of ethnic Germans from southeastern Poland in 1940, from Bosnia and Slovenia in 1942, from the Ukraine in 1943, and from Hungary in 1944. The estimated total of those affected is 1.1 million ethnic Germans (Kulski 1976: 99). Already in 1938, Hitler and Mussolini had agreed to allow the ethnic Germans of South Tyrol to 'choose' between emigration to Germany or assimilation in Italy.

4. There are, however, some examples of population transfers in the first half of the twentieth century in the Balkans after the Balkan wars and the territorial reorganisation of the region after the First World War between 1919 and 1923. The first instance in this context was the Bulgarian–Turkish exchange of populations agreed by the two states in an Annex to the Peace Treaty of Constantinople on 15 November 1913. In 1919, the Treaty of Neuilly also included a convention that effected a population exchange between Greece and Bulgaria, which was implemented over a period of thirteen years and involved the migration of 92,000 Bulgarians and 46,000 Greeks. The Convention Concerning the Exchange of Greek and Turkish Populations of 30 January 1923 resulted in approximately 1.1 million Greeks from Asia Minor and Eastern Thrace being expelled to Greece and between 350,000 and 500,000 Moslems, primarily from the Greek provinces of Macedonia and Epirus, being expelled to Turkey.

5. In April 1999, a resolution was passed by the European Parliament in which the members called 'on the Czech Government, in the same spirit of reconciliatory statements made by President Havel, to repeal the surviving laws and decrees from 1945 and 1946, insofar as they concern the expulsion of individual ethnic groups in the former Czechoslovakia' (European Parliament 1999). Prior to this resolution of the European Parliament, the US House of Representatives passed a resolution on 13 October 1998 in which members of the House demanded that the formerly Communist countries in Central and Eastern Europe 'return wrongfully expropriated properties to their rightful owners or, when actual return is not possible, to pay prompt, just and effective compensation, in accordance with principles of justice and in a manner that is just, transparent and fair'

(House of Representatives 1998). In contrast to the Austrian Parliament, the *Österreichischer Nationalrat* (1999), which passed a resolution in May 1999 asking the Austrian government to use its influence to bring about the repeal of the relevant Beneš Decrees, the German Parliament supported a motion introduced by the SPD and Alliance 90/The Greens in October 1999 in which members were asked to welcome the statement by Chancellor Schroeder and Czech Minister-President Zeman of 8 March 1999 that 'neither government will re-introduce property issues [into their bilateral relationship] either today or in the future' (Deutscher Bundestag 1999).

References

Blumenwitz, Dieter, 'Die Beneš-Dekrete aus dem Jahre 1945 unter dem Gesichtspunkt des Völker-rechts', *Deutschland und seine Nachbarn*, no. 6, February 1993, pp. 5–19.

Brubaker, Rogers, *Citizenship and Nationhood in France and Germany*. Cambridge, MA, Harvard University Press, 1992.

Deutscher Bundestag, 'Antrag der Fraktionen SPD und Bündnis 90/Die Grünen: Weiterentwicklung der deutsch-tschechischen Beziehungen', *Bundestagsdrucksache 14/1873* (26 October 1999), Bonn, 1999.

European Parliament, 'Resolution on the Regular Report from the Commission on the Czech Republic's Progress towards Accession', (COM(98)0708–C4-0111/99), Brussels, 1999.

Geiss, Immanuel, 'Die deutsche Frage im internationalen System', in *Die deutsche Frage als internationales Problem*, ed. Hans-Jürgen Schröder. Stuttgart, Steiner, 1990, pp. 15–37.

Holdsworth, Nick, 'Eyewitness', *Times Higher Education Supplement*, no. 1457, 13 October 2000, p. 9.

House of Representatives, 105th Congress, Second Session, 'House Resolution No. 562' (HRES 562 IH), Washington, 1998.

Kulski, Wladislaw W., *Germany and Poland. From War to Peaceful Relations*. Syracuse, NY, Syracuse University Press, 1976.

Marcus, Lucy P., 'The Carpathian Germans', in *German Minorities in Europe. Ethnic Identity and National Belonging*, ed. Stefan Wolff. Oxford and New York, Berghahn, 2000, pp. 97–108.

Österreichischer Nationalrat, 'Entschließung des Nationalrates vom 19. Mai 1999 betreffend Aufhe-bung der "Beneš-Dekrete" und der "AVNOJ-Bestimmungen"', *Stenographisches Protokoll der 169. Sitzung des Nationalrates* (XX. GP), Wien, 1999, p. 69.

Stricker, Gerd, 'Ethnic Germans in Russia and the Former Soviet Union', in *German Minorities in Europe. Ethnic Identity and National Belonging*, ed. Stefan Wolff. Oxford and New York, Berghahn, 2000, pp. 165–179.

Part I

Refugees, Expellees and *Aussiedler* in the
Federal Republic of Germany:
Historical, Social, Political and Legal
Dimensions of the Integration Process

Chapter 1

Integrating Ethnic Germans in West Germany: The Early Postwar Period

Daniel Levy

Introduction

This chapter provides an overview of the various forms of, and decisive moments in, the integration process of ethnic Germans from Central and Eastern Europe during the first two postwar decades. The immediate postwar period is of particular importance because it sets the political agenda for their integration and it provides the foundational images for the interpretation of the history that follows. Integration is a key concept, both in the sense of their actual incorporation into the West German model and as a metaphor for the subsequent (and retrospective) assessment of the genesis of the Federal Republic. As many of the following chapters show, this experience was by no means a uniform story. Analysing the integration of ethnic Germans provides a framework through which we can observe the contested trajectory of the new West German state and its national self-understanding.[1]

Key stages in the Integration of Ethnic Germans

Settlements of Ethnic Germans before and after the Second World War

In order to grasp the scope of ethnic German postwar migration it is indispensable to look at the prewar constitution of this group. The largest concentration of ethnic Germans before 1939 was in the eastern provinces of the German Reich – Silesia, Pomerania and East Prussia – with about nine million (*Reichsdeutsche*). The total of ethnic Germans outside the boundaries of the Reich (*Volksdeutsche*) amounted to 8.6 million (Reichling

1986). In 1939 there were about 1.4 million ethnic Germans living in Russia, many concentrated along the Volga River, near the Black sea and other settlements. The German population of Romania, who arrived there as early as the twelfth century, numbered 780,000 in 1939. There were 1.2 million Germans living in Poland, 3.5 million in Czechoslovakia, 600,000 in Hungary and half a million in Yugoslavia (Reichling 1986). Altogether the population of Germans in the eastern provinces, Central, East and Southeast Europe before the Second World War amounted to eighteen million people (see Table 1.1). This demographic configuration changed drastically during and after the Second World War. The incorporation of ethnic Germans into the Federal Republic of Germany can be divided into three stages. In 1945 the three allied powers signed the Potsdam Agreement sanctioning large population transfers that had already begun during the war years. Altogether a total of about twelve million ethnic Germans fled from Eastern Europe.[2] They are referred to as expellees (*Vertriebene*). The Soviet Union expelled about one million German citizens from Eastern Prussia, but did not expel the ethnic German minorities residing on its territory to the west. Instead they had become subject to internal deportations to remote areas such as Siberia, Kazakhstan, and Kyrgyzstan.[3] Of the twelve million who were expelled or fled, about eight million settled in West Germany, four million in East Germany, five hundred thousand in Austria and other countries (see Table 1.2). As the result of expulsion or flight, about two million Germans lost their lives. Approximately 20 percent of the population in the nascent Federal Republic consisted of expellees and refugees (Bade 1994).[4]

After the expulsion measures ended, about four million ethnic Germans remained in their traditional regions of settlement, primarily in Poland, Romania, Hungary and some in Czechoslovakia, as well as the 1.5 million Russian Germans (*Russlanddeutsche*) who were forcibly resettled within the Soviet Union. Of those four million, about two million emigrated to Germany between 1950 and 1987. They are referred to as *Aussiedler*. The pattern of their emigration was largely determined by political changes in their host-countries. Periods of liberalisation in selected countries of the Communist Bloc and the use of exit permits for ethnic Germans as leverage for economic assistance determined their flow to West Germany. During this period the majority of ethnic Germans came from Poland (62 percent) and Romania (15 percent). Despite their larger numbers in their host-country, only 8 percent came from the Soviet Union (see Table 1.3).

A third immigration wave followed thereafter. The opening of the Iron Curtain precipitated large-scale migrations of ethnic Germans from Central and Eastern Europe. There was a dramatic increase in the number of *Aussiedler*. From an annual average of 38,000 since the mid-1960s, the number jumped to 200,000 in 1988 and almost 400,000 in 1990. Those ethnic Germans coming to the Federal Republic after 1993 are referred to as *Spätaussiedler*. Between 1988 and 1996 a total of almost 2.3 million ethnic Germans emigrated. In contrast to the two earlier periods, the majority of *Aussiedler*, about 66 percent, now arrived from the former Soviet Union, followed by Poland with 25 percent and Romania with 9 percent (see Table 1.4).

The Federal Republic perceived itself as the historical and juridical successor to the German Reich. Consequently it granted citizenship to both Germans who formerly lived on German state territory in the east (and had thus had German citizenship) and those ethnic Germans living outside of its borders. The central legal foundation for the incorporation of ethnic Germans was laid down in Germany's provisional constitution, the Basic Law (*Grundgesetz*) in 1949. Based on Wilhelminian law of 1913, the incorporation of ethnic Germans was facilitated by the principle of *jus sanguinis*, according to which being German is a matter of descent. Article 116 of the Basic Law conferred automatic citizenship rights to 'a person who possesses German nationality or who has been admitted to the territory of the German Reich within the frontiers of 31 December 1937 as a refugee or expellee of German stock [*Volkszugehörigkeit*] or as the spouse or descendant of such person.' This definition allowed for the broad inclusion of two categories: one relates to those who had been nationals of the former German Reich (*Staatsangehörige*); the other includes those who had German ancestry but were citizens of other Eastern European countries from where they had been expelled. Thus citizenship rights were extended to so-called 'Status Germans' on the basis of their *Volkszugehörigkeit*. This latter category was further extended in the Federal Expellee law of 1953. However, ethnic Germans are not a culturally homogeneous group. Indeed, ethnic German minorities are a rather heterogeneous group who over the last two centuries have developed different cultural attributes and a variety of German dialects. Some have maintained ethnic traits and preserved German traditions while others have been highly assimilated (Münz and Ohliger 1997). It is a legally sanctioned ethnonational self-understanding that defines them as German – no matter how feeble their 'ethnicity' in terms of culture or language – rather than a set of uniform cultural practices. It was the legally privileged access to citizenship of ethnic Germans that institutionalised descent as a definition of Germanness.

The Political Integration of Ethnic Germans in the Federal Republic

To understand the relative success of their integration, it is essential to look briefly at the institutional power ethnic Germans wielded at the time. They were a pervasive presence in politics and society. Early on, mostly to prevent their radicalisation, the British and the Americans included them in the advisory committees (*Beratende Ausschüsse*) where policy recommendations for the occupying forces were articulated. However, since the military government initially did not allow them to form political parties – fearing this would have a destabilizing effect and hoping that they would participate in existing parties – they formed 'Regional Associations' (*Landsmannschaften*). Together with informal networks and help from the churches, expellees found new means of representation through the *Landsmannschaften*, based on their regional origins. These provided an organisational infrastructure for political organisation, social aid measures and the preservation of cultural customs, a framework to keep alive collective memories of the old *Heimat*. However, they also sought social parity with the resident population and continuously emphasised the reintegration of the lost territories into a unified German state.

Many of the expellees' informal and regional associations formed the basis of political organisations that sprang up after the Allies lifted their ban on the formation of expellee parties (Weiss 1985). Most prominent was the Central Association of Expelled Germans (*Zentralverband vertriebener Deutscher*, or ZvD). It soon became an informal umbrella for other expellee organisations and its charter was officially endorsed by most of them. In 1950 expellees formed a national party, the Bloc of Expellees and Disenfranchised (*Bund der Heimatvertriebenen und Entrechteten*, or BHE) which focused on the social integration of expellees. Essentially it sought to fulfil the demands of the ZvD Charter: 'Equal right as citizens, not only before the law, but also in the reality of every-day life. Just and reasonable distribution of the burden of the last war on the entire German *Volk* ... Reasonable integration of all professional groups of expellees in the life of the German *Volk*' (Lemberg and Edding 1959: 662).

Their first electoral success came in state elections in Schleswig-Holstein in July 1950 where they received the second largest vote (23.4 percent) after the Social Democratic Party (SPD). A series of electoral successes in the *Länder* culminated in the BHE's entry into the federal parliament (*Bundestag*) in 1953 with 5.9 percent of the vote. They set the agenda and their initial electoral successes required that other parties respond to it. Adenauer invited them into his coalition and ably co-opted much of the BHE's agenda. Domestically they were instrumental in developing legislative measures to alleviate the difficult social and economic conditions of their constituency. But the scope of expellee interests extended far beyond the realms of the BHE, as the generic term 'expellee parliamentarians' (*Vertriebenenabgeordnete*) indicates.

Many expellees joined existing parties and acted as political pressure groups. The licensed parties recognised the opportunities to absorb them and make their platform attractive to the vast numbers of expellee voters. Parties formed special interest groups for expellees within their organisational structures. Expellees exercised an important agenda-setting function. Their pervasive presence, and the parties' recognition that they were a significant portion of the electorate, made them politically a formidable lobby. After the first elections to the *Bundestag* in 1949, seventy-seven representatives were expellees or refugees: thirty-three in the SPD, fifteen in the governing Christian Democratic Union (CDU), thirteen in the Free Democratic Party (FDP), and sixteen in other parties. After the second elections in 1953 18 percent of all members of parliament were expellees (Schönberg 1970).

They were also well represented on the state level. By 1959, more than 20 percent of civil servants in High Federal Employment (*Obere Bundesbehörden*) positions were expellees. The percentage of expellees was even larger – 27 percent – among the Highest Federal Employment (*Oberste Bundesbehörden*) civil servants (Schönberg, 1970).[5] The recognition of expellees was also expressed in the formation of the Ministry for Expellees, Refugees and War-Damaged (*Bundesministerium für Vertriebene, Flüchtlinge und Kriegsgeschädigte* – BMV) after Konrad Adenauer's first election victory in 1949. Thus, the new West German state had a significant number of officials whose identities were shaped by their status as expellees and refugees, and they wielded considerable political power.

The refugee problem was a major concern of the new state. As the contributions by Senders and Klekowski von Koppenfels in this volume show, recognition of the expellees' fate was institutionalised in the legal realm and citizenship legislation, providing material and moral support for ethnic Germans. A host of laws provided the basis for an expansive approach towards *Vertriebene*, and later towards *Aussiedler* and *Spätaussiedler* as well. Two central legislative measures addressed the status of ethnic Germans: Article 116 of the Basic Law and the 1953 Federal Expellee and Refugee Law (BVFG). However, the integration of ethnic Germans was not confined to the formal political realm and citizenship issues. State policies supported the preservation of ethnocultural awareness and provided the financial foundations for the dissemination of ethnic German cultural values (*Kulturgut*). Paragraph 96 of the BVFG directly addressed the preservation of cultural values of expellees and refugees, and sponsorship of scientific research (*Pflege des Kulturgutes der Vertriebenen und Flüchtlinge und Förderung der wissenschaftlichen Forschung*). The government established archives, libraries and research institutes dedicated to the preservation and study of the history of Germans in Eastern Europe. By law, the federal and state governments were encouraged not only to keep the culture and traditions of those expelled alive but also their memories of expulsion and of the eastern territories. There still is, for instance, an annual celebration day of homeland (*Tag der Heimat*), emphasising the integral relationship of ethnic Germans to the lost territories east of the Oder–Neisse line. It is an occasion that simultaneously confirmed the ethnic foundations of German nationhood, embedded the political claims to these territories, and expressed hostility to Communism. Government-sponsored activities were complemented by voluntary actions organised by the *Landsmannschaften*. Ethnic Germans would congregate during *Heimatabende* and circulate *Heimatblätter* (circulars) based on their regional affiliation. This history was an integral part of school curricula (Ohliger 2000). Through geography focused on one's own region (*Heimatkunde*) memories of these groups were preserved in the educational system. Following its constitutional obligation under paragraph 96 to keep alive the cultural values of the Eastern territories the state was a sponsor of films that focused on the misery of expulsion, integration into a new society and memories of the *Heimat* (Kurth 1959).[6] These were complemented by documentary films about public events and demonstrations organised by the expellees to celebrate and commemorate their homeland (so-called *Heimatkundgebungen*). Most of these film projects were supported by the Ministry of Expellees or *Länder* governments focusing on the fate of expellees in their respective states.

State sponsorship of the study of Eastern Europe (*Ostkunde/Ostforschung*) continued a scholarly tradition that had flourished under the Nazis who had drawn upon it for their *Lebensraum* policies. Scholarly institutes for *Ostforschung* offered academic legitimacy for alleged historical continuities supporting irredentist claims to the territories east of the Oder–Neisse line (Burleigh 1988). The West German state used this kind of research to rectify aspects of the Potsdam Agreement by creating awareness of the suffering of expellees and to lay the foundations for reclaiming their homes and property.

Most notable was a multi-volume project commissioned by the government and published by the Ministry of Expellees. The eight-volume study, entitled Documentation of the Expulsion of Germans from East Central Europe (*Dokumentation der Vertreibung der Deutschen aus Ost-Mitteleuropa*), was conducted by Theodor Schieder and other eminent historians who were part of the *Königsberger Kreis*, a centre of Germany's *Ostforschung* prior to 1945. The first volume was published in 1953, and reissued as a paperback in 1984. Primary emphasis was put on the miseries of expulsion and the brutality experienced at the hands of the Red Army. Testimonies of eyewitnesses offered detailed accounts of brutal expulsion measures. The political purpose of this work was unmistakable (Beer 1998). It created awareness of the suffering of Germans and established factual foundations for the return of property. The editors of the documentation project made these goals explicit: 'Through this documentation future German governments will have materials that might become relevant. Therefore, all contributions, especially factual reports [by eye witnesses] are notarized' (cited in Beer 1998: 358). However, aside from the political instrumentalisation of the expellees' fate it was, first and foremost, their socioeconomic integration that marked the postwar decade.

Contentious Socioeconomic Integration

While cultural references initially continued to play a role in the adherence to a unified concept of the nation – despite, or maybe because of its division into two states and loss of territorial sovereignty – the integration of expellees and *Aussiedler* unfolded mostly along the axis of socioeconomic considerations. One-fifth of the West German population were expellees and refugees. Their precarious economic situation raised many problems. It was an important issue testing the political reliability and economic viability of the new West German state. Ethnic German expellees were the central group around which this discourse of integration was constructed.[7] They were identified with distinctive hardships and integrative measures were created for them. The immediate purpose of integration policies was to create the material conditions for a successful and rapid incorporation of expellees, especially with respect to housing and employment. There was general agreement that the expellees should be integrated, but the terms of integration were contested. Contrary to the celebratory official rhetoric about the successful postwar integration of ethnic Germans that has frequently dominated contemporary political occasions, the first decade after the war was marked by an ongoing antagonism between ethnic Germans and the long-time resident population.

Formal adherence to descent-based citizenship regulations could not mask the tensions between these two groups. Faced with great economic problems, unemployment and severe housing shortages, conflicts between natives – the term used then was *Einheimische* – and expellees were a prominent theme on the political agenda. Tensions rose once it became apparent that expellees would remain. International political developments – such as decisions by the Council of the Allied Foreign Ministers in 1947 and the Communist takeover of Czechoslovakia – reinforced a sense that expellees would not return to their home countries. Domestically, the Currency Reform of 1948 exacerbated the disadvantages of expellees *vis-à-vis* the native population and sharpened antagonisms.

In the summer of 1948, the Western Allies told German politicians to address the discrepancies between the two groups and devise a system of burden-sharing. This resulted in the passing of a provisional law, the Immediate Aid Law (*Soforthilfegesetz*, or SHG) of 8 August 1949. It provided a monthly payment of 70 DM to refugees and expellees, and financial assistance in the form of grants for housing, education and business initiatives (Schillinger 1985). The SHG hardly eliminated economic discrepancies between the two groups, but was an important step in recognising the needs of expellees and laid the groundwork for later legislation on their behalf.

Conflicts over the distribution of expellees and concerns over integration dominated many parliamentary debates and legislation on behalf of ethnic Germans. The rhetoric of integration and actual integration policies stood in a complex relationship to each other. Rhetorically, integration was an indispensable frame of reference for the formation of national solidarity. Time and again, parliamentarians pointed to national unity as based on the equality of all members. Acknowledging the actual divisions and discrepancies between *Einheimische* and newcomers defined both a problem of distributing expellees and one of national identity.

Many political debates centred on questions of distributive justice and persisting problems of social envy between *Einheimische* and expellees. Competition for resources and antagonism between the resident population and newcomers undermined the quest for national solidarity.[8] Confessional divides, a predominantly rural background, different dialects and clear economic disadvantages allowed for the identification of expellees as a distinctive group. Two major cleavages emerged. One reflected the antagonism between long-time resident and ethnic German newcomers. Objections to fiscal privileges for expellees were particularly heated in debates revolving around tensions between expellees and the rural population. The second cleavage relates to the large flight of Germans to the Federal Republic from the Soviet Occupied Zone (SBZ) which would become the German Democratic Republic (GDR).

Social envy and antagonism were particularly strong in the rural areas where many expellees were sent upon arrival. As a result of complicated negotiations among the Allies, the distribution of these expellees was uneven and led to a disproportionate concentration in some areas.[9] In contrast to the destroyed cities, rural areas often had no war damage or food shortages. When these newcomers demanded their share and equal rights, hostilities between them and the the rural population intensified. Rainer Schulze explains this conflict as follows: 'Different standards and ways of life, temperaments and casts of mind, political traditions and established customs had a more damaging effect on the prospects for co-existence than was the case in urban industrial areas which had always encouraged a higher degree of social mobility and had acted as a melting pot' (Schulze 1997: 67). Confessional divisions were more significant in the predominantly Catholic rural context, as the majority of expellees were Protestants.

Schulze documents the deep suspicions with which the native population treated the expellees. The 'infiltration of foreign elements' was a common fear among the rural native population who felt their customs threatened. These views were mostly sustained by prejudices about the hygiene and morality of expellees. 'The native rural population still had almost everything: homeland, housing, possessions, an established occupation and employment, their own land to provide food, and, above all, an accepted social status and a secure identity. All this had now to be shared with the refugees ... The refugees had corrupted a world which had previously remained intact and isolated, and had brought with them other ways of life, models, and standards. In consequence, the native inhabitants grew to regard them as threat to their own existence, both material and philosophical' (ibid: 67).

Nevertheless, or perhaps precisely because of the aforementioned antagonism, the Equalisation of Burden Act (*Lastenausgleichsgesetz*, or LAG), which was passed in May of 1952, was a key piece of social legislation in the early Federal Republic. It was aimed at millions of refugees, who were to be compensated for lost property, homes, businesses and other assets. It affected mainly Germans from the territories east of the Oder–Neisse line who, facing expulsion, had to leave behind most of their belongings. The LAG legislated large financial transfers by prescribing a tax on assets in West Germany. The levy was stretched over a thirty-year period so that it would not be too great an expense. Minor losses were fully compensated. Major losses were compensated in a ratio of 1 to 10 between the old and the new currency. Claims were scrutinised by special committees. Because of the cumbersome nature of the verification process and the large number of applicants many years passed before payments were made. By the time claimants received their money the actual value of the financial compensation was far lower than the original estimated value (Schillinger 1985).

However, the LAG significantly contributed to the moral rather than material integration of ethnic Germans. Implemented when unemployment was high and the effects of economic recovery not evenly distributed, the LAG was important in legitimating the new order. It is widely regarded as the key moment for the integration of expellees, and politicians celebrate it as an exemplary piece of social policy. Even though the LAG aid was not substantially higher than earlier welfare provisions, it marked a significant symbolic shift from treating expellees as welfare recipients to their participation in the recovering economy (Schillinger 1985). As such it became emblematic for the spirit of reconstruction that would later provide the new foundation for national identification in the absence of more traditional modes of national integration, such as national symbols and a military establishment.

Successful Integration

Ultimately, however, it was the successful integration of ethnic Germans that marked the 1950s, emblematic for the social and political reconstruction of the Federal Republic of Germany. National identity was no longer identified with the chauvinistic hyperbole that had characterised it since the last quarter of the nineteenth century. It was now shaped through more universal patterns of consumption and work (Carter 1997; Moeller 1997). Pride in economic accomplishments became the new frame for collective identification. Expellees embodied the resilience of Germans and the successful process of economic reconstruction. Their initial disadvantages underscored the virtues of hard work, discipline and economic success. More than any other group, they represented the success story of the new Germany. However, compared with the *Einheimische*, their standards of living remained lower for much longer and initial unemployment was much higher.[10]

Eventually, expellees would share in the general prosperity that reached Germany in the mid-1950s. With the consolidation of a new economic identity, expellees showed more concern for becoming West German than for *völkisch* concepts of the nation. To be sure, continuous emphasis on economic themes did not eliminate ethnocultural considerations but it weakened their political relevance. The pervasive official emphasis on the economy as a source of national revitalisation offered categories in terms of which the population could identify itself. Once the ethnic idiom was depreciated at the expense of economic reconstruction, opposition against ethnocultural accounts of nationhood was readily available. The very success of integration and its subsequent mythologisation had diverse consequences for the articulation of national identity.[11] In the aftermath of the passage of the BVFG in 1953, with sharply improving economic conditions, the integration of ethnic Germans was perceived as a social, economic and cultural accomplishment. Studies showed that, by the mid-1960s, expellees could no longer be distinguished as a separate social group (Hinst 1968). Integration measures encouraged ethnic Germans' participation in the Federal Republic and, conversely, their participation further promoted integration. Initial antagonisms were replaced by the common project of reconstruction and economic success.

The socioeconomic integration of the mid-1950s was followed by a political and psychological integration. Writing in 1970, Dieter Strothmann noted that 'twenty years after the big expulsion the fate of the expellees is resolved. It is no longer an economic or social problem; it has lost its political relevance ... The previously common distinction between "natives" and "expellees" no longer exists. The expellees of 1945 are the natives of 1969' (Strothmann 1970: 305, 312). There had also been a considerable generational turnover. And by now, West Germany was the dominant frame of reference for the majority of young ethnic Germans, whose formative political socialisation took place in the Federal Republic.[12] They no longer shared the actual experience of expulsion. The public perception of the 'expellee problem' also changed. As early as 1959, *Der Spiegel* no longer saw expellees as an impoverished group, a status now attributed to refugees from the GDR. This process was completed with the arrival of foreign labour migrants (guestworkers) from the mid-1950s on. The outsider function was assumed by the new group. The 'refugee problem' was replaced by the 'foreigner problem'; in both cases, the terms refer to problems the native population had with the newcomers (Bausinger 1987).

The flow of *Aussiedler* continued throughout the 1960s and especially during the early 1970s after Brandt signed a bilateral treaty with Poland. However, the overall influx was much lower compared with almost ten million in the aftermath of the Second World War and the dramatic increase to almost 400,000 after 1989. Between 1960 and 1975 a total of 361,000 *Aussiedler* came to West Germany, averaging about 22,500 a year. In contrast to earlier experiences, they were a non-topic in the public sphere and their absorption unfolded without much public notice (Schlau 1979).[13]

Political Marginalisation

With an improving national economy, broad legal recognition and social integration, the BHE's electoral basis steadily eroded, leaving it out of the federal parliament. In the 1957 elections its share of the vote declined to 4.6 percent. In 1961 it joined with the *Deutsche Partei* (DP) to form the *Gesamtdeutsche Partei* (GDP) but received only 2.8 percent of the vote. The BHE, despite its attempts to appeal to a broader electorate, had always been an interest party lobbying on behalf of its expellee constituency. The very success of the BHE destroyed the social foundation for its existence as a political party. Furthermore, as ethnic Germans were firmly incorporated into West Germany and most legislation on their behalf passed, expellee votes became politically dispensable. Adenauer no longer had to court organised expellee groups.[14]

Deprived of their domestic agenda, expellee organisations focused on foreign policy issues. They continued to demand territorial revisions in the east and the return of their properties in those 'lost territories'. To be sure, there was nothing novel about these demands. However, against the political background of reconciliation with the east and an increasingly vocal postwar generation, the foreign policy stance of expellee organisations was now regarded as retrogade.[15] Ethnic Germans did not cast their votes according to a foreign policy agenda that envisioned the return to the old *Heimat*.[16] This re-imagination of expellee organisations as a disruptive radical voice was shaped amidst the official endorsement of a new foreign policy agenda during the mid- and late 1960s. Negative perceptions of expellees' official rhetoric intensified as social and political forces sought reconciliation with the East.[17] In the face of growing popular support for Brandt's *Ostpolitik* (his *détente* with Eastern Europe), expellee organisations were isolated. The public came to perceive of expellees' political views as anachronistic (Rautenberg 1997). This negative perception was expressed, among other ways, in the derogatory description of them as *Ewig Gestrige* (eternally stuck in the past). Ethnocultural values were frequently dismissed as *Deutschtümelei*, a negative expression of nationhood with a secretive, conspirational connotation. The decline of expellees' influence was also reflected in the abolition of the 'Ministry for Expellees'. During his inaugural speech in 1969, Brandt announced its absorption into a subdivision of the Ministry of the Interior.

Conclusion

The purpose of this chapter has been to provide a broad overview of the various dimensions of the social, political and legal integration of ethnic Germans in the postwar period. From a sociocultural perspective the integration of expellees and *Aussiedler* has played an important role in the re-formation of German nationhood. However, ultimately the main source of cohesive identity in the Federal Republic was sustained economic growth and pride in it. National solidarity was predicated on economic success. Official discourse about integrative measures for ethnic Germans contributed an important foundation for a new and shared identity articulated in economic terms. To be sure, conceptions of integrative policies toward ethnic Germans have been transformed in the context of changing political, cultural and economic circumstances. In this respect, the integration of ethnic Germans in the post-Cold War period differs markedly from the one discussed in this chapter (Levy, forthcoming). Integration measures have been circumscribed by distinctive political exigencies involving domestic as well as foreign policy considerations.

The integration of ethnic Germans as privileged immigrants into the West German body politic can be viewed as a model for immigration. It is simultaneously an example of massive state-sponsored efforts to assist in the integration process and it reveals the difficulties immigrants face while adjusting to a new environment. The implications of ethnic German immigration are not confined to the history of Germany. The story of ethnic German immigrants – expellees as well as *Aussiedler* – to the Federal Republic raises broader issues of ethnic persistence, pressures of assimilation, changing conceptions of home (*Heimat*) and corresponding notions of diaspora. In the following chapters we learn how these and other aspects of ethnic German immigration manifest themselves in the political, legal, social and cultural realms of the Federal Republic.

Table 1.1: German Population in the Eastern Territories of the Reich, Central, East and Southeastern Europe before the Start of the Second World War

Countries/Provinces as of 31 December 1937	German Population in September 1939
German Eastern Territories	9,575,000
Poland	1,200,000
Czechoslovakia	3,544,000
Yugoslavia	536,000
Romania	782,000
Hungary	600,000
Baltic States	250,000
Free City of Danzig	380,000
Total	16,867,000

Source: Reichling (1986)

Table 1.2: Number of Expellees

Expelled from	Expelled to West Germany	Total of Expelled To West*	Deported to Soviet Union **	Died as a result of expulsion or deportation
German Eastern Territories	4,520,000	6,987,000	350,000	870,000
Poland	785,000	1,405,000	460,000	174,000
Czecho Slovakia	1,935,000	3,055,000	30,000	220,000
Yugoslavia	135,000	283,000	40,000	106,000
Romania	65,000	133,000	80,000	75,000
Hungary	175,000	210,000	30,000	84,000
Baltic States	50,000	72,000	10,000	3,000
Total	7,665,000	12,450,000	1,000,000	1,532,000

* Includes FRG, GDR, Austria and other countries
** Between 1941 and 1944, 700,000 Russian Germans were deported from European settlement regions to Asian parts of the Soviet Union.
Source: Reichling, (1986).

Table 1.3: *Aussiedler* who Immigrated to the Federal Republic of Germany between 1950 and 1987

	1950-4	1955-9	1960-4	1965-9	1970-4	1975-9	1980-4	1985-7	Total 1950-87
Former USSR	1,802	11,639	4,455	3,617	15,941	40,644	14,858	15,701	**108,657**
Poland	43,557	248,626	49,832	60,786	61,075	141,637	144,551	97,686	**847,750**
Former CSSR	17,169	3,192	7,514	48,219	8,836	3,939	7,277	2,474	**98,620**
Hungary	248	4,152	1,450	2,365	2,419	1,338	2,591	1,650	**16,213**
Romania	1,228	2,361	9,241	7,053	29,802	41,615	72,824	42,048	**206,172**
Former Yugoslavia	24,707	32,805	12,238	8,870	4,862	1,361	1,061	529	**86,433**
Other Territories	2,392	1,160	57	76	67	69	80	44	**3,945**
Total of Aussiedler	**91,103**	**303,935**	**84,787**	**130,986**	**123,002**	**230,603**	**243,242**	**160,132**	**1,367,790**

Source: Bundesverwaltungsamt, Köln

Table 1.4: *Aussiedler* who Immigrated to the Federal Republic of Germany between 1988 and 2000

	Rate of Immigration													Total
	1988	1989	1990	1991	1992	1993	1994	1995	1996	1997	1998	1999	2000	
Former USSR	47,572	98,134	147,950	147,320	195,576	207,347	213,214	209,409	172,181	131,895	101,550	103,599	94,558	1,438,703
Poland	140,226	250,340	133,872	40,129	17,742	5,431	2,440	1,677	1,175	687	488	428	45	593,032
Former CSSR	949	2,027	1,708	927	460	134	97	62	14	10	15	11	0	6,378
Romania	12,902	23,387	111,150	32,178	16,146	5,811	6,615	6,519	4,282	1,777	1,005	855	27	218,992
Former Yugoslavia	223	1,469	961	450	199	120	182	178	77	33	14	19	0	3,859
Other Territories	801	1,698	1,432	991	442	45	43	53	20	17	8	4	0	5,525
Total	202,673	377,055	397,073	221,995	230,565	218,888	222,591	217,898	177,751	134,419	103,080	104,916	95,615	2,266,489

Source: Bundesverwaltungsamt Köln

Notes

1. Elsewhere, I have demonstrated how state officials used the integration of expellees to emphasise the need for national cohesion and how, once ethnic Germans were successfully integrated, government officials celebrated their experience as evidence for a new emerging identity based on economic accomplishments (Levy, forthcoming).

2. Previous expulsions were sanctioned ex post facto by the Potsdam Agreement. Many ethnic Germans had fled or been evacuated with the retreating German armies from Eastern and Southeastern Europe.

3. Already in 1941 Stalin had ordered their deportation to Siberia and Central Asian parts of the Soviet Union.

4. An additional group of Germans who emigrated to West Germany came from the German Democratic Republic (GDR). They are referred to as *Übersiedler*. Already prior to the formation of the two German states, about 730,000 people moved from the Soviet Occupied Zone to the Western zones. After the creation of the GDR in 1949 and until the construction of the Wall in 1961, another 3.9 million people migrated to the Federal Republic (Münz and Ohliger 1997).

5. Expellees were able to ensure legal quotas for their employment. Thus the Federal Expellee Law of 1953 had a provision (paragraph 77) according to which the federal office of employment had to assign a certain percentage to each profession (BT- 2/25/1953).

6. For a comprehensive discussion of the representation of expulsion and ethnic Germans in the media (press, film, radio) see Kurth (1959).

7. A series of films documented their hardship and the difficulties they had upon arrival in West Germany. These paid particular attention to the expellees' reconstructive efforts in the economy, emphasised their determination to help themselves, and pointed to integrative measures implemented to ameliorate their suffering (Kurth 1959).

8. Opinion surveys conducted by the Office of Military Government U.S. (OMGUS) between 1945–1949 show that the native inhabitants resented the expellees: 46 percent of the native population foresaw trouble with the expellees and some 78 percent of a sample in Württemberg-Baden saw expellees as an economic burden in 1946. Nevertheless, 'the share of natives who perceived of expellees as German citizens rose from 49 percent in early 1946 to 67 percent in late 1947, during which period those viewing them as foreigners dropped from 28 to 18 percent' (Merritt and Merritt 1970: 20). However, these numbers changed once again when severe food shortages and economic crises grew and, most importantly, when it became clear that the expellees would not return home. 'Throughout the entire occupation years roughly 90 percent expected that the expellees would return to their homelands if they were permitted to do so' (ibid: 20). The perception of expellees differed markedly. Their desire to return to their homelands declined steadily. In 1948 , 64 percent of the expellees believed that they would not get along with the native population. 'The share of those expressing actual dissatisfaction with their treatment by local populations rose from 7 percent in March 1946 to 50 percent in June 1948' (ibid: 20). 'Two-fifths of those who were dissatisfied with their reception stated that, instead of regarding them as Germans, the natives considered them to be human beings of inferior value, foreigners, or even beggars' (ibid: 113).

9. Attempts to negotiate quotas for specific zones were complicated through the refusal of the French to allow expellees into their zone. Most of the expellees were thus directed to the American and British zones. The three states with the highest percentage of expellees were Schleswig-Holstein (33 percent), Lower Saxony (27.2 percent) and Bavaria (21.2 percent). Politicians from these states were particularly vocal in their demands for more financial support.

10. In an OMGUS report from December 1947 it is noted that 'the economic situation of the expellees was considerably worse than that of the *Einheimische*. A third (34 percent) of the expellees received

less than 70 Reichsmark a month as compared to 19 percent of the native population. Conversely, as few as 15 percent of the new arrivals had monthly incomes above RM 200, whereas 34 percent of native Germans received this sum every month. Twice as many [expellees] were working as unskilled laborers' (Merritt and Merritt 1970: 190).

11. The degree to which the integration of ethnic Germans was in fact a success has become a topic of controversy. See for instance Lutz Niethammer (1987), who has claimed that 'successful integration' is a misleading term as it is superimposed from the perspective of the pride taken in this success as it solidified in the 1960s. Integration is deemed successful in as much as there has not been a permanent malaise and no radicalisation among expellees. See also Lüttinger (1986).

12. In a 1972 survey, when asked whether the children of expellees born in the Federal Republic should also be considered as expellees or whether their *Heimat* was the FRG, 74 percent perceived them as natives, while only 14 percent referred to them as expellees (Noelle-Neumann 1981: 528).

13. Another indication of declining public attention to ethnic German expellees and *Aussiedler* is revealed in changing opinion-survey categories. An examination of the keyword index of the annual *Allens-bacher* survey shows no direct references to ethnic Germans from the late 1960s to the mid-1980s.

14. The situation differed in the various *Länder*. In some, politicians continued to court the conservative *Landsmannschaften*. This is particularly relevant in Bavaria, and until the late 1970s and early 1980s this was also the case in Lower Saxony and Schleswig-Holstein.

15. The discrepancy between the BHE's political agenda and the concerns of its constituency are evidenced in a public opinion survey from 1958. Asked about the importance of the 'national question' (i.e. unification and the revision of the Oder–Neisse line) in people's decision to vote for the BHE, 9 percent of BHE voters named it as primary reason in 1953, a number that declined to 3 percent by 1957 (Noelle-Neumann 1967).

16. The broad consensus about the Oder–Neisse line was sustained in the first postwar decade. Asked whether the government should concede the new German–Polish border, in 1951 80 percent responded that one should not yield these territories. Asked in 1953 whether they thought these territories would again belong to Germany one day, 66 percent still agreed (Noelle-Neumann 1967: 315). In a survey conducted in 1959, refugees and expellees were asked: 'If tomorrow your *Heimat* belonged to Germany again, would you return or is that out of the question?' Thirty-eight percent said they would certainly, 27 percent responded 'maybe', while 30 percent refused categorically (ibid: 505). By 1969, the number of those who would return was down to 11 percent for the entire population and 29 percent among ethnic Germans (ibid: 526).

17. While in 1951 a firm 80 percent had refused to yield the 'lost territories', the number drastically declined in the following years, going down to 50 percent in 1962 and dropping to a mere 18 percent by 1972 (Noelle-Neumann 1981: 525). Conversely the number of those approving the new German–Polish border grew from a mere 8 percent in 1951 to 61 percent in 1972 (ibid: 525).

References

Bade, Klaus, *Ausländer Aussiedler Asyl*, München, Beck'sche Verlagsbuchhandlung, 1994.

Bausinger, Hermann, 'Das Problem der Flüchtlinge und Vertriebenen in den Forschungen zur Kultur der unteren Schichten', in *Flüchtlinge und Vertriebene in der westdeutschen Nachkriegsgeschichte*, ed. Helga Grebing, Rainer Schulze and Doris von der Brelie-Lewien, Hildesheim, Verlag August Lax, 1987, pp. 180–95.

Beer, Mathias, 'Im Spannungsfeld von Politik und Zeitgeschichte, Das Grossforschungsprojekt 'Dokumentation der Vertreibung der Deutschen aus Ost-Mitteleuropa', *Vierteljahreshefte für Zeitgeschichte* 3, 1998, pp. 345–91.

Burleigh, Michael, *Germany Turns Eastwards, A Study of Ostforschung in the Third Reich*. Cambridge, Cambridge University Press, 1988.

Carter, Erica, *How German is She? Postwar West German Reconstruction and the Consuming Woman.* Ann Arbor, University of Michigan Press, 1997.

Hinst, Klaus, *Das Verhältnis zwischen Westdeutschen und Flüchtlingen. Eine empirische Untersuchung.* Bern, Verlag Hans Huber, 1968.

Kurth, Karl O., 'Presse, Film und Rundfunk', in *Die Vertriebenen in Westdeutschland. Ihre Eingliederung und ihr Einfluss auf Gesellschaft, Wirtschaft, Politik und Geistesleben,* vol. 3, ed. Eugen Lemberg and Friedrich Edding, Kiel, Ferdinand Hirt, 1959, pp. 402–34.

Lemberg, Eugen and Friedrich Edding, *Die Vertriebenen in Westdeutschland, Ihre Eingliederung und ihr Einfluss auf Gesellschaft, Wirtschaft, Politik und Geistesleben,* Kiel, Ferdinand Hirt, 1959.

Levy, Daniel, 'The Politicization of Ethnic German Immigrants, The Transformation of State Priorities', in *Ethnic Migration in 20th Century Europe, Germany, Israel and Russia in Comparative Perspective,* ed. Rainer Münz and Rainer Ohliger. London, Frank Cass (forthcoming).

Levy, Daniel, 'Coming Home? Ethnic Germans and the Transformation of National Identity in the Federal Republic of Germany', in *Immigration and the Politics of Belonging in Contemporary Europe,* ed. Andrew Geddes and Adrian Favell. Aldershot, Avebury, 1999, pp. 93–108.

Lüttinger, Paul, 'Der Mythos der schnellen Integration, Eine empirische Untersuchung der Integration der Vertriebenen in der Bundesrepublick Deutschland bis 1971', *Zeitschrift für Soziologie* 15, 1986, pp. 20–36.

Merritt, Anna J, and Richard L, Merritt, (eds), *Public Opinion in Occupied Germany: The OMGUS Surveys, 1945–1949.* Urbana, University of Illinois Press, 1970.

Moeller, Robert, 'Introduction' *West Germany under Construction, Politics, Society, and Culture in the Adenauer Era,* ed. Robert Moeller. Ann Arbor, University of Michigan Press, 1997, pp. 1–30.

Münz, Rainer and Rainer Ohliger, 'Long Distance Citizens, Ethnic Germans and their Immigration to Germany' in Peter Schuck and Rainer Münz, eds, *Paths to Inclusion, The Integration of Migrants in the United States and Germany.* Providence, Berghahn Publishers, 1997, pp. 155–201.

Niethammer, Lutz, 'Flucht ins Konventionelle? Einige Randglossen zu Forschungsproblemen der deutschen Nachkriegsmigration', in *Flüchtlinge und Vertriebene in der westdeutschen Nachkriegsgsgeschichte,* ed. Helga Grebing, Rainer Schulze and Doris von der Brelie-Lewien, Hildesheim, Verlag August Lax, 1987, pp. 316–23.

Noelle-Neumann, Elisabeth, ed., *The Germans: Public Opinion Polls 1947–1966.* Allensbach, Verlag für Demoskopie, 1967.

Noelle-Neumann, Elisabeth, ed., *The Germans: Public Opinion Polls, 1967–1980.* Westport, Conn., Greenwood Press, 1981.

Ohliger, Rainer, 'Representing Ethnic Migrants – Comparing National Others, "Return" Migrants, "Repatriates" and Expellees in Dutch, French and German Post-war Textbooks', paper presented at the European Social Science History Association, Amsterdam, 2000.

Rautenberg, Hans Werner, 'Die Wahrnehmung von Flucht und Vertreibung in der deutschen Nachkriegsgeschichte', *Aus Politik und Zeitgeschichte B53/97,* 1997, pp. 34–46.

Reichling, Gerhard, *Die deutschen Vertriebenen in Zahlen.* Bonn, Kulturstiftung der Deutschen Vertriebenen, 1986.

Schillinger, Reinhold, 'Der Lastenausgleich', in *Die Vertreibung der Deutschen aus dem Osten,* ed. Wolfgang Benz. Frankfurt, Fischer, 1985, pp. 183–92.

Schlau, Wilfried, 'Die Eingliederung aus gesellschaftlicher Sicht', in *Aus Trümmern wurden Fundamente,* ed. Hans Joachim von Merkatz. Düsseldorf, Walter Rau Verlag, 1979.

Schönberg, Hans W., *Germans from the East, A Study of Their Migration, Resettlement, and Subsequent Group History since 1945.* The Hague, Martinus Nijhoff, 1970.

Schulze, Rainer, 'Growing Discontent, Relations between Native and Refugee Populations in a Rural District in Western Germany after the Second World War', in *West Germany under Construction, Politics, Society, and Culture in the Adenauer Era,* ed. Robert G, Moeller. Ann Arbor, University of Michigan Press, 1997, pp. 53–73.

Strothmann, Dieter 'Die Vertriebenen', in *Nach 25 Jahren, Eine Deutschland-Bilanz.* ed. Karl Dietrich Bracher. Munich, Kindler, 1970, pp. 300–21.

Weiss, Hermann, 'Die Organisationen der Vertriebenen und ihre Presse', in *Die Vertreibung der Deutschen aus dem Osten,* ed. Wolfgang Benz. Frankfurt, Fischer, 1985, pp. 193–208.

Chapter 2

The Struggle of Past and Present in Individual Identities: The Case of German Refugees and Expellees from the East

Rainer Schulze

At the end of the Second World War, millions of Germans lost their homes in Central, Eastern and Southeastern Europe. They either fled from the Red Army alongside or behind the retreating German troops and were not allowed to return after the end of the war, or they were officially expelled by the new authorities who now ruled these territories, and forcibly resettled into Potsdam Germany (the four zones of occupation) under the provisions of Article XIII of the Potsdam Agreement. Most came from areas where Germans had settled for generations, and they had developed strong regional identities, customs and dialects which differed quite significantly from those living within the borders of Potsdam Germany. The latter often regarded the Germans living further east as almost Slavs, even though the majority lived in areas which had been exclusively or predominantly settled by Germans, and many had little or no contact with non-German populations. In particular those from areas which had been part of interwar Poland, such as West Prussia and Posen, were classified as half Polish, but this notion often also included those German populations who lived in regions which had remained part of Germany after the Versailles peace settlement and which only became part of the new state of Poland after 1945, such as Pomerania and Silesia. It is estimated that approximately eleven to thirteen million Germans were affected by the compulsory transfer of population from east to west. By the end of 1950, when the expulsion measures had all but come to a close, approximately 16.5 percent of the population of the Federal Republic of Germany (the three western zones) and almost 25 percent of the population of the German Democratic Republic (the Soviet zone) were either refugees or expellees from outside the borders of Potsdam Germany (Frantzioch–Immenkeppel 1996: 5).

Obviously, this enormous influx of population caused huge problems for the receiving areas, and most urgent among them was providing the newcomers with accommodation, food and employment. In the years immediately after the war, the problems facing Germany as a result of this influx of millions of people were judged to be so serious that it was feared it might take a generation or more to overcome them, and contemporary observers predicted a volatile start for the new postwar German body politic. Yet, contrary to all these grave predictions, the newcomers were absorbed into the polity, economy and society of the two German states relatively quickly and without causing much, if any, political upheaval and radicalisation in the medium and long term. This fact is generally regarded as one of the great success stories of Germany's postwar history. The policies towards the refugees and expellees in Eastern Germany, where they were almost immediately referred to as *Umsiedler* (resettlers) and then as *Neubürger* (new citizens) by the new authorities, are set out in the next chapter. This chapter focuses on Western Germany, although its conclusions will go beyond it.

There was wide agreement amongst the Allies over the necessity of a forced resettlement of German populations east of the Oder–Neisse line after the end of the war; indeed, Churchill defended this policy publicly in a speech in the House of Commons as early as December 1944. The occupying powers considered the problem of the reception and integration of the German refugees and expellees as a purely internal German matter. They only organised and conducted the transfers of the refugees and expellees to the reception areas. All further responsibilities for dealing with the practical problems were delegated to the German authorities, and they were instructed to integrate the refugees and expellees as quickly as possible and to avoid any provisional measures and special treatment of the newcomers. The aim was their complete political, economic and social assimilation in the reception areas. Accommodation in camps was only allowed as a temporary emergency measure and a last resort. The old communal and regional associations of the newcomers, if they had survived flight and expulsion, were to be broken up by a deliberate dispersion of the refugees and expellees to different reception areas. This was to ensure that old identities and solidarities would disintegrate as quickly as possible and to prevent potentially unruly *irredentas* from emerging (Donnison 1961: 341, 351–2).

It was only when the Western powers became increasingly worried that the newcomers' discontent could lead to actual unrest in their zones and possibly make them 'an easy prey to Communist blandishments' (British Military Governor Brian Robertson, 26 February 1949, Public Record Office, [PRO], FO 1030/119), that the three Military Governors set up a Tripartite Working Commission on German Refugees in late 1948 (which later became a permanent committee under the Tripartite Board) to deal with the refugee problem in conjunction with the German authorities.

Apart from discussing the possible emigration of German refugees, the advice to the West German authorities was to bring about a marked improvement of the living conditions of the refugees and expellees by way of economic integration (PRO, FO 371/76533), a policy which the British Military Governor believed had obvious benefits: 'If the problem of economic integration can be solved, the political and psychological considerations would lose much of their importance' (Robertson, PRO, FO 1030/119). After the establishment of the Federal Republic this became the overall *leitmotif* of all measures taken in West Germany. When the economy started to take off in the 1950s, the refugees and expellees provided a much needed, highly motivated, mobile and flexible labour force, and with their increasing integration into the labour market, they also participated in the rising standard of living enjoyed by the majority of the population. On average, the newcomers remained always one step behind the natives, but the most pressing hardships of the refugees and expellees could be relieved during the general boom of the West German economy in the 1950s without much direct conflict. The improvement of the economic situation of the newcomers through employment, combined with some element of compensation for the losses sustained – an equalisation of burdens, as it became known – laid the foundations for the process by which native and refugee populations gradually grew together (Schulze 2000).

However, despite their active participation in the reconstruction of West Germany, refugees and expellees kept being officially referred to as *Vertriebene* (expellees) or even *Heimatvertriebene* (expellees from their homes), and during the period of the Cold War both the Western powers and the West German government found it opportune to support the hopes of many refugees and expellees that a return to their former homes would be possible. Official maps, including those used in schools, continued to show Germany with the borders of 31 December 1937 and labelled the territories east of the Oder–Neisse line as 'temporarily under Polish administration'. The West German government insisted that it required an official peace treaty for the definite settlement of Germany's postwar borders, and that until such a peace treaty was concluded the future of the territories east of the Oder–Neisse line had to be regarded as open under international law. In their manifestos and official speeches, refugee and expellee organisations, which had been allowed to form in the Western zones from the late 1940s, made propaganda for the right of the refugees and expellees to return to their homes in the east (*Recht auf Heimat*) and, with the exception of the Communists, all the main political parties and pressure groups officially supported this view (Schwartz 1997: 182–9).

The organisations of the refugees played an important role in the emerging Federal Republic. They often appeared quite radical in their public statements, but in the main this was verbal radicalism only. For all practical purposes they acted as pressure groups to improve the living conditions of their members. By the 1960s, and definitely by the 1970s, even though refugee organisations still continued to hold their rallies, it seemed that almost everywhere differences between the newcomers and the natives had all but disappeared, and that the *Heimatvertriebene* had become fully integrated into West German society, on an equal standing and with no significant difference to those people who had lived there for generations.

As far as political, economic and legal equality are concerned, this was certainly the case. However, important as it is, this only refers to their official status and not automatically to their social and mental reality as well. Interviews conducted with refugees and expellees from the East who are still alive today show that there are important areas where differences have remained between natives and newcomers. Among those differences which the refugees and expellees feel still set them apart as a group until the present day, more than fifty years after flight and expulsion, are the struggle of past and present in their individual identities, and the difficulty of constructing a comprehensive life narrative which not only combines the two, but which they feel they can link to a common narrative of the receiving areas.

The extensive historiography on the integration, or absorption, of the refugees and expellees into the polity, economy and society of postwar Western Germany has focused mainly on the political, economic and legal aspects and the impact the influx of people had on the receiving areas (Lemberg and Edding 1959; Frantzioch 1987; Krallert-Sattler 1996). As a result, the individual memories and specific experiences of the refugees and expellees have remained largely ignored or discussed only in so far as they counteracted or delayed the process of integration. By maintaining that a full integration has taken place historiography has so far – consciously or unconsciously – not offered this population group a proper place in the collective history of the receiving areas in the West.

Based on fieldwork carried out in *Landkreis* Celle, a rural district in northwest Germany,[1] this chapter argues that despite all apparent success in their lives in the West, which makes the refugees and expellees today appear just like the natives, the experience of their forced loss of home and their struggles to settle into a completely new environment is something that is still very prevalent in the life of those who had to undergo it, and that many find that it continues to have an important bearing on their lives and keep them different from the natives. The chapter is based on narrative interviews and other testimonies of refugees and expellees who were born east of the Oder–Neisse line, were forced to leave their homes – either by flight or expulsion – at the end of the Second World War, and eventually settled in *Landkreis* Celle. Since all of them are still alive, no one over the age of forty at the time of flight and expulsion is included; the oldest was born in 1906, the youngest in 1940. In order to protect their anonymity, the names of the refugees and expellees whose testimonies are quoted here have been replaced by letters.[2]

Professional Careers

Almost all refugees and expellees interviewed in *Landkreis* Celle did achieve something with their lives in the West and were relatively success-ful in their professional careers. Indeed, they were probably more suc-cessful, in material terms, than they would have been had they not been forced to leave their old homes in the East. Herr I. is in no doubt about this: 'We would have never been able to achieve there what we achieved here ... From that point of view it was actually a good thing that we were forced to leave ... Almost 99 percent had better chances here than they would have had at home.' Quite a number became teachers, others re-established their businesses from the East in Celle, or became respected craftsmen, such as roofers, car mechanics or joiners. One refugee took over the local refuse collection in the village where he settled, another one ran, as a leaseholder, all the canteens on the military premises of Faßberg in the north of the *Landkreis*. Many also achieved leading positions in voluntary work, such as Herr D., who became the leader of the local postal workers' union, or Frau C., who is still active in the community work of the local church and in the Red Cross. The vast majority gained a reasonable level of prosperity so that now, after fifty years, there is little if any difference in terms of material well-being as compared to the native population. Many refugees and expellees built their own houses in the late 1950s or 1960s, or bought their own flats; many have children who went to university and received an academic degree – all of these things are generally taken as an indication that the integration was successful.

However, even though the majority of the refugees and expellees became respectable and respected *Neubürger* in *Landkreis* Celle and were, from today's standpoint, reasonably successful in their 'new' lives after flight and expulsion, they themselves do not always share this view when looking back. Instead, many point out that they were not able to find employment in their old professions and had to retrain; others emphasise that they had to commute in order to get to their workplaces – and they stress that this made them different from most of the native population. Whilst these forms of work-mobility are regarded as normal today, they were seen as quite exceptional at that time; in the 1950s there was still talk of a 'stopgap job', or a 'fallback job' whereas the ideal was that of lifelong 'job loyalty'. Many refugees and expellees, therefore, regard their new jobs as some form of social decline, even though most express pride in what they achieved nonetheless. Many also cite lack of job prospects and fewer chances of promotion in comparison with the natives; or the fact that they are convinced that they had to work much harder than the natives in order to enjoy the same benefits. The interviews also show the emphasis which refugees and expellees put on education, if not for themselves then at least for their children, in order to get ahead again: 'That was something which I impressed upon my children from the cradle,' says Frau C., for example, 'we cannot give you anything else but the chance of a decent education. After all, we didn't have anything ourselves here in Celle – no connections, no money, no influence.'

Social and Mental Situation

Many refugees also point out that admission to the natives' associations, in particular to the prestigious voluntary fire brigade associations, village church choirs, rifle associations and bowling clubs which were important in the social life of rural areas, was only granted hesitantly, and that in some places these traditional bastions of native rural elites often remained closed to them for decades. In fact, even today when entry is open to all of these associations, distinctions are sometimes still made. Herr O., who was born in 1938 in Bobersberg (today Bobrowice) in Neumark, eastern Brandenburg, and who has lived in the same village in *Landkreis* Celle since his arrival with his family in February 1945, recalls an incident during the annual prize shooting in his local rifle association (*Schützenverein*) only four or five years ago: 'I, too, was going strong, as were a number of natives, and then a lady came up to me whom I actually knew quite well, and said, I should go a bit easy: after all, the natives should become *Schützenkönig* (champion marksman) first, and I wasn't a real Beedenbostler, but – well, she didn't say refugee, but I wasn't a real Beedenbostler, and therefore I should let the natives go first if they wanted to become *Schützenkönig*.' In the end, Herr O. actually did not try as hard as he could have done in the final round, and he did not become *Schützenkönig*. He is married to a native and considers himself well integrated into the life of the village, 'but when there's actually something at stake, that one could perhaps be a bit more in the public eye, then there are still people who are envious, and then references to the time of flight and expulsion are still being made ... That is so, and there are also other things where one senses that.'

Other utterances still underline that many refugees and expellees continue to feel that, despite all apparent success in their lives in the West after flight and expulsion, it still makes a difference that they were not born in the region where they live now. There is still a lingering feeling that they have remained somewhat a stranger, an outsider, not quite 'belonging' there. This can be traced back to experiences right after their arrival in the West. Almost all remember in great detail how difficult it was to settle in *Landkreis* Celle. Frau C., for example, reports: 'We were strangers, and they did not accept us. But the difference was that they did not know where Breslau was, but we knew about the Lüneburg Heath – Herman Löns, that was something we had learnt in school.'[3] The refugees and expellees not only realised very quickly, in their first encounters with the natives of *Landkreis* Celle, that they were regarded as different and, therefore, inferior – Frau C. also recalls that she and her family were often called 'Polacken' (a common German word of abuse for the Poles) – but they gave it a positive twist: yes, they were different, but instead of inferior they were actually superior to the natives; they were better educated, they had a better sense of German history and traditions, and the natives in the rural regions in the West were only too backward and unsophisticated themselves to realise this. Or, as Herr K. put it in a speech commemorating the fiftieth anniversary of the day when the German population fled from Kreis Altburgund-Schubin (today Szubin) in the Wartheland (the old Prussian province of Posen): 'Remember, there we were not only the farmers from Groß-Nebau or Schubin, we were Germans. Yes, we were not only Germans, we were Europeans, we were the Occident.' ('Der 21. Januar 1945' 1995: 5–6)

Memory and Loss

It is the difference in experience and memory which is the most important aspect setting off the refugees and expellees on the one hand against the natives on the other. Apart from the memory of the the difficult new beginning after 1945, almost all refugees and expellees still have very vivid memories of their flight and expulsion and of the atrocities and the hardships which they suffered – memories and experiences which they feel they could not, and still cannot, really share with the natives in rural Celle. All refugees and expellees interviewed in *Landkreis* Celle also have distinct and extremely detailed memories of their former homes in the East, including those who were still children at the time of flight or expulsion. These memories are basically positive. They remember the house or the flat they grew up in, the church, the school, the tree with the swing in the garden, the playgrounds, the meadows and the forests where they played, their parents' allotments where some spent many afternoons in the summer, the way to the zoo. Herr M. explains: 'It is part of one's self. One does not have to "preserve" it – it is simply there. It does not require any effort.' Similarly, Frau L. states: 'In my mind I still often walk the old paths and streets which I am pretty sure have changed beyond recognition now.' These are, of course, to a certain extent normal childhood memories, but for most the memories of their homes go further than this and include elements which are quite specific to their region of origin – the particular landscape, the 'high skies', the different climate, the regional dialect, the food and special dishes and recipes, the peculiar ways of communicating and socialising – all of which they associate with the warmth, familiarity and security of home, of *Heimat*.

For the majority it took until the late 1940s or even early 1950s before they began to accept that their loss of home was not temporary but permanent and that it would be impossible to return there. Their reaction to this realisation was usually one of sadness and resignation, but many mention that this also mobilised new energies and the will to become their own masters again, if not in their former homes, then at least in their new environment. They were determined to improve their material situation as quickly as possible or, as Frau C. put it, 'to roll up our sleeves, work and make sure that we get out of this desperate situation again.'

Even though most refugees and expellees succeeded in doing this, most state now that they had to pay a price for this which natives in a similar position of economic hardship did not have to. 'We had to adapt', says Frau F. 'I simply gave up [many of my habits and customs]. If I have got to live here, I just have to conform to the people here.' Herr K. adds, 'We were glad that we had saved our lives.' However, many now feel, especially since reaching retirement age, that despite all their economic success something is missing. As Frau E. put it, 'Material possessions were there, that's what I had worked hard for – but I wasn't really able to relate to them.'

Most if not all believe that the region where they were born has left some form of an impression upon them, even though they left this region more than fifty years ago, and that they have kept until today certain qualities or peculiarities from their region of origin. Almost all state, for example, that they still regularly, and in particular for special occasions, use recipes from their region of origin when cooking and baking. Many refugees and expellees also affirm that they have kept certain customs and rituals which they had brought with them. Nearly as often articulation and ways of speaking are mentioned. Frau S. adds: 'In Lower Silesia, people used to chat quite a bit, and that's something I still do today – unlike most natives here.' Quite a few have not completely lost their regional accent until the present day, and there are those, such as Herr I., who still speak their specific German dialect when meeting with relatives or friends from their former homes: 'Then we speak our mother tongue which is something the natives can't comprehend.' On the other hand, there are very few refugees and expellees who have learnt to speak the type of Low German which is particular to the Celle region, even though most understand it now.

Flight and expulsion also meant that for most their old village communities and neighbourhoods were torn apart. School friends, neighbours, the family doctor, the pastor, the keeper of the corner shop – they were now likely to be scattered all over the four zones of occupation, and the individual refugees and expellees lost the social networks in which they had grown up. Many mention that even today they still feel somewhat envious that most of their native neighbours have these networks, which not only provide important social and emotional support but can also be of importance in terms of connections and influence. To make up for this, almost all refugees and expellees tried to trace and keep in touch with their relatives, former neighbours and friends after their arrival in the West. Many joined refugee organisations, like the *Landsmannschaften*, the *Bund der Ver-*

triebenen or the various *Heimatvereine* (associations of refugees and expellees coming from the same district) when those were allowed to be formed in Western Germany in the late 1940s or early 1950s, in order to meet other people from their region of origin and exchange memories as well as news, or attended the so-called *Heimattreffen*. The vast majority still subscribe today to the newsletter of their region of origin. However, overall this also contributed to keeping them 'different', or at least to a certain extent separate, from the natives, who often regarded the refugee organisations as somewhat inward-looking and peculiar.

Most refugees and expellees not only have their memories of their old homes in the East; the majority have been back to their regions of origin for a visit at least once. Some went as soon as such visits became possible in the early 1970s, and quite a few have been back many more times. For most, these visits were full of emotions and left a lasting impression. The first reaction was usually sadness, often mixed with anger, which then generally gave way to feelings of joy, happiness and gratitude which most found difficult to describe. Herr H., born in 1933 in a small village near Bromberg (today Bydgoszcz), says simply: 'This meant a great deal to me', and his wife, who grew up in a neighbouring village, recalls that the only thought she had was: 'This is so beautiful here!'

Even more than fifty years after flight and expulsion, more than half of all the refugees and expellees interviewed in Landkreis Celle still consider as their home – their Heimat – the place where they were born. Frau B., for example, who was born in 1926 in Marienwerder (today Kwidzyn), declares without hesitation: 'My home is Marienwerder.' Herr M., who was born in 1924 in Schmenzin (today Smecino) in Pomerania, leaves no doubt either: 'I am a Pomeranian – of course! ... New roots are not possible, they only exist there.' Herr I., who was born in 1928 in Brigidau, Galicia, says just as clearly: 'I am a Galician ... For me, there is only one home, and that is Galicia ... One has grown old here [*Landkreis* Celle], the children were born here, one has built up something for the children here, but somehow one is still very attached to it [Galicia]. One simply cannot give it up so easily ... It is similar to birds of passage; they, too, always return to their place of origin.'

For some, it was only when they visited their place of birth again that they realised that this was still their home. Frau E., born in 1934 in Bartenstein (today Bartoszyce) in East Prussia, waited until 1990 before she felt ready to go back to Bartenstein for a visit, and even then she would not go alone and took two friends with her. She visited the old Lutheran church where her father had been choirmaster, and one of her friends was allowed to play the organ: 'And this was when I realised that this was home for me, when she [her friend] played the organ ... This was the first time that I truly felt, this is home.' She needed a second visit, one year later, before she could actually visit the house where she and her family had lived before their flight. She was led around the house where she grew up by the Polish family who live there today. She still weeps when she recalls, seven years after this visit: 'And then, when I left, I could not help crying. And then it was so nice of this Pole, at this moment he put his arm around me, like a friend and protector. And it was only then that I finally said goodbye to my old home, at that very moment, I am pretty sure of that.' For her, it is now clear: 'I have found my home. I have found it again, but it was only at this point that I recognised that this really is where my home is ... It did not matter to me that this was now Poland or whatever, it was simply my home. Other people live there now who speak a different language; it is a different country, but it remains my home, my emotional home.' For Herr R., who was born in 1931 in Petrigau (today Piotrków Borowski) in Silesia, the experience was similar. He deliberately waited with his first visit to Silesia until 1985 when he felt he would be able to go back just like a normal tourist, but when he arrived there he felt like fifteen or sixteen again and it was as if the forty years he had spent in the West were completely eradicated: 'I wanted to continue where I had left off [in 1945–6].' Like Frau E., he confirmed: 'You know, it was really only then that I realised fully that I did not have any emotional ties here [to Celle]. Only when I was back home in Silesia in 1985 did I realise fully what emotional ties really mean.' He had 'somehow' felt before, deep inside, that his real home was still Silesia, but it took this visit to make this clearly visible: 'I had no idea what effect this still had, how deeply implanted it is still in me.'

Others feel not quite as strongly about their place of birth in the East, but their utterances, too, show that that they are still attached to it in some way or other. Herr N., who was born in 1930 in Steinau/Oder (today Scinawa) in Silesia and who has become a respected local historian of Celle, calls himself 'a Lower Saxon who was born in Silesia', and Frau A., who was born in 1938 in Königsberg (today Kaliningrad), similarly defines herself as 'a naturalised East Prussian'. Others use words such as *Rucksack-Celler* (alluding to the fact that they had arrived in Celle with little more than a backpack or a suitcase) or *Beute-Celler* (describing themselves as Celle's war booty).

There is hardly anyone who answers the question as to whether they have become a Celler with an unqualified and unreserved 'Yes'. Frau G., born in 1926 in Stolp (today Slupsk) in Pomerania does say, 'For me, Eschede [a small place in *Landkreis* Celle] has become my home, even though it has been difficult. Today you would not be able to make me move again.' However, she adds immediately: 'But somehow one is still a bit of an outsider ... One does not belong here 100 percent.' Herr D., the leader of the postal workers' union in Kreis Celle for many years, fudges the issue in a way which is typical for many refugees and expellees: 'Actually, I would say that I feel more or less European ... Well, German, yes, but more towards European. But Celler? No ... I like it in Celle, Celle is a nice town. ... But I cannot really say that I feel rooted in Celle in one way or another, that it is only Celle and nothing else, no, I don't think so, not really.'

Old Home versus New World

For all, even for those who state that they have found new roots and a new home in *Landkreis* Celle, the old home in the East is still very much present and plays an important part in their lives, and this sets them apart, as a group, from the natives up until the present day. Even Herr P., who was only born in 1940, admits that no matter how much he considers himself a 'real' Lower Saxon there is still something else making up his identity. His parents had to leave Galicia, where the family had lived since the late eighteenth century, after the Hitler–Stalin Pact, and were eventually resettled in a small village near Dietfurt (today Znin) in the Wartheland. He himself was born in Saaz (today Zatec) in the Sudetenland when his parents were still in a transit camp for Galician expellees there. In early 1945, when he had not even turned five, they fled to Hambühren in *Landkreis* Celle. And still, when he went back to the place of his childhood in 1987, he had the feeling of 'having returned somehow', and he concludes that, perhaps unconsciously, he still has some roots in this region where he spent the first years of his childhood. At the same time he still feels strong affinities to his parents' Galician heritage; for example, until the death of his father they still spoke their regional dialect at home. For many years, he was the chairman of the choral society of Hambühren, the oldest association in the village, which had been founded in 1869, but even now he has not learnt to speak the regional dialect, the Celler *Platt*. This peculiar feeling of simultaneousness of the 'old' home, which exists in memory, family traditions and in a distant country, and the 'new' home, which even after more than fifty years still holds some degree of strangeness, this multiple intertwining of past and present so typical for many refugees and expellees, is summed up by Frau L. when she says that she considers Lustgarten (Wesolkach), which was part of Poland when she was born in 1928, her home (Heimat), because this is the place where she grew up. However, after living here for more than fifty years, she now feels at home (*zuhause*) in *Landkreis* Celle.

The interviews demonstrate that, despite all the outward successes which make the refugees and expellees appear just like the natives, the integration and assimilation in the West, the new *Heimat*, has not yet been fully achieved and probably never will be. There are, of course, big differences as to how much the refugees and expellees remained in their 'old world' and how far they fitted into their 'new world'. However, independent of the degree of their adaptation or lack of it, it holds true for all refugees and expellees that their former homes and the forced loss of these were a formative influence, and moulded their identities up until the present day. What is different is only the overall importance that this experience holds in their lives, how much it overshadowed their new lives in the West, and how scarred and complicated their life biographies became because of this. For some, the memories of their old home are merely memories of their childhood and youth which come back to them more vividly and about which they tend to speak more often now that they have reached old age, but which they do not necessarily regard as harrowing any more. For others, however, they still today represent injury and pain, and some even explain their lack of self-confidence by this forced break in their biography which denied them the chance to live the kind of life which they had seen mapped out for them as children. Frau A., for example, who became a vocational teacher in Celle, is convinced that if flight and expulsion had not happened to her, 'I could have become a secondary school teacher with a better salary. I also think that with my talents I could have done something in the area of interior design or something like that – I could have pursued a completely different career. In that respect, I am sure, war has left its mark on me which is still today branded somewhere on me.'

Dimensions of Identity

Owing to the loss of their original home and the necessity of settling into a new environment, 'region' has lost importance for the make-up of their identity for many refugees and expellees. They point out that they are now much less tied to a region than natives of the same age, and they define themselves much more through their profession and their personal interests or through their family networks, which for many refugees and expellees seem to have taken the place of 'home'. From today's perspective the experience of the refugees and expellees can be seen as an anticipation of a general social development, caused by (often forced) work-mobility, which is characterised by an increasing loss of a sense of 'home' (*Heimatverlust*) and a 'de-regionalisation' of identity (Krockow 1989: 40–50). However, as the forerunners in this general social development the refugees and expellees were basically left on their own to come to terms with this and to make some sense of it. This happened to a large extent out of overriding political considerations which were perhaps well meant, but ultimately misplaced. Both in the period of the Cold War as well as in the following period of *détente*, it was not only the grief itself over the loss of their 'old' home which remained a purely private matter, but also the ways of dealing with this grief which remained private as postwar German society, both West and East, did not offer the refugees and expellees any collective patterns or 'cushions' for dealing with this kind of experience. They had to come to terms with the loss of their former homes almost outside the public domain.

In the Federal Republic, the formation of refugees and expellee organisations was encouraged, almost all West German towns and districts were twinned with a town or district in the former German territories east of the Oder–Neisse line (*Patenschaften*),[4] and the *Bundesvertriebenengesetz* (Federal Expellee Act) of 1953 included a provision (paragraph 96) which placed an obligation on the federal government and the state governments to preserve the German cultural heritage of the refugees' and expellees' regions of origins. However, whilst special museums and research institutes for the history of the Germans in Central and Eastern Germany, as well as various *Heimattreffen* and general cultural activities of the refugees and expellees, were funded under this programme, the commitment remained superficial and hardly more than formal. The overall result was not the establishment of some form of shared past of native and refugee population; instead, it meant that the experience and memory of the refugees and expellees could be shunted off into a special niche, separated from the generally accepted collective history of Western Germany which was basically that of the natives. At the same time it gave the native society the comforting feeling it was doing its bit to acknowledge the past of the refugees and expellees.[5]

As far as the natives were concerned, it was taken for granted and almost expected, even though it was never explicitly stated, that in the course of their successful settling into postwar Germany the refugees and expellees would give up, or 'shed' the old collective identities and mentalities as well as the specific experiences and individual memories which they brought with them from the East. When representatives of the refugees and expellees, like Peter Paul Nahm, insisted that 'wealth and economic advancement are no compensation for home, justice and all the real and metaphysical things connected with this sphere of our order ... The assumption or expectation that the home of an individual can be replaced by general economic advancement is a fallacy borne out of a purely materialistic outlook on life' (Nahm 1959: 153), they were often all called 'cold warriors' and 'revanchists' and located on the right wing of the political spectrum, and they were also accused of being totally out of touch with reality, especially since the 1960s when the period of *détente* was ushered in.

However, utterances like these already indicated that the pain and injuries which the refugees and expellees suffered with the forced loss of their old homes in the East, and the mental and emotional problems caused by the experience of flight and expulsion remained – and often still remain – very real despite an overall 'successful' political and economic integration. They continued to have an impact on the life biographies of those affected by this experience, and could not be overcome by the political measures passed and enacted since the late 1940s alone. The old collective identities and mentalities, the specific experiences and individual memories which the refugees and expellees, to a varying degree, brought with them from their former homes did not disappear or wither away the longer they stayed in their new environment. They lingered on and, while the pain and injuries which the refugees and expellees suffered with the forced loss of their old homes in the East could perhaps be marginalised or even suppressed by such a 'politically correct' attitude towards the utterances of refugee representatives like Nahm, there was no serious attempt to come to terms with, and accept, the specific experiences and individual memories of the refugees and expellees as an integral part of German public memory. Herr R., since 1988 the chairman of the local group of the *Bund der Vertriebenen* in Celle, affirms this when he says he regrets that the native population hardly goes to those cultural events which the refugees and expellees put on in Celle to celebrate their heritage from the East, whereas their own cultural events celebrating the local heritage are well attended, by natives and refugees and expellees alike. He finds it 'quite sad' that Lower Saxony was not more ready to take in the culture of the former homes of the refugees and expellees, and he would like the natives 'to be more open' and to make more of an effort 'to take note of the culture and heritage of those who came to Celle after the end of the Second World War ... to take note of the whole of German history, not only the history of one side.'

Such a demand by refugees and expellees has often been branded as just another form of revisionism or revanchism, but Herr P. emphasises that for him this accusation is only a lame but often welcome excuse for the natives to shy away from including the refugees and expellees in a commonly shared past. He says he cannot understand 'that today Breslau and Königsberg and Stettin and all these cities – Danzig – which have a German heritage that goes back centuries – that this all of a sudden is not to be the case any more.' He stresses he finds it important 'that one keeps alive the memory, that one makes people aware of how it was ... What I find very distressing is that it is automatically assumed that one has a desire for revenge or something like that – that is absolutely not true!' Many refugees and expellees feel hurt when they are officially told that they were born in Wroclaw (rather than Breslau) or Kwidzyn (rather than Marienwerder), and they regard this as an attempt to deny them their personal history. As Herr P. points out: 'The only thing I mean is that what one should not do to people is to take away their history – that must not happen! That one simply, as is the case in the schools, does not teach about it, that the children do not even know any more that there was something like Königsberg – and that is, in my opinion, taking away history, and that is bad, that must not be done.' On the one hand, this failure to incorporate the historical experience of all sections of the population into the overall public memory makes it impossible for the refugees and expellees to connect their personal past to the collectively acknowledged past of the German nation. Not surprisingly, many still feel they do not really 'belong', and it might also go some way to explain why their representatives often react with slogans and demands which seem to confirm all suspicions of revisionism and revanchism. On the other hand, this failure also denies the natives a chance to acknowledge the enrichment of the social, cultural and mental fabric of the receiving areas, both positively and negatively, which the influx of the refugees and expellees brought about, and which had an important impact on their lives as well.

Conclusion

Landkreis Celle is by no means an exceptional case. There are indications in other studies which point in a similar direction (Wagnerová 1990; Lehmann 1991; Müller-Handl 1993; see also Schulze 1997). The findings for *Landkreis* Celle highlight the general phenomenon that so far the specific experiences and memories of the refugees and expellees have largely remained excluded from the common German historical consciousness and collective memory. The newcomers were expected to integrate into the German postwar polity, economy and society without being offered a proper place in the collective history of the receiving areas. The collective consciousness of postwar Germany was shaped (and narrowed) still further by the political necessities of first the Cold War and then the period of *détente*, which meant that the refugees and expellees had even less of a chance of their experiences and memories becoming a part of it.

During the period of the Cold War the biographies of the refugees and expellees were reduced to the themes of flight and expulsion, and in Western Germany their suffering was instrumentalised to emphasise that Germans, too, were victims of the Second World War and that the crimes committed against them were in some way comparable to the crimes committed against the Jews (Moeller 1996: 1,017–32; Schwartz 1997: 189–94). Representations of refugees and expellees in popular films similarly reduced them to people who were innocent victims and lost everything in 1945 but ultimately settled successfully in a new home in the west (Bliersbach 1985: Schraut 1996: 367–73; 32–49; Wilharm 1998). It is only this aspect of their biographies that became part of West Germany's public memory. With the onset of *détente* even this theme was regarded as increasingly embarrassing and therefore discarded and renounced as 'revanchist'; once again the real memories of the refugees and expellees were subordinated to political considerations (Rautenberg 1997: 35–40).

The vast majority of refugees and expellees settled successfully in postwar Germany and played an important part in the development of both Western and Eastern Germany since 1945. What has been widely overlooked, or even consciously ignored, is the fact that in this process the cultural assets and values and the specific experiences of the refugees and expellees became de facto part of the historical roots of the Federal Republic, albeit without being incorporated into the public memory, without being consciously and properly acknowledged. This lack of acknowledgement was all the easier because for a long time the majority of the refugees and expellees themselves were more concerned with re-establishing their lives in the West and getting their share in the general affluence of postwar German society than with drawing attention to the fact that they were a section of the population with historical experiences and individual memories which were different from those of the natives.

Today's German society is a society of natives *and* refugees and expellees, and the heritage of the refugees' and expellees' regions of origin is an integral part of the overall German heritage, even though Germany's political boundaries do not include these territories any longer. This means that the experiences and memories of the refugees and expellees are just as much part of the historical roots of the Federal Republic as those of the natives. This fact still needs to be incorporated into a new consciousness of the foundations of the German body politic, a consciousness which would then finally comprise the whole of the German heritage but in such a way that it constitutes a 'founding myth' which no longer threatens any of Germany's neighbours. This would also mean a further step towards not only accepting the effects of war and defeat superficially or rationally, but whole-heartedly and emotionally as well.[6] A history of the refugees and expellees which is not revanchist or revisionist in character, but which does take the specific heritage and the individual and collective experience and pain of the refugees and expellees seriously, could make an important contribution to such a change in the foundations and character of the German state.

It seems that the majority of the German refugees and expellees who are still alive today are not only ready for such a changed consciousness and the resulting 'broadened' public memory, but more often than not have already travelled some distance along that path. As Frau B. put it: 'We are, after all, the bridge between those who live there now and those who are here in the West. If we do not build and preserve the bond and continuity between the two, who else would be able to do this?' Indications are that it is mainly the natives who still have to come to terms with this.

Notes

1. Landkreis Celle is situated north of Hanover on the southern edge of the Lüneburg Heath in what is today the federal state of Lower Saxony (Niedersachsen). From early 1945, large numbers of German refugees from the eastern territories began to enter the Landkreis, and by April 1948 there were more than 42,000 refugees and expellees from the territories east of the Oder–Neisse line in Landkreis Celle (including Stadt Celle), compared to a 'native' population of about 86,000. Today, refugees and expellees, or their descendants, still make up more than a third of the population of this district. Landkreis Celle can be regarded as a typical (rural) reception area of refugees and expellees in Western Germany. For more detail see Schulze 1991: 13–47.

2. The letters used here correlate with those used in Schulze 1997.

3. Hermann Löns (1866–1914) is the most famous poet of the Lüneburg Heath. He was actually born in Culm (today Chelmno), which belonged to West Prussia from 1772/1814 until 1920.

4. *Landkreis* Celle was twinned with *Kreis* Belgard in Pomerania, and it set up the *Heimatarchiv* Belgard-Schivelbein which still exists today and collects documents, photographs and other materials relating to the history of the district of Belgard.

5. On this point I disagree with Robert G. Moeller who argues in his otherwise very thoughtful discussion that the testimonies of the refugees and expellees became part of West Germany's public

memory (Moeller, 1996: 1021; see also Schwartz 1997: 188–9, 193, and Rautenberg 1997: 34–46, esp. 37).

6. Richard von Weizsäcker, President of the Federal Republic of Germany 1984–94, had already included a short reference to that respect in his speech of 8 May 1985 commemorating the fortieth anniversary of Hitler-Germany's unconditional surrender and the end of the Second World War (Weizsäcker 1994: 48–50; see also Grebing 1987: 2).

References

Primary Sources

Taped narrative interviews with German refugees and expellees from the East, in possession of the author.

'Der 21. Januar 1945. Ansprache unseres Kreisältesten auf der Jahreshauptversammlung des Heimatkreises am 21. Januar 1995 in Bergen, Kreis Celle', typed Manuscript, 1995, in possession of the author.

Public Record Office, Kew/London (PRO): FO 371, FO 1005, FO 1030.

Books and Articles

Bliersbach, Gerhard, *So grün war die Heide. Der deutsche Nachkriegsfilm in neuer Sicht.* Weinheim, 1985.
Donnison, F.S.V., *Civil Affairs and Military Government North-West Europe 1944–1946.* London, 1961.
Frantzioch, Marion, *Die Vertriebenen. Hemmnisse, Antriebskräfte und Wege ihrer Integration in der Bundesrepublik Deutschland. Mit einer kommentierten Bibliographie.* Berlin, 1987.
Frantzioch-Immenkeppel, Marion, 'Die Vertriebenen in der Bundesrepublik Deutschland', *Aus Politik und Zeitgeschichte* Heft B 28/96 (1996), pp. 3–13.
Grebing, Helga, 'Begrüßung und Einführung in das Symposion', in *Flüchtlinge und Vertriebene in der westdeutschen Nachkriegsgeschichte,* ed. Rainer Schulze, Helga Grebing and Doris von der Brelie-Lewien. Hildesheim, 1987, pp. 1–5.
Krallert-Sattler, Gertrud, 'Kommentierte Auswahlbibliographie zur neuzeitlichen Geschichte des Ost- und Südostdeutschtums bis zum Zusammenbruch 1944/45 und zum Vertriebenen- und Flüchtlingsproblem in West- und Mitteldeutschland (Literatur 1987–1995)', in Die Ostdeutschen. Eine dokumentarische Bilanz *1945–1995,* ed. Wilfried Schlau, Munich, 1996, pp. 183–279.
Krockow, Christian Graf von, *Heimat. Erfahrungen mit einem deutschen Thema,* 2nd edn. Stuttgart, 1989.
Lehmann, Albrecht, *Im Fremden ungewollt zuhaus. Flüchtlinge und Vertriebene in Westdeutschland 1945–1990.* Munich, 1991.
Lemberg, Eugen and Edding, Friedrich (eds), *Die Vertriebenen in Westdeutschland. Ihre Eingliederung und ihr Einfluß auf Gesellschaft, Wirtschaft, Politik und Geistesleben,* 3 vols., Kiel, 1959.
Moeller, Robert G., 'War Stories: The Search for a Usable Past in the Federal Republic of Germany', *American Historical Review* 101 (1996), pp. 1,008–48.
Müller-Handl, Utta, *'Die Gedanken laufen oft zurück ...' Flüchtlingsfrauen erinnern sich an ihr Leben in Böhmen und Mähren und an den Neuanfang in Hessen nach 1945,* Wiesbaden, 1993.
Nahm, Peter Paul, 'Der Wille zur Eingliederung und seine Förderung', in *Die Vertriebenen in Westdeutschland. Ihre Eingliederung und ihr Einfluß auf Gesellschaft, Wirtschaft, Politik und Geistesleben,* ed. Eugen Lemberg and Friedrich Edding, vol. 1. Kiel, 1959, pp. 145–55.
Rautenberg, Hans-Werner, 'Die Wahrnehmung von Flucht und Vertreibung in der deutschen Nachkriegsgeschichte bis heute', *Aus Politik und Zeitgeschichte* Heft B 53/97 (1997), pp. 34–46.

Schraut, Sylvia, 'Das Flüchtlingsbild im westdeutschen Nachkriegsfilm der Besatzungszeit', in *Die Flüchtlingsfrage in der deutschen Nachkriegsgesellschaft*, ed. Sylvia Schraut and Thomas Grosser. Mannheim, 1996, pp. 349–75.

Schulze, Rainer, 'Growing Discontent: Relations between Native and Refugee Populations in a Rural District in Western Germany after the Second World War', *German History* 7: 3 (1989), pp. 332–49 (reprinted in *West Germany under Construction. Politics, Society and Culture in the Adenauer Era*, ed. Robert G. Moeller. Ann Arbor, Michigan, 1997, pp. 53–72).

Schulze, Rainer, 'Nachkriegsleben in einem ländlichen Raum', in *Unruhige Zeiten. Erlebnisberichte aus dem Landkreis Celle 1945–1949*, ed. Rainer Schulze, 2nd edn. Munich, 1991, pp. 13–47.

Schulze, Rainer, 'Alte Heimat – neue Heinat – oder heimatlos dazwischen? Zur Frage der regionalen Identität deutscher Flüchtlinge und Vertriebener – Eine Skizze', *Nordost-Archiv* N.F. 6 (1997), pp. 759–87.

Schulze, Rainer, 'The Newcomers from the East and the Creation of a Western German Identity', in *Expulsion, Settlement, Integration, Transformation: The Consequences of Forced Migration for the post-war History of Central and Eastern Europe*, ed. Philipp Ther and Ana Siljak. Boulder, CO, 2000.

Schwartz, Michael, 'Vertreibung und Vergangenheitspolitik. Ein Versuch über geteilte deutsche Nachkriegsidentitäten', *Deutschland-Archiv* 30 (1997), pp. 177–95.

Wagnerová, Alena, *1945 waren sie Kinder: Flucht und Vertreibung im Leben einer Generation*. Cologne, 1990.

Weizsäcker, Richard von, *Demokratische Leidenschaft: Reden des Bundespräsidenten*, ed. Eberhard Jäckel. Stuttgart, 1994.

Wilharm, Irmgard, 'Der Heimatfilm in Niedersachsen', in *Von der Währungsreform zum Wirtschaftswunder. Wiederaufbau in Niedersachsen*, ed. Bernd Weisbrod. Hanover, 1998, pp. 47–56.

Chapter 3

Expellee Policy in the Soviet-occupied Zone and the GDR: 1945–1953[1]

Philipp Ther

After the Second World War, the GDR (earlier the Soviet-occupied Zone) was the state in Europe most affected by the flight of refugees and expellees. By 1948, when the massive shifts in population were to a great extent already over, expellees made up almost one quarter of the entire population in the Soviet Zone. This exerted an influence on politics and society in the GDR right up to its demise, but above all in the 1950s. Deep divisions, not only amongst the various social classes as in other countries, but between people of different origin marked its society.

The presence of 4.3 million expellees changed society as well as politics. Already in 1945, the government was forced to react spontaneously to the huge influx of people and to consider their long-term integration. The means of achieving this were above all an active social policy, the redistribution of accommodation and land reform. This was not only a step towards communism, as the West later claimed, but was also intended to help integrate the expellees. The latter also played an important part in GDR foreign policy and in establishing the state's identity. True, as the smaller of the two German states, the GDR did not have legitimacy as a nation-state anyway, but because of, amongst other things, the expellees in their country, the Communists were not able to instrumentalise nationalism for their particular ends as the Polish Workers Party did. That would have immediately strengthened the desire of expellees to return to their old homes and also raised doubts about the Oder–Neisse border. Recognition of the latter in 1950 met with more opposition than any of the other political measures taken by the young GDR. However, despite the great burden which the expellees did become, the government profited from their presence in other respects. As Krystyna Kersten (1991: 308 and 318) has shown in the case of Poland, the instability and lack of cohesion in postwar society facilitated the establishment of Communist power. This finding also applies to the Soviet Zone/GDR. Moreover, as in West Germany, the expellees provided the reservoir of workers needed to support the dynamic reconstruction of industry in the 1950s.

But we are here less concerned with the significance of the expellee problem for the Soviet Zone/GDR than with policies employed to deal with expellees. These can be divided into three areas: social-charitable, redistributive and social-revolutionary policies. With its social-charitable policy, the government tried above all to alleviate the greatest hardships of the expellees. The redistributive policy sought to pass on property directly from indigenous Germans to expellees, in order to address the latters' immediate needs for accommodation. With social-revolutionary policy, measures taken to integrate expellees were directly linked to radical changes in the prevailing order such as the land reform. For purposes of comparison we may note that in West Germany it was above all the social-charitable policy which was put into practice, and that there was little direct redistribution and no social-revolutionary policy at all in favour of expellees. In East and West Germany and amongst the Allies, however, there was one common goal: to integrate the expellees as quickly and permanently as possible.

To appreciate the historical lead-up to this and the initial conditions behind the expellee policy, however, we now need to move away from a strictly German perspective or one focusing on the later GDR. The mass compulsory migrations in Europe were not a phenomenon concerning Germans alone and they did not begin in 1945 either. Hitler set the massive shifts in population in motion during the decade from 1938 to 1948 with the conclusion of the repatriation agreement for expatriate Germans, the annexation of the Sudetenland and, related to that, the partial expulsion of its Czech population. With the Second World War, he proceeded towards his comprehensive ethnic and racial reorganisation of Europe. In Western Poland, the Germans expelled over a million people between 1939 and 1940, just under a half of whom were ethnic Poles and just over a half Polish Jews who were later murdered in concentration camps. In other occupied areas, too, such as Slovenia, Central and Southern Poland, and in Bohemia and Moravia, hundreds of thousands of people had to leave their homes. If production for the war had not taken precedence over the expansion of so-called racially pure German Lebensraum, the terror would have been even more extensive (Luczak 1993: 145ff.; Aly 1995: 65).

Hitler changed the territorial order of Europe as well as its ethnic map. In the pact with Stalin, he arranged things in such a way that the Soviet Union got the eastern half of Poland and the Baltic States. Stalin was allowed to keep most of these areas towards the end of the war, which was to have tragic repercussions for the Germans in the east. At Germany's expense, Poland was shifted two to three hundred kilometres westwards.

Moreover, the Allies were in agreement that the European postwar order should be based on homogeneous nation-states. They consciously took on board the fact that this would entail the expulsion of over 20 million people. On 15 December 1944, in his speech about the future of Poland in the House of Commons, Churchill declared: 'There will be no mixture of populations to cause endless trouble ... A clean sweep will be made.' (Churchill 1974: 7,069) Churchill ended his argument for the expulsions with the prediction that, thanks to modern technology, these would be much easier to carry out than ever before. From our perspective today, the question arises as to what is more shocking about this speech: the condescending and negative attitude towards his ally, Poland, the contempt for humanity apparent even in the choice of the words 'clean sweep' – as if human beings could be swept up – or the misjudgement in believing that the 'transfer' of millions of people would be easy to organise.

The first victims of the ethnic and territorial reorganisation of Europe were the two million or more Poles who fled or were transported to the West from the now Soviet areas of Eastern Poland between 1944 and 1946 (Ther 1998: 71–87). From spring 1945, they were mostly transported to the former eastern territories of Germany where the expulsion of the Germans now began. The General Secretary of the Polish Communists, Wladyslaw Gomulka, issued the following policy statement at a session of the Politburo: 'The Germans are to be thrown out. For those who are there, conditions are to be made so bad that they will not wish to stay.' (Quoted from *Dokumenty* 1992: 42–3). Even before the Potsdam Agreement in August 1945, the Polish Army drove up to 300,000 Germans across the Oder and the Neisse. The Czechs went about things in similar fashion in the Sudetenland. At the time, the Görlitz pastor Frank Scholz (1984: 51) noted in his diary: 'The Germans have ceased being subjects with rights. Their honour, their bodies and their lives are at the merciless disposal of high-spirited victors.' By 'bodies' Scholz meant above all women who were raped on a massive scale.

The Potsdam Agreement was supposed to end this 'unauthorised expulsion' and at the same time it legalised the forced resettlement of Germans in the eastern part of Central Europe. But 'that any transfers that take place should be effected in an orderly and humane manner', as prescribed in the Agreement, remained a fiction. Before crossing the future border, the expellees were often robbed of everything and arrived in the Soviet Zone/GDR completely impoverished and often sick as well. Just as devastating in their effects were the destruction left by the war, the bottlenecks in supplies, the wind and the weather (for the destruction see Osêkowski 1994: 28 ff.). In many cases, the expellees had to wait for weeks, even months, to be transported; they were exposed to extremes of heat and cold in the rail trucks, often without any food, and in many cases they died of cold, exhaustion or mass epidemics.

As reports from the Soviet Zone show, their misery was by no means over when they crossed the border. The Brandenburg authorities in charge of administering expellees wrote in 1946: 'There is hardly an example in history comparable to this migration of a people. Cities like Frankfurt/Oder and Küstrin which became the gateway for hundreds of thousands of people – themselves mostly destroyed, without any provisions, without any water-supply, without medical help, without medicine, without anywhere to stay, without any means of transport and without enough people who could have helped – became the scene of a dreadful tragedy' (Brandenburg Main State Archive, Potsdam [BLHA]. Ld,. Br. Rep. 203, No. 1074, p. 1). Along the entire southern and eastern border of the Soviet Zone, epidemics quickly broke out. In August and September 1945 alone, official statistics recorded more than 30,000 cases of typhoid. In towns near the border such as Görlitz, epidemics were particularly frequent, with expellee reception camps often the centres (Wille 1993: 39; Bundesarchiv, Außenstelle Berlin Lichterfelde [BAB], DO 1–10, Nr. 4, p. 28; Sächsisches Staatshauptarchiv, Dresden [SHSA], MdI, Nr. 170.). In view of their wretched plight, a mood of despair spread amongst expellees. In Frankfurt (Oder) in June 1945, a large number of new arrivals committed suicide, and in Schwerin in December 1945, when food and supplies failed to be delivered, one expellee demanded: 'It would be better for you to take a machine gun and shoot us to pieces, for then our plight would at least be at an end.' (*Dokumentation der Vertreibung 1953–1961*, Vol. I/2, 687; BAB, DO 1–10, Nr. 11, p. 236.)

The authorities in the Soviet Zone, the Soviet Military Administration for Germany (SMAD) and the German administrative units, were literally overrun by the first wave of expellees. Even as early as summer 1945, approximately 2 to 2.5 million refugees and unofficial expellees had arrived in the Soviet Zone. In July, the SMAD issued its first order as to how these people were to be distributed throughout the Soviet Zone. All new arrivals from areas east of the Oder and Neisse were to be taken to the northeast of Mecklenburg and to some eastern districts of Brandenburg, the Sudeten Germans to the eastern districts of the Prussian province of Saxony (later to become the state Saxony-Anhalt, and not to be confused with the state of Saxony). The state of Saxony, on the other hand, even though it bordered on Bohemia and Silesia, was not a designated reception area and was actually barred from accepting refugees from October 1945 to March 1946.

The attempts to direct and channel the flood of expellees were, from the outset, unrealistic and continually being overtaken by events. In the Western Zones of Germany, the situation was similar (Schraut 1995: 33–43). The local administrative districts and authorities were no less overtaxed than the wider authorities operating at zonal and regional state level. Even by summer 1945, many areas were completely overcrowded because the Soviet Zone was functioning as both transit and host country. Local authorities were sending new arrivals hither and thither from town to (wider) administrative district since no one wanted to take on additional boarders in times of general hardship. In autumn 1945, the authorities in Saxony had several thousand refugees put on rafts, leaving them to drift down the Elbe, or transported them on lorries to neighbouring German states (Jahn 1995: 231). Already close to despair, therefore, the Central Administrative Authority for *Umsiedler* (ZVU) demanded on 2 October 1945: 'All this wandering and travelling around has to stop. Every chief district adminis-trative officer and every mayor must use police force to prevent this con-tinual wandering around, with people being shunted from one place to another.' (BAB, DO 1–10, Nr. 1, p.7).

The setting up of the ZVU in September 1945 is evidence of the fact that the SMAD and the east German authorities recognised that the general administrative authorities were unable to cope with the expellee problem. So a few months before the Americans did so in their zone, the Soviets ordered the setting up of the ZVU. The states and local authorities quickly followed suit, also forming special expellee administrative bodies and com-mittees. With the setting up of this administration, the authorities created a new term – '*Umsiedler*'. With this word they wanted, for one thing, to demonstrate to indigenous Germans and to expellees, who were at this time usually labelled 'refugees', that their flight was over and their accep-tance in the locality final, and also to underpin the choice of words used in the Potsdam Agreement, according to which it was not a question of cruel expulsion contrary to international law, but of a legal and planned reset-tlement.

By the start of 1946, the authorities were slowly getting to grips with the first intake. They had already built 358 reception camps across the whole Soviet Zone in which up to 350,000 peple could be accommodated (Wille 1993: 37). In the camps, as far as supplies would allow, new arrivals were given medical treatment and then sent on to the places where they were to settle. There were intake quotas for the individual states and districts which were set according to accommodation available, with the aim of providing the expellees with a roof over their head. This was most likely to be in small towns and villages, almost half of the expellees being accommo-dated in villages with less than 2,000 inhabitants. This also explains the marked differences in terms of percentage of expellees in the individual states in the Soviet Zone. Whilst in industrialised Saxony 17 percent of the population were expellees – corresponding to the West German average – the figure in Mecklenburg was 43.4 percent. Although many communities were very reluctant to accept more expellees, the local German population did eventually get used to the idea of having to take people in. If need be, the Soviet or German authorities simply put their foot down. However, this alleviation of the worst deprivation still left the question open as to what was to be done with these *Umsiedler* in the long run. And here the foun-dation was laid for an expellee policy which looked beyond the immediate future. Experts from the American State Department declared in Autumn 1945 that they were aiming for a total political, social and economic assimilation of the refugees in all the communities accepting them 'in order to avoid the growth of dangerous minority-problems in the states affected' (cited from Schraut 1995: 44).

The SMAD had similar ideas even if they usually talked about 'integrating them'. Despite the approaching Cold War, there was a consensus amongst the victorious powers about the territorial status quo of the postwar order of things. The solution of the expellee problem was seen as an important basis for this, in order to prevent any emergence of the sort of irredentism or revisionism that emerged after the First World War.

The first precondition for any integration of the expellees was the need to give them legal equality with indigenous citizens. On 30 September 1945, Saxony declared all citizens registered there to be Saxons. Brandenburg and the other eastern states soon followed suit until finally, in 1948, regulations concerning citizenship were then put in force throughout the Soviet Zone. The authorities were unusually generous in two respects: giving expellees legal equality included the right to food ration cards and welfare aid, and it was also virtually free from restriction until an amendment in 1948. Whoever wanted to be a German at that time could be one, without having to undergo language tests or offer proof of nationality, as is the case today (BLHA, Ld. Br. Rep. 203, Nr. 1115, pp. 364ff.; Nr. 1163, p.3ff.; cf. draft bill for giving stateless ethnic Germans equality, 14 February 1948 in BLHA, Ld. Br. Rep. 203, Nr. 727). In the West, the policy was similar in principle but there were restrictions for expellees coming from states not included in the Potsdam Agreement, for instance Yugoslavia.

The next thing which the authorities in the Soviet Zone wanted to do was to give expellees social equality. In 1946 the ZVU declared: 'We have to carry out a really big solidarity-campaign, and poor as we are, we have to help the *Umsiedler* who have even less than we do'. (BAB, DO 1–10, Nr. 1, p. 13; cf. also BAB, DO 1–10, Nr. 50, p. 50ff.) The first legal measure to be taken in this direction was SMAD order 304. Needy *Umsiedler* could make one application for a donation of 300 Reichsmarks per household and 100 Reichsmarks per child. This was generous in view of the prevailing conditions at the time and the very limited financial scope that the government had. Not until 1949 was there a similar flat-rate donation in West Germany via the emergency aid law. With SMAD order 304, though, there was a difference between the draft legal bill and its practice. As SED-Politburo member Paul Merker complained, 'in many cases, stubborn bureaucracy prevented aid from getting through quickly' (Merker 1947: 19). In February 1947, Brandenburg Social Minister Schwob of the Christian Democratic Union felt obliged to write to all the districts to demand 'special empathy' with the fate of expellees: 'It simply won't do, reproaching them with their misfortune and the administrative authorities explaining to them that they are a burden to the communities supposed to be their home and that, for this reason, aid will be denied to them' (BLHA, LD. BR. Rep. 206, Nr. 3312, p. 16). The limitations of the social-charitable policy towards expellees can be judged from these orders. Extensive measures in favour of expellees, justifiable though they may have been in view of their plight, met with resistance from the indigenous population who had also suffered in the war. Nonetheless, up to 1948 almost half of all expellees in the Soviet Zone received a donation on the basis of SMAD order 304 (Schwartz 1997: 179).

Because the Soviet Zone could financially only afford special laws such as SMAD order 304 for a limited time, it began to involve social organisations and the churches in its social-charitable policy from 1946 onwards. In 1946, collections for expellees were organised at regional and local level, and these played a central role early on in the ZVU's plans for integrating expellees (BAB, DO 1–10, Nr. 1, p. 13). With reference to the solidarity campaign stage-managed by the state, the ZVU declared: 'Our initiative has to work miracles and create enthusiasm and sympathy in all sections of the population such as we have never hitherto experienced in Germany' (BAB, DO 1–10, Nr. 1, p.13). In 1947, the collections were extended to the whole of the Soviet Zone. They culminated in the so-called *Umsiedler-Wochen* (resettler weeks) which were organised at great expense. In Thuringia they produced only 110 pairs of shoes, 132 saucepans and 10 big cookers; in Saxony , though, 32,000 pairs of walking-shoes, 15,800 pieces of furniture; and in Brandenburg, 23,232 pairs of shoes (BAB, DO 1–10, Nr. 27, p. 214 and Nr. 26, p. 161; SHSA, MinAS, Nr. 28, pp. 28–32; BLHA, Ld, Br. Rep. 332, Nr. 574. pp. 84–6 and Nr. 575, pp. 57–120). The best statistics were not able to disguise the fact that the results of the collections did not meet expectations. Moreover, the *Umsiedler-Wochen* in 1948 revealed a new tendency in expellee policy: the SED saw the campaign as the keystone for the overall success of its integration policy. It therefore began to gloss over the integration problem and solve it through denial.

Even if, thanks to the SED's active social policy, hunger became less of a problem for expellees, they were short of many other essential goods. Many expellees had been temporarily housed in attics, stables and other accommodation ordered to be given to them. The head of the ZVU, Rudolf Engel, realising that accommodation was the central problem of integration, declared in 1946: 'At the present stage, the decisive problem for *Umsiedler* is the question of getting somewhere to live. Only when *Umsiedler* have their own place to live in their new homeland, and be this ever so modest, can they begin to feel at home' (BAB, DO 1–10, Nr. 4, p. 69). However, not having somewhere to live applied not only to expellees but also to those bombed out of their homes, as well as to many other indigenous Germans. In 1947, the Soviet Zone was short of a million homes. Per capita, people were living in a space of only 8.1 square metres, and expellees a good deal less (BAB, DO 1–10, Nr. 31, ibid., pp.176–78; Nr. 23, p. 4; Nr. 13, p. 90).

Unlike shoes and household equipment, homes could not simply be acquired through donations or be built quickly. The authorities therefore developed a new kind of expellee policy, that of direct redistribution (cf. Ther 1998: 204–16). At first, basing their actions on the 'Law of the Allied Control Council No. 18' of 18 March 1946, they confiscated the homes of former Nazis. In 1947 began the general checks on homes, and these were extended in 1948. If homes were not fully – or inappropriately – occupied, tenants or owners could expect either to have to accommodate expellees or to face a compulsory exchange of home. However, statistics from Brandenburg in 1948 show that of the 600,000 homes throughout the state, only 25,000 were checked and only in 1,500 cases could more places for expellees actually be obtained (BLHA, Ld., Br. Rep. 203, Nr. 1104, p. 6; Nr. 1115, p. 292). Moreover, opposition increased steadily amongst the indigenous population. The local authorities, who were in touch with the mood in the country, delayed the process wherever they could, hiding behind bureaucratic procedures. As the Saxon Social Ministry observed in March 1949, they were carrying out checks in a lax manner 'in order to avoid the allocation of *Umsiedler* to their communities' (SHSA, MinAS, Nr. 27, p. 71).

Despite these difficulties, the Soviet Zone/GDR had, in the area of accommodation, taken some important steps in the direction of achieving equality for expellees. According to surveys carried out in Saxony, in 1949 indigenous Germans had on average 8.73 square metres of living space, expellees 8.29 square metres. Particularly striking is a comparison with the year 1947. Indigenous Germans had to take a drop of 1.52 square metres of living space per capita, whereas expellees had on average over one square metre more (all figures from Just 1985: 105). Here, the efforts on behalf of expellees were more effective than in the West where even former Nazis were not stopped from living in big homes, whilst hundreds of thousands of expellees had to live for years in huts. However, redistributive measures such as the checks on homes continued to put pressure on the already poor relations between indigenous Germans and expellees. Particularly marked was the opposition between expellees and local Germans in small village communities.

Perhaps the most important effect of the redistributive expellee policy was the speedy closure of the camps. According to a GDR-wide survey of April 1950, 93 percent of expellees lived in a fixed abode, 43,085 or 6.4 percent still lived in huts and housing of lightweight construction, 4,039 or 0.6 percent in emergency accommodation (BLHA, Ld. Br. Rep. 203. Nr. 1150, p. 75). By way of comparison: in the British Zone, 276,000 expellees were in camps and other forms of mass accommodation at the end of 1948; in the American Zone the figure was 115,200, with 110,000 of these in Bavaria. On 1 April 1953, 82,065 expellees were still living in camps and emergency accommodation in Bavaria (cf. Sallinger 1991: 70; Schraut 1995: 253).

The limitations of redistributive policy in the GDR can be seen in the 1947 debate about a *Lastenausgleich* ('burden sharing': according to a special law, a tax was levied on the indigenous population to financially compensate expellees for losses suffered as a result of the Second World War or to make possible other redistributive measures in favour of the expellees). When an appropriate law was introduced in the state parliament in Saxony, the following argument was put forward: 'The State Government of Saxony takes the view that an enforced seizure [of accommodation, furniture, household goods etc.] is not possible. We cannot afford lowering morale amongst the population' (BAB, DO 1–10, Nr. 31, p. 202). This discussion shows that those in power were generally not able to disregard the wishes of the majority of the population and could thus not act against the interests of indigenous Germans.

On account of its close connection with changes in the distribution of property and in the class structure of society, the third important area of expellee policy can be termed social-revolutionary (Ther 1998: 171–88). From May 1945, the Communist Party of Germany (KPD) pointed the finger at big landowners as the really guilty party behind Hitler's seizure of power and the outbreak of war. With a piece of historical trickery going back to the Peasant Wars, the KPD announced that the post-1500 expropriation of peasants' land was to be reversed in the villages and a more just and, moreover, anti-fascist order established. The propaganda for the land reform was at first directed at the indigenous small farmers and agricultural workers, with the aim of triggering off a social revolution in the countryside. By summer 1945, however, the situation had drastically changed as a result of the arrival of over two million expellees. They too now – at least from a Marxist perspective – were part of the village proletariat and, as a group of foreign origin, were moreover to be integrated into society. Norman Naimark has shown that it was the integration of the expellees, together with the intention of the KPD to achieve political control in the countryside, which led to the land reform (Naimark 1995: 144). At the beginning of September 1945, the state and provincial governments enacted the land reform laws in which the expellees along with agricultural workers and small farmers were expressly named as recipient group. Up to 1949, expellees received 43.3 percent of all new farmsteads and 34.9 percent of the land redistributed, considerably more than their 24.2 percent share of the population (cf. statistics in Meinicke 1993: 63; Bauerkämper 1994: 126). In absolute figures, this meant that, in the land reform, 91,155 expellees were allocated farmsteads, and, including family members, approximately one in every ten expellees in the Soviet Zone was able to earn a living as a farmer.

The integrating effects of the land reform were nevertheless limited. This was above all because of structural problems in the changeover from large-scale landowning to smallholdings. Even at the end of 1946, three-quarters of the *Neubauern* (new farmers) had to work without horses which were absolutely essential for tractive power and manure, and only one third of the land reform farmers owned a cow. Only one farmstead in four was equipped with a plough, one in five with iron harrows and only one in fourteen with reapers and threshing machines (cf. Bauerkämper 1994: 303 and 306). For the so-called *Umsiedler-Neubauern* (resettler-new farmers), things were even more difficult because as expellees they had no capital at their disposal and no possessions to barter with. Many therefore went bankrupt or gave up. Even in 1948, only about one expellee in seven who had received land in the reform was financially successful enough not to have to worry about the future (cf. statistics in Meinicke and von Plato 1991: 6; BLHA, Rep. 203, MdI, Nr.1166, p.15).

The government responded to the problem by pumping even more resources into the countryside. Above all in 1946, it sent out cattle all across the Soviet Zone so that every farmer owned at least one cow, and distributed all agricultural implements still to be found. As local statistics show, expellees often came away empty-handed here because they lacked the necessary connections in the villages. Two years after the start of the land reform, therefore, the Soviet Zone took the most sweeping of all the measures so far in favour of the 'new farmers'. SMAD order 209, issued on 9 September 1947 and also known as the new-farmer programme, stipulated that 37,000 new farmers' houses were to be built by the end of 1948. This meant that the Soviet Zone was investing almost all its building resources and a considerable part of its financial resources in the villages, for which there was no parallel in the Western Zones. SMAD order 209 was aimed at all new farmers, but had a component specially related to expellee policy. For one thing, between 1947 and 1948 almost 60 percent of the residential buildings were to be built in Mecklenburg and Brandenburg, i.e., in the two states in which over two-thirds of the *Umsiedler-Neubauern* were operating. For another, supplementary guidelines for the new-farmer programme, issued in 1949, contained a passage which stated that *Umsiedler* were to be given preferential treatment when deciding upon the urgency of building projects (BLHA, Ld. Br. Rep. 206, Nr. 2845, p. 105).

However, the new-farmer building programme suffered from the outset in terms of difficulty of coordination amongst the authorities and, above all, a catastrophic lack of building materials. This is best verified via local and regional data. At the beginning of the building season in 1948 in Brandenburg, there was an estimated demand for 22,000 building stones and a supply of 11,902. Instead of the required 10,000 roof-tiles, only 1,085 had been delivered. There was no lime, cement, roofing-felt or nails at all (BLHA, Ld. Br. Rep. 206, Nr. 2845, p. 197). There were therefore huge building delays. Although administrative districts with their antiquated procedures dressed up the figures and even counted rabbit hutches as building units, realistic counts reveal that they were only able to build approximately one-third of the farmsteads planned. Despite the preferential treatment of expellees, even up to 1950, only about one *Umsiedler-Neubauer* in four profited from the special building programme (BLHA, Ld. Br. Rep. 203, Nr. 311, p. 420; Nr. 2845, p. 99). In addition to this, in summer 1949 it turned out that the state could no longer afford the programme. Because all investment monies had already been used up by the end of July, the authorities imposed a halt to all building projects, which was not lifted until 1950 (BLHA, Ld. Br. Rep. 206, Nr. 2845, p. 32ff.).

Overall the Soviet Zone paid a high economic and political price for SMAD order 209. Investments in the new farms required nearly all building resources to be steered in the direction of the countryside. As a result, building work in the cities was brought to a standstill even though the need for action was just as great as in the country because of the war damage, the shortage of housing and the increasing demand for labour (BLHA, Ld. Br. Rep. 203, Nr. 1104, p. 6). SMAD order 209 also jeopardised the attempts of expellees to build a life for themselves outside agriculture. The cooperatives and private businesses founded by expellees suddenly had to stop all building work and investments in 1947 and 1948. Meanwhile, the loans kept on running and many businesses got into difficulties with their repayments as a result. For the East German state, the failure of many *Umsiedler-Neubauern* therefore meant a misguided policy of prioritising limited economic resources and of expellee policy in the countryside where integration was moving along more slowly than in the cities.

Social-revolutionary expellee policy in the Soviet Zone/GDR can be judged from two different standpoints. In relation to original expectations and to the input of resources, it must be viewed as having failed. Including all family members, approximately one expellee in ten profited from the land reform, of whom however approximately one in two either gave up their business completely or only had enough for a bare subsistence. Compared with the West, however, this failure has to be seen in relative terms. There, too, the occupation authorities had at first believed that the future of the expellees lay in the country, not the town. Evidence of this can be seen in a letter from the American General Erich Fischer to the leader of the military government in the American zone, General Clay: 'If food cannot be brought to the cities, at least city dwellers can be moved to the food; and pay for their board by their labour in producing more food. If further studies show that this would be impractical, at least sending a preponderance of German expellees to rural areas would seem to be indicated' (cited from Schraut 1995: 42). As land reform had been rejected in the West for ideological reasons, the only thing expellees could do was to enter service as farm-workers. The failure to integrate expellee-farmers was one of the focal points of expellee policy in West Germany right up to the 1960s, whereas in the Soviet Zone/GDR, through a mixture of good luck and skill, at least those expellees who really wanted to continue to practise their old profession were able to establish themselves as farmers.

In general terms, though, it remained difficult to integrate expellees professionally. True, the ZVU, the state governments and the employment exchanges recognised in autumn 1946 that not only living space, but also the criteria of the labour market would have to play a part in the reception of expellees (cf. BAB, DO 1–10, Nr. 4, pp. 40, 43 and 80). But by this time, most expellees had already arrived. Only in 1947 were expellees in Saxony registered in quarantine-camps according to professional occupation so that they could be allocated by the state employment exchange to the individual districts according to demand (BAB, DO 1–10, Nr. 23, p. 89). In the Soviet Zone too, therefore, most expellees had to accept professional downgrading, as in West Germany. Despite the land reform, many more expellees were farm-workers rather than farmers, others at first taking up lower positions in the railway, the post office and other areas, and if there was a crisis, they were the first to be dismissed. Only slowly and through very hard labour were they able to work their way up to better positions.

Whilst the presence of expellees in business/industry gradually increased, it remained at a low level in the sphere of politics where ideological and not technical reliability counted. In the local districts, the states and the Socialist Unity Party (SED), expellees were clearly underrepresented. In Saxony, for instance, only three of 120 state parliamentary representatives, 4.25 percent of the town councillors and just over 7 percent of the district assembly representatives were expellees, and even in Brandenburg only 6.5 percent of the town councillors and district assembly representatives were expellees, hence in each case they made up only about one-quarter of what corresponded to their share in terms of the total population (Just 1985: vol. 2, 85; BLHA, Ld. Br. Rep. 203, Nr. 1104, p. 20). This weakened the position of expellees in dealing with everyday conflicts with the indigenous German population, in legislative assemblies and in the areas of law and order. In addition, because of this, the authorities responsible for *Umsiedler* became in effect almost the only lobby for expellees, despite the ambivalent position they occupied between party and expellee interests.

To sum up, the results of the three areas of expellee policy were at best mixed. Measured in terms of what was financially viable in the Soviet Zone, much had been achieved, but not in terms of the ambitious, sometimes even naive goals of integration policy. Yet the quantitatively measurable successes of expellee policy were in any case only one side of the coin. Just as important was the reception of this policy amongst indigenous Germans and expellees, as well as its effects on relations between the two groups of the population. In this respect, the SED found itself in a no-win situation: if it did not support the expellees enough, social tensions would increase, together with the risk that a permanent underclass would be established. If it supported expellees enough to bring their standard of living slowly up to that of the indigenous German population, then the latter would resist this either directly or via the control of local committees and administrations. The experience of the West German government in 1952 was similar with the introduction of the *Lastenausgleich* (burden sharing) law, which also met with strong resistance from the indigenous German population. Attempts to achieve a balance between measures deemed objectively necessary for integration and resistance to these offered no way out of this dilemma because then, frequently, neither indigenous Germans nor expellees were satisfied. The SED increased people's dissatisfaction by promising the expellees more than it could offer them in practice. Examples of this were SMAD order 304 and the new-farmer programme which were, it is true, exclusively or partly aimed at expellees, but then missed their targets by a long way. Moreover, the SED had monopolised expellee policy by bringing all social and political institutions into line in 1947 and 1948. If something did not work, then people logically blamed the SED before all else. In the Soviet Zone, the tendency not to solve but to suppress expellee problems increased after 1948 at both local and zonal level. This change was caused by the dim prospects for expellee policy and by a change in attitude to the expellees. The social-charitable approach, as the poor overall results show, had exhausted itself by the time of the Umsiedler-Wochen of 1948. Even the stock of 'wrongly occupied' accommodation had become exhausted as the years went by. At first, the greatest potential for integration lay in the social-revolutionary approach. As the land had long since been redistributed by 1948, however, further initiatives could not be expected here. On the contrary, the integration of expellees within the bounds of the land reform was accompanied by structural problems which the Soviet Zone/GDR was unable to clear up on account of financial bottlenecks. In addition, a series of resultant problems had arisen which were almost insoluble.

In conclusion, while it is true that expellee policy in the Soviet Zone up to 1948 did have limited success, such as the dissolution of almost all the expellee camps and the accommodation of expellees in flats, the effectiveness of all three approaches either could not be increased any further or had already noticeably diminished. At the same time, the demands of expellees became ever more prominent. This can be seen from the discussion about compensation for losses suffered in the Second World War which political rivals from the SED, the CDU and the LPD were already exploiting. As far as the domestic authorities were concerned, too, the ZVU became an increasingly self-confident rival to the SED, with its claim to be the sole political power and decision maker of expellee policy, a key area of social policy. In autumn 1947, the ZVU openly tried to convene a *Zentraler Umsiedler-Beirat* (Central Resettler Advisory Council) which was to 'co-evaluate' the laws of the state parliaments with regard to their acceptability in terms of expellee policy (see BAB, DO 1–10, Nr. 4, p. 51; Nr. 31, pp. 70ff.; Nr. 50, pp. 32ff.; see also Wille 1993: 43). The idea behind this was for a committee for expellees at zonal level to have the right to raise objections, and this committee would thus have given expellees real representation in the state and its policies. For the SED, this was very definitely going too far and it promptly rejected the *Umsiedler-Beirat* (BAB, DO 1–10, Nr. 50, p. 57; BAB, DO 1–10, Nr. 31, p. 74).

On a local level, the mood *vis-à-vis* expellees slowly began to change in 1947, with the ever acute problems now seeming insoluble. The question was increasingly posed as to whether the expellees themselves were not the main cause of these problems, especially as corresponding connections such as the link between the new-farmer building programme and the general halt to building projects were easy to establish. The complaints of the expellees which had earlier evoked sympathy now brought rejection. A good example of this change of mood is provided by a 1947 speech in the county assembly in Hoyerswerda, Northern Saxony, which broached the expellee problem in the following manner: 'There must not be criticism of things which cannot be changed. We have to work actively and positively' (SHSA, Kreistag/Kreisrat [KT/KR] Hoyerswerda, Nr. 2, p. 4).

In 1948, the call to 'eliminate the term *Umsiedler*' was heard for the first time at central level (BAB, DO 1–10, Nr.1, pp. 89ff.). It was argued the expellee problem had been largely solved. Similar self-deceptive statements were made in connection with the *Umsiedler-Wochen*, but these should be regarded not just as propaganda as they were also to be found in the internal expellee discussions in both party and government. Whereas at the end of 1948, a spade was still being called a spade as far as these problems were concerned, in 1949 they were regarded as solved (BAB, DO 1–10, Nr. 27, pp. 288ff.). People proudly pointed to the drastically reduced number of complaints made by expellees without asking the real reason why these had gone down in number (BAB, DO 1–10, Nr. 27, p. 303; BLHA, Ld. Br. Rep 202G, Nr. 136, pp. 334 and 354).

This change in attitude had direct repercussions for the *Umsiedler* administration, for if the very term 'Umsiedler' was to disappear, then consequently there was no longer any need for a central administration for *Umsiedler*. On 1 July 1948, the ZVU was dissolved and a follow-on authority, with drastically reduced personnel and merely called *Hauptabteilung Umsiedler* (Main Department for Resettlers), was attached to the Deutsche Verwaltung des Innern (German Administration for Internal Affairs – DVdI). The *Umsiedler* authority in Brandenburg warned in 1948: 'In order to make the term "*Umsiedler*" disappear, we cannot just dissolve the corresponding departments, so leaving the Umsiedler entirely to their own devices' (BLHA, Ld. Br. Rep 332, Nr. 574, p. 89). But the General Secretariat of the SED decided to close the various state *Umsiedler* authorities and the local Umsiedler committees too. They gave the following as their reason for so doing: 'The continued existence of a special central administration for Umsiedler and special offices for Umsiedler in the states and districts would hinder the process of fusion by giving prominence to special Umsiedler interests' (cf. BLHA, Ld. Br. Rep 332, Nr. 574, p. 20; see also BAB, DO 1–10, Nr. 4, p. 130). In autumn 1949 it was further stipulated that in official buildings, all public notices which contained the word *Umsiedler* were to be removed (BLHA, Ld. Br. Rep 206, Nr. 2243, p. 4).

The dissolution of the *Umsiedler* authorities reinforced the impression that 'special *Umsiedler* interests' (at this point in time, this was an unequivocally negative labelling of the demands of expellees as particularist interests) were no longer on the agenda of the state and party leaders in Berlin. The significance of the end of the ZVU as a caesura can therefore not be underestimated (cf. Schwartz 1995: 93). Formally, the general administration and the SED were now supposed to take the interests of the expellees into consideration. Yet as numerous petitions and complaints verify, this was only the case to a very limited extent. The Hauptabteilung *Umsiedler* in the DVdI (i.e., the follow-on organisation from the ZVU) made the following observation after the abolition of the *Umsiedler* committees: 'From the complaints of our new citizens, which come in daily, it is obvious that hitherto the main authorities, right up to those inside the government, have not yet fought for the interests of the new citizens in the way that is required' (BAB, DO 1–10, Nr. 23, pp. 150 and 171; cf. also a similar assessment of the situation in BAB, DO 1–10, Nr. 27, pp. 4ff.). Financially, too, the dissolution of the *Umsiedler* authority made itself felt. In 1948, the SMA in Brandenburg demanded of the state government that it cut the funds in the state budget for *Umsiedler* from 5.5 to 3.4 million Marks (BLHA, Ld. Br. Rep 332, Nr. 574, p. 91).

When coming to a judgement on these events, we must not overlook the fact that during the same period, for instance, expellee authorities in West German states were also closed and integrated into the general administration. The dismantling of special administrations therefore reflects a basic tendency in administrations towards standardisation and centralisation. In West Germany, though, a ministry with responsibility for expellees was kept on during the 1950s and 1960s at federal level. In addition, the expellee associations were able to lobby on behalf of their members. Thus, the reaon that the dissolution of the special administration in the GDR had such sweeping consequences was because it had been the only institution representing the interests of the expellees.

Expellees were not allowed to found interest-group associations in the Soviet Zone/GDR. At first, the basis for this was (as in the Western zones) the ban on coalitions. But as this was slowly relaxed in the West, the ZVU, in 1947, declared the founding of 'special *Umsiedler* organisations' to be undesirable. Nevertheless, expellees attempted to found either local groups which were orientated towards their old home country or interest-group associations for any Germans born in East Central Europe (cf. BAB, DO 1–10, Nr. 13, p. 88; BAB, DO 1–11, Hauptverwaltung der deutschen Volkspolizei, Nr. 886, pp. 12–14 and 110–33). But in 1948, the SED issued the already more sharply-worded order: 'Attempts to form special *Umsiedler* organisations, their concentration into regional groups, supported above all by church organisations, and any effects of agitation filtering through from the Western Zones are to be eliminated' (BLHA, Ld. Br. Rep 332, Nr. 574, p.10). The policy of the SED towards the expellee associations in East and West Germany was devious. Outwardly, the Party condemned the expellees as revanchists, but behind closed doors, the Head of the Department for Provincial Policy in the Central Secretariat, Anton Plenikowski, declared: 'Our position vis-à-vis the *Umsiedler* problem in the West is different. There, because of their unequal treatment, their classification as refugees, we are in favour of the formation of special representation groups which help in the struggle for their interests. In the West, you have the struggle for equal rights for these people, in the East, however, you already have their assimilation' (BLHA, Ld. Br. Rep 332, Nr. 574, p. 131).

The more the regime faced unresolvable problems in its attempts at a constructive solution to the expellee problem, the more strongly it resorted to taboos and the methods of a police state. Thus, for instance, the Brandenburg information service kept expellees under surveillance, suspecting them of 'reactionary tendencies'. At GDR state level, spying on expellees and their surveillance reached a new high in the run-up to the GDR's recognition of the Oder-Neisse border. In a circular of 13 January 1950, Lust, the head of the main department for permits with the *Volkspolizei*, announced a ban on all *Umsiedler* associations and organisations as 'all attacks on the peaceful German-Polish border in word, text or image and via the formation of anti-democratic unions ... are a crime, contrary to article 6 of the Constitution of the German Democratic Republic ... The Constitution of the German Democratic Republic proclaims equal rights for all its citizens so there can be no talk of persons who have resettled from the former German Eastern territories constituting a special group within the German people. Resettled persons are given every opportunity, through social institutions and through the redistribution of land in the land-reform, to build a new life for themselves' (cf. BAB, DO 1–11, HDVP, Nr. 886, p. 24). In concrete terms, this meant that even complaints about problems of integration could lead to police investigations. In 1950, even as far as cultural life was concerned, the Interior Ministry prohibited any public reference to the former home country. At the end of 1950, the authorities crushed several secret meetings held by expellees (BAB, DO 1–11, HDVP, Nr. 886, pp. 12–21, 134 and 159) and continued to suppress even informal gatherings thereafter.

At the same time as the regime resorted to drastic measures against expellees' attempts at collective associations, the 'law for the further improvement of the situation of former *Umsiedler*' was passed. This lumped together all preceding areas of expellee policy into one last move. By far the most important single measure was the provision of interest-free credit of 1,000 Marks per family for the purchase of consumer goods, single-person households being able to claim up to 600 Marks. The law further provided cheap credit for building homes and working quarters, a lowering by 50 percent of the quotas for products to be delivered to the state by *Umsiedler-Neubauern*, and credit for expelled former craftsmen and Neubauern. This meant in effect that in the GDR there was a sort of preferential *Lastenausgleich* which did, however, lag behind the law passed in the West in 1953 in two respects. It firmly avoided acknowledging any special burden carried by the expellees as a consequence of the war. On the contrary, the latter saw themselves increasingly exposed to the stigma-tisation of having been Hitler's fifth column. The regime thus missed the chance of giving moral and psychological support to the expellees and their integration.

Moreover, as was already the case with the previous laws, social-politi-cal claims and economic reality were poles apart. As with the previous measures, the *Umsiedler* law created expectations which it could not fulfil. There was no adequate supply of goods to satisfy the great demand trig-gered off by the credits. On 17 December 1950, the GDR regime applied the emergency brakes and amended the law by indicating a top limit to income. According to this, those who received credit were not allowed to earn a monthly income of more than 250 Marks in the large cities, and 200 Marks in the country. Credit was only paid out in two instalments of 500 Marks each, so potential recipients were correspondingly annoyed (Just 1985: 129). Yet despite the above-cited cost-cutting measures, there was not enough money. In the district of Hoyerswerda, for instance, people had applied for 1,126,000 Marks by February 1951, but only 80,000 Marks of credit had been transferred from Berlin. Hoyerswerda did not want to apply for the sums allocated to be raised and explained it away by telling expellees that there would be a wait of up to two years (SHSA, KT/KR Hoyerswerda, Nr. 26). At a conference in the Interior Ministry of the GDR in October 1952, it turned out that only about half of the *Umsiedler* had profited from the law, receiving only about 500 Marks each (SHSA, Rat des Bezirkes [RdB] Dresden, Nr. 6071, pp. 36ff.). The disappointment was again correspondingly huge, evidence of permanent deficiencies in GDR social policy. On the other hand, the *Umsiedler* law shows that the GDR completely exhausted the limits of its modest financial resources ear-marked for *Umsiedler*, doing all that it could. The Stalinist metaphor of 'the stick and the carrot' seems particularly appropriate for the GDR, which was a mixture of welfare- and police-state. The 'carrot' only applied, though, up to 1953 when the most important achievements of the law were brought to a halt. Already in 1952, the government interrupted the distrib-ution of credit authorisations at Christmas of all times, from 15 to 31 December. On 9 September 1953, i.e. exactly three years after the law came into force, the Department for Population Policy in the Interior Min-istry of the GDR ordered an end to credit payments (SHSA, RdB Dresden, Nr. 6071, pp. 33 and 11). Despite continuing differences between indige-nous Germans and expellees in standard of living and in household bud-get provision, no further special laws were passed or continued in favour of expellees. Here the GDR and the Federal Republic clearly developed in separate ways. Whilst the GDR was able to keep up with and surpass the West up to 1952 in its provision for expellees, it brought this policy to a halt at the same time that extensive special payments for expellees got under way in the Federal Republic with the *Lastenausgleich*.

Summary

In the early days of the GDR, expellee policy soon diminished in significance, despite the *Umsiedler* law. Economic and social elements of Stalinism, such as the expansion of heavy industry and emigration to the cities, changed the lives of expellees more than the specific preceding policies. Here, too, the GDR and the Federal Republic grew apart from each other. As verified by *Lastenausgleich*, by the resettlement of expellees within the Federal Republic and by their integration into various governments under Adenauer, expellee policy in West Germany at the beginning of the 1950s became more dynamic. The GDR, on the other hand, brought its expellee policy completely to a halt in 1953 with the phasing out of the last of its special measures for *Umsiedler* and made the whole question of expellees a taboo subject in public discourse for more than two decades until the publication of Christa Wolff's novel *Kindheitsmuster*.

Considering the very concrete goal of integration and the extensive political and economic resources employed by the Soviet Zone/GDR to realise it, it is striking how very limited their expellee policy was in terms of its effectiveness. True, the social-charitable policy enabled the expellees to survive on an extremely modest level, but it did not allow them to be brought into line with the rest of the population. Statistically, they owned considerably fewer basic goods such as household utensils and furniture. True, they were able to make good some of the material losses that they had suffered in being expelled, but only a few expellees managed to do this completely by 1953. Perhaps the most important success of the redistributive expellee policy was the emptying of the camps, which the GDR managed several years earlier than the Federal Republic. But there was only very limited success in achieving real parity for the expellees in terms of living space because of opposition from the indigenous German population, the increasingly tight room for manoeuvre with redistribution and the initially very small amount of building work going on. The government did make it very clear early on, though, through its defence of parity for the expellees, that any open discrimination against them or ill-treatment of them would be against the political credo of the Soviet Zone. Here policy in the East differed from that in the West. As Franz Bauer, in his monograph on the expellees in Bavaria (1982), has shown, the government there repeatedly distanced itself from the 'refugees' – with corresponding consequences for their treatment by the indigenous German population. On the other hand, the reasons why the social-revolutionary policy was not very effective were quite different. In this area, it was not opposition from other sections of the population that were the greatest obstacle but the inert economic and social structures which prevailed before 1945. The transformation from a system of big landowners to an agrarian structure based on smallholders proved extremely difficult. The expellees were the ones who suffered most from structural deficiencies such as the shortage of farms, cattle and machines. They were therefore only able to benefit in a very limited fashion from the social-revolutionary policy, even though this was particularly aimed at them.

This was why expellee policy clearly reached a crisis point in 1948. Acceptance of expellee policy diminished both amongst expellees themselves and amongst the indigenous German population, who became increasingly more vehemently opposed to the redistributive measures. The structural problems in agriculture appeared insoluble; expellees in particular gave up their farms in droves or remained completely dependent on the indigenous German population. The expellee law of 1950 again brought a number of benefits to expellees, but from 1948 onwards, this 'carrot' was accompanied by increasingly stronger ideological and cultural repression and deep mistrust of 'former *Umsiedler*'. The integration of expellees into GDR society was therefore fragmentary, and the relationship between state and party and most expellees remained a very distant one. The expellees, though, were also able to benefit from the economic upturn in the 1950s and 1960s, and they were therefore only rarely externally recognisable as expellees in the later years of the GDR. The amount of integration achieved was, however, largely the result of general policy or economic change, not of any policy specifically directed at expellees.

Note

1. Translated by David Rock. For refugees and expellees in the GDR, the official term used was *Umsiedler* (resettler). This term will be used in all quotes from and references to East German policy documents. Otherwise, the term expellees (*Vertriebene*) will be used.

References

Archival Sources
Brandenburgisches Landeshauptarchiv Potsdam (BLHA)
Ld. Br. Rep. 203 (Ministerium des Innern)
Ld. Br. Rep. 206 (Ministerium für Wirtschaft)
Ld. Br. Rep. 332 (Sozialistische Einheitspartei Deutschlands)
Ld. Br. Rep 202G (Amt für Information beim Ministerpräsidenten)
Bundesarchiv, Außenstelle Berlin-Lichterfelde (BAB)

DO 1-10 (Zentralverwaltung für deutsche Umsiedler)
DO 1-11 (Hauptverwaltung der deutschen Volkspolizei [HDVP])
Sächsisches Hauptsstaatsarchiv Dresden (SHSA)
MdI (Ministerium des Innern)
MinAS (Ministerium für Arbeit und Soziales)
KT/KR (Kreistag/Kreisrat Hoyerswerda)
RdB (Rat des Bezirkes Dresden)

Other Sources

Aly, Götz, '*Endlösung*'. *Völkerverschiebung und der Mord an den europäischen Juden*. Frankfurt am Main, Fischer-Taschenbuch-Verlag, 1995.

Bauer, Franz J., *Flüchtlinge und Flüchtlingspolitik in Bayern 1945–1950*, Stuttgart, Klett-Cotta, 1982.

Bauerkämper, Arndt, 'Von der Bodenreform zur Kollektivierung. Zum Wandel der ländlichen Gesellschaft in der Sowjetischen Besatzungszone Deutschlands und DDR 1945-1952', in *Sozialgeschichte der DDR*, ed. Hartmut Kaelble, Jürgen Kocka and Hartmut Zwahr, Stuttgart, Klett-Cotta, 1994, pp. 119–143.

Bauerkämper, Arndt, 'Problemdruck und Ressourcenverbrauch. Wirtschaftliche Auswirkungen der Bodenreform in der SBZ/DDR 1945–1952', in *Wirtschaftliche Folgelasten des Krieges in der SBZ/DDR*, ed. Christoph Buchheim. Baden-Baden, Nomos-Verlags-Gesellschaft, 1995, pp. 295–322.

Winston S. Churchill: His complete speeches 1897–1963, ed. Robert Rhodes James, vol. VII 1943-1949, New York and London, Weidenfeld & Nicolson, 1974.

Dokumentation der Vertreibung der Deutschen aus Ostmitteleuropa, ed. Theodor Schieder, Bonn, Bundesministerium für Vertriebene, Flüchtlinge und Kriegsgeschädigte, 1953–1961, vol. I/1-3 'Die Vertreibung der deutschen Bevölkerung aus den Gebieten östlich der Oder-Neisse'.

Dokumenty do dziejów PRL, no. 1, Protokol obrad KC PPR w maju 1945 roku, ed. Aleksander Kochñski. Warsaw 1992.

Jahn, Manfred, 'Kriegsende 1945: Zur Vertreibung der Deutschen aus der Tschechoslowakei und zu ihrer Aufnahme in der Sowjetischen Besatzungszone Deutschlands', in *Odsun. Die Vertreibung der Sudetendeutschen*. Munich, Sudetendeutsches Archiv, 1995, pp. 213–40.

Just, Regine, *Die Lösung der Umsiedlerfrage auf dem Gebiet der DDR, dargestellt am Beispiel des Landes Sachsen 1945 - 1952*, Ph.D. Dissertation, Magdeburg, Technische Universität, 1985.

Kersten, Krystyna, *The Establishment of Communist Rule in Poland, 1943–1948*. Berkeley, University of California Press, 1991.

Luczak, Czeslaw, *Polska i Polacy w drugiej wojnie œwiatowej, Poznañ* , Wydawnictwo naukowe uniwersytetu im. Adama Mickiewicza, 1993.

Meinicke, Wolfgang, 'Die Bodenreform und die Vertriebenen in der SBZ und in den Anfangsjahren der DDR', in *Sie hatten alles verloren. Flüchtlinge und Vertriebene in der sowjetischen Besatzungszone*, ed. Manfred Wille, Johannes Hoffmann and Wolfgang Meinicke. Wiesbaden, Harrassowitz, 1993, pp. 55–86.

Meinicke, Wolfgang and von Plato, Alexander, *Alte Heimat–Neue Zeit. Flüchtlinge, Umgesiedelte, Vertriebene in der Sowjetischen Besatzungszone und in der DDR*. Berlin, Verlags-Anstalt Union, 1991.

Merker, Paul, *Die nächsten Schritte zur Lösung des Umsiedlerproblems*. Berlin, Dietz, 1947.

Naimark, Norman M., *The Russians in Germany: A History of the Soviet Zone of Occupation*. Cambridge, MA, Harvard University Press, 1995.

Osêkowski, Czeslaw, *Spoleczeñstwo Polski zachodniej i pólnocnej w latach 1945–1956*, Zielona Góra, Wyzsza Szkola Pedagogiczna, 1994.

Sallinger, Barbara, *Die Integration der Heimatvertriebenen im Landkreis Günzburg nach 1945*, Munich, Vögel, 1991.

Scholz, Frank, *Wächter, wie tief die Nacht. Görlitzer Tagebuch 1945/46*. Eltville, 1984.

Schraut, Sylvia, *Flüchtlingsaufnahme in Württemberg-Baden 1945–1949. Amerikanische Besatzungsziele und demokratischer Wiederaufbau im Konflikt*. Muncih, Oldenbourg, 1995.

Schwartz, Michael, 'Zwischen Zusammenbruch und Stalinisierung. Zur Ortsbestimmung der Zentralverwaltung für deutsche Umsiedler, ZVU, im politisch-administrativen System der SBZ', in *Von der SBZ zur DDR. Studien zum Herrschaftssystem in der Sowjetischen Besatzungszone Deutschlands und in der Deutschen Demokratischen Republik*, ed. Hartmut Mehringer. Muncih, Oldenbourg, 1995, pp. 43–96.

Schwartz, Michael, 'Vertreibung und Vergangenheitspolitik. Ein Versuch über geteilte deutsche Nachkriegsidentitäten, *Deutschlandarchiv*, No. 2, March/April 1997, pp. 177–95.

Ther, Philipp, *Deutsche und Polnische Vertriebene. Gesellschaft und Vertriebenenpolitik in der SBZ/DDR und in Polen 1945–1956*. Göttingen, Vandenhoeck & Ruprecht, 1998.

Wille, Manfred, Hoffmann, Johannes, and Meinicke, Wolfgang, 'Flüchtlinge und Vertriebene im Spannungsfeld der SBZ-Nachkriegspolitik', in *Sie hatten alles verloren. Flüchtlinge und Vertriebene in der sowjetischen Besatzungszone*, ed. Manfred Wille, Johannes Hoffmann and Wolfgang Meinicke. Wiesbaden, Harrassowitz, 1993, pp. 12–26.

Wille, Manfred, 'Die Zentralverwaltung für deutsche Umsiedler – Möglichkeiten und Grenzen ihres Wirkens, 1945–1948', in *Sie hatten alles verloren. Flüchtlinge und Vertriebene in der sowjetischen Besatzungszone*, ed. Manfred Wille, Johannes Hoffmann and Wolfgang Meinicke. Wiesbaden, Harrassowitz, 1993, pp. 27–54.

Wille, Manfred, Hoffmann, Johannes, and Meinicke, Wolfgang, eds., *Sie hatten alles verloren. Flüchtlinge und Vertriebene in der sowjetischen Besatzungszone*. Wiesbaden, Harrassowitz, 1993.

Chapter 4

The Integration of Ethnic Germans from the Soviet Union

Andreas Heinrich

Introduction: the Concept of Integration

Integration is a long-term process to absorb migrants into the social structures of an existing society that includes more than just one generation. Integration encompasses all areas of everyday life and aims at providing migrants with equal opportunities to access economic, social, political and cultural resources in their new host-society. During the integration process, migrants adopt culturally specific values and norms of the host-society without necessarily giving up their own distinct cultural identity (Berry 1996: 171–86). Integration is a two-way process in as much as the host-society responds to, and changes during, the migration process as well. Thus, integration prevents the existing social system from becoming unstable and ensures its continued functioning as a unity.

Aussiedler generally intend to stay permanently in the Federal Republic. Thus, if integration does not succeed, dangers arise not only in terms of their personal life, but also society at large.

In the following chapter, I will examine the social-structural aspects of integration – how far patterns of social stratification among *Aussiedler* resemble those of German society and whether they are afforded equal opportunities in everyday life.

Emigration Context

For decades, the authorities of the former Soviet Union discriminated against everyone who intended to leave the country. The Soviet Emigration Law of 1959, and its amended versions of 1970 and 1986, did not give any legal and enforceable guarantees, but merely provided for the possibility of emigration in order to reunite families. Permission to leave the country was granted at the discretion of the state and depended upon internal quotas, bilateral agreements, pressure from the West, and the general state of international relations. In addition, the difficult and lengthy application procedure was restricted to four population groups – Jews, Germans, Armenians and Greeks (Biermann 1992:31).

The 1986 revision, which became effective as of 1987, was a fundamental improvement of the emigration procedure. While the reunification of first-degree relatives continued to be the legal basis of emigration, the pressure exerted by authorities on potential émigrés decreased sharply and applications were processed much faster. Thus, from 1987, the number of ethnic Germans migrating from the Soviet Union increased significantly (see Table 4.1). Another, more liberal, version of the Emigration Law was passed in 1990, but the dissolution of the Soviet Union prevented it from coming into effect. Emigration issues are now handled by all the successor states individually (Dietz and Hilkes 1993: 98, 112–4).

Table 4.1: Ethnic German Migrants from the Former Soviet Union

1986	1987	1988	1989	1990	1991	1992	1993
753	14,488	47,572	98,134	147,950	147,320	195,576	207,347
1994	**1995**	**1996**	**1997**	**1998**	**1999**	**2000**	
213,214	209,409	172,181	131,895	101,550	103,599	94,558	

Source: *Infodienst Deutsche Aussiedler* no. 91 (1997) and no. 110 (2000) and various Press Releases of the Bundesinnenministerium of 1998, 1999 and 2000.

According to the results of the last official census in the Soviet Union in 1989, some two million ethnic Germans were then living in various parts of the country. The actual figure is likely to be somewhat higher, probably 2.5 million, as many ethnic Germans, fearing discrimination, did not reveal their nationality. In 1996, the largest group of ethnic Germans (700,000) lived in the Russian Federation, followed by Kazakhstan (660,000) (Gassner 1997: 128).

The motivation of ethnic Germans to leave their traditional homelands arises mostly from the following sources: the almost complete collapse of economic structure and struggle against individual social decline, the breakdown of public order, disappointment about the progress of democratisation, the resurgence of old nationalisms, the desire to live as Germans among Germans, lack of religious freedom, reunion of families, and indirect pressure of the mass exodus that has occurred since the late 1980s.

Apart from the declining numbers of *Aussiedler* arriving in Germany, fewer ethnic Germans who have been recognised as *Aussiedler* exercise their right to migrate to Germany partly because of the improved minority rights situation in the former Soviet Union and partly because of the aid programme administered by the German government to provide ethnic Germans in their homelands with an alternative to emigration. (Waffenschmidt 1997a: 4; 1998: 3)

Areas of Integration

Language

Language competence is one of the essential factors that determine whether an *Aussiedler* will be accepted by 'domestic' Germans as a member of their in-group or not. Furthermore, a sufficiently developed ability to communicate in German is a crucial criterion for success in the labour market. Ethnic Germans from Russia are aware of this situation (Boll 1993: 41; Dietz and Hilkes 1994: 47).

Over the years, the number of those who registered German as their mother tongue in census questionnaires in the former Soviet Union has declined dramatically. In 1959, 74 percent of all those who declared their nationality as German also described their mother tongue as German. Within three decades, this figure had dropped to 49 percent. Yet not even these figures give an accurate picture of the actual language competence, as the declaration of one's mother tongue was also used as a manifestation of ethnic origin.

Today, German is used primarily in a family context and in a local variety, rather than in its standard form. It is difficult to paint an overall picture of the situation, as significant differences occur between the various settlement areas in the successor states of the former Soviet Union. In general, language competence is better developed among the older generation and in areas with compact German settlements and functioning community institutions. (Dietz and Hilkes 1993: 49, 55; 1994: 21, 50, 54)

Irrespective of their ability to speak German, upon arrival in the Federal Republic, *Aussiedler* are legally entitled to a language course. The length of the course was cut in half between 1976 (when it could last up to twelve months) and 1993. In this year, the funding structure changed, too. Until the end of 1992, language courses for *Aussiedler* were financed by the Federal Labour Agency. From January 1993 onwards, the exclusive source of funding had been resources provided directly by the federal budget, which has led to severe cut backs over the past five years.

Apart from developing the language skills of *Aussiedler*, these courses are also supposed to advance knowledge of the Federal Republic and to facilitate integration in general. This requires qualified teaching staff, who are not always available. Another problem is that there is normally no ranking of course participants according to their level of language competence. This and the fact that the courses cannot make allowances for initial adjustment to new teaching methods, which is particularly difficult for the older generation, has resulted in a decline in target attainment by *Aussiedler* (Dietz and Hilkes 1994: 27–9; Michel and Steinke 1996: xi).

The motivation of *Aussiedler* to learn German is generally high, notwithstanding an increasingly visible motivational deficit among the younger generation, especially amongst twelve- to fifteen-year-olds, who did not always volunteer to migrate to Germany. In this context, it is also important to realise that the Russian language retains its function as preserving the identity of, and solidarity within, the group of *Aussiedler* from the former Soviet Union. Especially for younger *Aussiedler*, the means of communication with friends and relatives is Russian; (Koller 1996: 12; Rakhkochkine 1997: 13).

A survey of fifteen- to twenty-five-year-old *Aussiedler* who arrived in Germany between 1990 and 1994 revealed that three-quarters of them had participated in a language course with an average length of eight months. Of those, only one-third considered their linguistic abilities to be good. They also belonged to those families that used German, at least partly, at home. Of all interviewees, only just under 8 percent spoke exclusively German, while the number of families using both Russian and German was 45 percent – the same number as those who spoke Russian only. Thirty-nine percent of those surveyed had one non-German parent. All this reflects the situation in the traditional settlement areas of *Aussiedler* in the former Soviet Union relatively accurately (Rakhkochkine 1997: 13).

While *Aussiedler* increasingly depend on their own initiative to enhance their knowledge of German, the language courses, nevertheless, significantly contribute to an improvement of the language skills, especially of younger *Aussiedler*, and thus promote acceptance among 'domestic' Germans.

Education

The Second World War generally limited educational opportunities in the Soviet Union, but ethnic Germans suffered additionally from the consequences of deportation and had, until the mid-1950s, hardly any chances of a proper education and were underrepresented at institutions of higher education until the late 1960s. Only in the two decades preceding the collapse of the Soviet Union could the educational deficit of Germans in comparison to other nationalities be overcome. The level of education of *Aussiedler* from the successor states of the Soviet Union, therefore, depends upon the generation to which they belong – younger *Aussiedler* often have a higher level of formal education than their parents' or grandparents' generation. (Dietz and Hilkes 1993: 37–9, 65; 1994: 20f., 33f.)

The unexpected increase in migration from the Soviet Union after 1987, and subsequently from its successor states, was met by the German government with the creation of the so-called 'guarantee fund' in 1988. Its main purpose is to provide financial aid for the educational, professional and social integration of young *Aussiedler*, but its funds have been cut over recent years as well – from 360 million Deutschmark in 1993 to 255 million in 1997 (Waffenschmidt 1997b).

Because of the educational autonomy of each of the *Länder* in Germany, there is no single way of integrating young *Aussiedler* into the German educational system. Some states provide specific preparation classes for *Aussiedler* prior to their integration into mainstream education, while others prefer immediate integration, occasionally with some additional tuition in German, depending upon the commitment of the respective school (Dietz and Hilkes 1994: 20, Michel and Steinke 1996: xvii). The Standing Conference of State Education Ministers has further recommended boarding schools with specific programmes to prepare *Aussiedler* for various school exit exams (which, however, do not facilitate contact with native German pupils), and day schools which offer special programmes to facilitate integration outside regular school hours.

Further difficulty arises from the fact that *Aussiedler* are often sent to types of school that do not match their capabilities because their educational achievements prior to migration are not considered adequate by the authorities.

Aussiedler who have already begun a university study, or are just about to enrol at an institution of higher education, can receive grants from the Otto Bennecke Foundation.

Cutbacks in funding since 1992/1993 have limited the range of services that can be offered to facilitate educational integration of young *Aussiedler* in the Federal Republic. Young *Aussiedler* thus lack crucial orientation in the general process of integration. On the other hand, the increasing emphasis on cross-cultural dimensions of learning in teacher training programmes in Germany has begun to provide better opportunities for the successful integration of *Aussiedler* in the mainstream education process (Dietz and Hilkes 1994: 29–31).

The Labour Market

The professional integration of *Aussiedler* is a basic precondition for their overall social integration into Germany. Until 1991, the situation in the German labour market made it easy for *Aussiedler* to find a job. In addition, their age and occupational structure facilitated job integration, in particular as *Aussiedler* filled an existing gap in blue-collar manufacturing jobs. Nevertheless, since the end of the 1980s, there has been a continuously high number of unemployed *Aussiedler*. This trend has worsened since the slowing of economic growth from 1993 onwards and has hit *Aussiedler* particularly hard as job offers in manufacturing decreased, and the only expanding sector – services – was mostly inaccessible for *Aussiedler* as a group because of their occupational structure. When, parallel to this, the number of available *Aussiedler* continued to increase throughout the first half of the 1990s, the professional integration of *Aussiedler* became harder.

The tense economic situation in Germany and the increased number of *Aussiedler* arriving in the country resulted in a per capita reduction of financial aid from the government. From 1 January 1990, *Aussiedler* of working age were entitled to so-called 'integration money' (*Eingliederungsgeld*), which, similar to regular unemployment benefit, was payable for up to twelve months, depending upon marital status. Attendance of a language course could increase the payment period by up to eight months. After that, *Aussiedler* were entitled to unemployment aid and subsequently to welfare benefits.

The 1993 War Consequences Consolidation Act introduced further cuts. *Aussiedler* were now entitled to nine months of integration benefits, which could be extended by up to six months if they attended a language course. The amount of money paid is means tested, all other income being taken into account. Further training and education are no longer financed by the Federal Labour Agency, but rather costs have to be covered by the individual *Aussiedler*. Similarly, it is no longer possible to combine two or more qualification measures, e.g., a language and a professional training course, so that *Aussiedler* now have to choose between the two. Since 1994, integration benefits have been paid up to a maximum of six months, without the possibility of extending it through participation in a language course. This makes further professional qualifications for *Aussiedler* very difficult.

Among those *Aussiedler* from Russia who have found a job, two-thirds are working in the manufacturing industry, and one-third have white-collar jobs. Women suffer more from unemployment than men, mostly because their professional qualifications do not allow them to continue working in their occupation without further training. This is particularly the case in social and educational jobs, but also in administration and organisation (Dietz and Hilkes 1994: 66–72). A lack of mobility, due to strong family ties, and a dependency on large-scale manufacturing as major employment sector have also added to the difficulties experienced by many *Aussiedler* from Russia in succeeding in terms of their professional integration.

The Housing Situation

Recognition of *Aussiedler* status implies at the same time allocation of accommodation in the Federal Republic. Initially, *Aussiedler* are brought to a central camp in Friedland, Lower Saxony, from where they are distributed to the various *Länder*, based on a negotiated quota.

Until the end of the 1980s, *Aussiedler* only stayed for a short time in provisional accommodation in the *Land* to which they had been allocated and were relatively easily able to find themselves accommodation to rent privately. Since then, however, the situation in the housing market and the increased numbers of *Aussiedler* have meant that provisional accommodation offered by the various *Länder* has very often developed into long-term options. This has led to increasingly poor living conditions for *Aussiedler*. There is very often not enough space to accommodate large families, halls of residence are usually in unattractive areas outside town centres, and *Aussiedler* accommodation has been attacked by right-wing extremists – all of which has increased social tensions among *Aussiedler* and between them and the local population. This, in turn, has not facilitated the social integration of *Aussiedler* at all. On the contrary, long-term 'provisional' accommodation (in 1996 between one-and-a-half and three years depending upon size of family and income) has increased ghettoisation and isolation of *Aussiedler* and has made them retreat into their families rather than reach out to the local population.

Since the mid-1970s, most *Aussiedler* from Russia have already had friends or relatives in Germany at the time of their arrival. Their permanent residence, rather than the situation in the labour or housing market, determines in the majority of cases where newly arriving *Aussiedler* want to settle down. Thus, these chain-migrations led to an over-proportionate settlement of *Aussiedler* from Russia in Lower Saxony, Hesse, Rhineland Palatine, and Baden-Württemberg between 1976 and 1992. An intervention by these and other strongly affected Länder resulted in the 1989 Law on the Determination of a Provisional Place of Residence for *Aussiedler* and *Übersiedler*, according to which *Aussiedler* have to settle in an allocated community for the first two years of their stay or lose all their entitlements to integration benefits. The only exception to this applies to *Aussiedler* who can prove that they have either a job or a place in a job-training programme or at a university in another community.

Even during the 1980s, when the situation in the housing market was much better than it was a decade later, *Aussiedler* from Russia found it difficult to fulfil their dream of buying a house or a flat. Aided by a special loan according to the *Lastenausgleichsgesetz* (burden sharing law), which was replaced by the War Consequences Consolidation Act in 1993, quite a substantial number of them managed to do so usually after several years. Since the beginning of the 1990s, this opportunity has almost completely vanished, because of the general economic downturn and the cut in integration support. Thus, it is not surprising that the gap between expectations of *Aussiedler* regarding their housing situation and the reality of it has steadily increased over the last decade.

Social Participation

Strongly influenced by their socialisation in a Communist system, *Aussiedler* from Russia have little or no knowledge about the political process and its rules in Germany. Therefore, *Aussiedler* are strongly influenced by the idea that the state should be responsible for the economic and social security of each individual citizen. A similar difference in comparison to the average 'indigenous' German exists in relation to the differentiation between a social and a private sphere, of which the latter has great importance for *Aussiedler* from the former Soviet Union. Individualisation, the lack of social structure to which *Aussiedler* had got accustomed in the Soviet Union, the social distance between them and 'indigenous' Germans, and the large number of foreigners in Germany, from whom they try to distinguish themselves clearly, make social participation of *Aussiedler* in Germany difficult and have contributed to an increasing lack of integration into mainstream society (Dietz and Hilkes 1994: 75ff.).

The integration process is further complicated by the rejection *Aussiedler* experience at the hands of the local population in their community, in their workplace, or by local authorities. Rejection is particularly often experienced by younger *Aussiedler*, who have more contact with 'indigenous' Germans, yet at the same time often lack sufficient communication abilities. This rejection, in turn, increases the difficulties of the integration process, as contacts with the local population are infrequent and often not of a positive nature, despite the fact that *Aussiedler* are aware of the need for social contacts with 'indigenous' Germans and generally seek to establish these. Whilst contact with other *Aussiedler* from the former Soviet Union and the creation and use of *Aussiedler* networks is an element of great importance in the integration process as a whole, an obvious danger is that this will remain the only contact and support for *Aussiedler*, leading to their marginalisation as individuals and as a group in German society.

Family and Religion as Factors in the Integration Process

The family is at the centre of the daily life of *Aussiedler* from the former Soviet Union. These families are primarily characterised by patriarchal structures, and there is a traditional division of roles between men and women. Strong family ties, on the one hand, provide important support to cope with the difficulties of the migration and integration process. On the other hand, however, these same strong family ties also hinder the individual development and integration primarily of young *Aussiedler*. Thus, conflict lines emerge within the families between the children and parental generations. These are further complicated by the fact that, in contrast to the earlier socialisation experience in the Soviet Union, education in Germany is not the exclusive domain of the state; parents are expected to take responsibility as well. The family therefore faces the double challenge of providing a support basis during integration as well as facilitating this same process, which very often creates conflicting aims and purposes.

The strong ties within families and among *Aussiedler* in part also result from the fact that religious activities in the former Soviet Union were usually confined to small and trustworthy circles of ethnic Germans. As religion was closely linked to their distinct ethnocultural identity, religious and customary traditions became closely intertwined and were passed down the generations (Dietz and Hilkes 1993: 87; 1994: 25, 103).

As there was no strict separation amongst the various religious communities of ethnic Germans in the former Soviet Union, *Aussiedler* from there participate in religious services near where they live rather than choose a church that corresponds to the religious community they belonged to in Russia or any of the other successor states. This obviously creates problems for the integration of *Aussiedler*, in particular also because they do not easily understand the religious separation between Catholic, Protestant and Free Churches and generally do not appreciate the anonymous, liberal and often political nature of religious services in German churches. All of these churches in Germany have made some effort to integrate *Aussiedler*, but their religious traditions and moral values do not fit in easily with church structures and the often more liberal approach to alcohol, cigarettes and sex in Germany. On the other hand, church activities that start at the time of the arrival of *Aussiedler* in Germany and include help in managing the bureaucratic complexities and psychological difficulties of the integration process are much appreciated by the *Aussiedler*.

Conclusion

The confrontation with German reality is experienced by many *Aussiedler* as a cultural shock and often leads to a withdrawal into the private community of other *Aussiedler*. On the one hand, this helps *Aussiedler* from the former Soviet Union to cope with the difficulties of the integration process. On the other hand, however, it leads to their isolation as a group, which is further increased by the rejection of *Aussiedler* as Germans from the indigenous population. Further complications in the integration process arise from decreasing opportunities for professional integration, from the tense situation in the housing market, and from cutbacks in government spending in various integration programmes at a time when the number of *Aussiedler* increased disproportionately.

Instead of a successful integration process, *Aussiedler* face increasing isolation. Few of their hopes for a better life in Germany have materialised. The only hope that remains for them is that their children will succeed in building a bridge between them and the 'indigenous' German population.

References

Berry, John W., 'Acculturation and Psychological Adaption', in *Migration, Ethnizität, Konflikt: Systemfragen und Fallstudien*, ed. Klaus J. Bade, Osnabrück, Institut für Migrationsforschung und Interkulturelle Studien, 1996.

Biermann, Rafael, 'Migration aus Osteuropa und dem Maghreb', *Aus Politik und Zeitgeschichte*, no. 9, 1992.

Boll, Klaus, *Kulturwandel der Deutschen aus der Sowjetunion. Eine empirische Studie zur Lebenswelt rußlanddeutscher Aussiedler in der Bundesrepublik*. Marburg, Kommission für ostdeutsche Volkskunde, 1993.

Dietz, Barbara and Hilkes, Peter, *Rußlanddeutsche: Unbekannte im Osten. Geschichte, Situation, Zukunftsperspektive*. Munich, Olzog, 1993.

Dietz, Barbara and Hilkes, Peter, *Integriert oder isoliert? Zur Situtaion rußlanddeutscher Aussiedler in der Bundesrepublik Deutschland*. Munich, Olzog, 1994.

Gassner, Hartmut, '*Aussiedler*politik', in *Migration und Flucht. Aufgaben und Strategien für Deutschland, Europa und die internationale Gemeinschaft*, ed. by Steffen Angenendt, Bonn , Bundeszentrale für Politische Bildung, 1997.

Koller, Barbara, '*Aussiedler* in Deutschland. Aspekte ihrer sozialen und beruflichen Eingliederung', in *Aus Politik und Zeitgeschichte* no. 48, 1996.

Michel, Manuela and Steinke, Jutta, *Arbeitsmarktintegration von Spätaussiedlerinnen und Spätaussiedlern in NRW*. Düsseldorf, Ministerium für Arbeit, Gesundheit und Soziales des Landes Nordrhein-Westfalen, 1996.

Rakhkochkine, Anatoli, 'Neue Heimat – neue Zukunft. Eine soziologisch-pädagogische Studie über die Integration der Kinder der *Aussiedler* aus den GUS-Staaten', in *Aus Politik und Zeitgeschichte*, no. 7–8, 1997.

Waffenschmidt, Horst, '*Aussiedler*politik 1997', in *Info-Dienst Deutsche Aussiedler*, no. 86, 1997a.

Waffenschmidt, Horst, 'Rede in der *Aussiedler*debatte am 13. November 1997 im Bundestag', in *Presseinformation des Bundesinnenministeriums*, 13 November 1997 Bonn, Bundesministerium des Innern, 1997b.

Waffenschmidt, Horst, Aktuelle *Aussiedler*politik. Bonn, Bundesministerium des Innern, 1998.

Chapter 5

Jus Sanguinis or *Jus Mimesis?* Rethinking 'Ethnic German' Repatriation

Stefan Senders

Nationalism is directly predicated on resemblance, whether biogenetic or cultural. The pivotal idea is that all citizens are, in some unarguable sense, all alike ...

(Herzfeld: 1997: 27)

The human is a creature who makes a picture of [itself] and then comes to resemble the picture.

(Murdoch 1957: 122)

When Liza Fechner, a former engineer from Siberia, arrived at the 'transit camp' in Bramsche, West Germany, she was immediately required to take a language test. Liza had come to Germany as an *Aussiedler*, an ethnic German, and her knowledge of German, it was reasoned, would confirm her German identity. With her few words she passed easily, and she was given a temporary status allowing her to travel to Berlin where she would be tested again and where she would stay. The man behind her in line, Liza told me laughing, did not make it through quite so easily. Unable even to muster a 'Ja' or a 'Nein', he was turned away by the testing official who grudgingly offered him another chance if he would try again later. 'He (the official) told him to come back the next day. He said that he had to learn six words of German by then, or he wouldn't let him through.'

It is easy to see why Liza laughed. The German government claims that 'Germany is not an immigration country', and that '*Aussiedler* are German'. Yet because *Aussiedler* do 'immigrate' (in German it is glossed as *zurück-wandern* (wander back), *zurückkehren* (turn around and come back), or *heimkehren* (come back home)) and foreigners ostensibly do not, distinguishing between them is critical. If all one need do to be a German is learn six German words, how seriously can the distinction between 'foreigners' and 'Germans' be taken? Liza was not the only one laughing; 'The only thing German about *Aussiedler*', the common joke goes, 'is that they have German Shepherds!'

What makes *Aussiedler* 'German'? In the literature concerning German citizenship, identity, and immigration law, a body of law which I will call simply 'identity law', one statement is ubiquitous – that German citizenship is based exclusively on the principle of *jus sanguinis*, the 'law of the blood'. Rogers Brubaker, for example, writes that the '1913 system of pure *jus sanguinis*, with no trace of *jus soli*, continues to determine the citizenship status of immigrants and their descendants today' (Brubaker 1992: 65).[1] Christian Giordano asserts that the 'exclusion of [second and third generation immigrants] and integration of [*Aussiedler*] come about by virtue of one's origin, which in the case of the '*Aussiedler*' must be biologically proven ... no reference whatsoever is made to the possibility of assimilation or integration: everything is inescapably defined by the family tree' (1997: 180). Nora Räthzel, in her 'One Race – One Nation?', argued that '... the concept of the German nation ... is constructed biologically. German nationals are defined by their origin: one can only be born a German' (1990: 41). And Jane Kramer writes that Germany is a 'country where *jus sanguinis* is still practised' (italics added) and she, like many others, seems to see Germany as a straggler in a global temporal order heading resolutely towards a republican *jus soli* (1996: xxi).

The widespread interest in and critique of German identity law stems from two sources. The first is concern for the rights and freedoms of Germany's large foreign population. Long-term Turkish residents, we are often reminded, rarely naturalise, and those who would do so find it difficult. The second is anger over Germany's willingness to include and embrace 'ethnic Germans' who are said to claim their German identity by virtue of descent or blood. The very mention of the word 'blood' is enough to link current policy to Nazi policy; *jus sanguinis* is inevitably polemical.

It is important to criticise Germany's lack of an adequate immigration law – Germany claims to have no immigrants at all – but the critique should not preclude analysis. Nor should the analytic distinction between *jus soli* and *jus sanguinis* be used to disguise or obscure political critique. What is wrong about German immigration policy is not that it 'defines Germanness by descent', but that it seeks to reproduce Germany *in Germany's own image*. It therefore excludes difference – and thus different people— from its narrative of national reproduction.

It is true that descent is granted central importance in German citizenship law. Yet the *meaning* of 'descent' is far from self-evident. While distinctions between 'blood and mud', as David Schneider is said to have put it, do allow us to characterise systems of identity law in relation to one another, they give us little insight into the ways the categories are actually made meaningful. Terms such as 'blood', 'descent', or even 'citizenship', form the starting points for analysis, not their conclusions.[2]

The role of descent in legal systems has long been of interest to anthropologists. In Sally Falk Moore's analysis of Lango jurisprudence, for example, she examines descent as concept and as jural-rule. Descent, Moore argues, is an 'ideology of identities, a model of relationships in the sense of homologies, not of behaviour ... It may be used symbolically to represent identities of interest or categories that, in fact, are not genealogical descent relationships at all' (1974: 380). In Germany the notion of descent serves to legitimate an unequal distribution of property, power, access, and inclusion. To be included in the German descent community, to be *deutschstämmig*, can mean access to citizenship, voting rights and retirement insurance, to name only a few benefits.

The most striking example of inclusion 'by descent' in Germany is that of 'ethnic Germans.' Most 'ethnic Germans' entering Germany since 1990 have come from areas of the former Soviet Union, including Kazakhstan, Siberia and Russia. Their privileged entry into Germany is based on the juridical assumption that they share in German identity, and their status is defined in two sets of laws. One is the 1949 *Grundgesetz* or 'Basic Law' which carries over the descent principle from the Weimar constitution of 1919. In the Basic Law the 'German' person is initially defined in article §116 which links German identity to both descent and history. The law, moreover, refers to yet another set of laws – the expellee laws – which were written to regulate the post-war influx of German 'refugees and expellees'.[3] The expellee laws constitute a right of return for those who can demonstrate ethnic German or *Volksdeutsche* identity.

In what follows, I examine one case in which the identity of an 'ethnic German' was legally challenged. The final decision, the determination of her identity, turned not on genealogical descent but on her purported sharing of experiences of suffering, repression and cultural identification. Yet, to be identified as a 'real' German in such cases includes the *attribution* of descent; there is no term distinguishing Germans-by-identification from Germans-by-descent. Descent, then, is not a biological or genealogical relation, but is an ideology used to legitimate identifications. It is a narrative strategy for designating a degree of likeness, of similarity, seen as necessary for full membership in the German nation. Such relationships of similarity and reproduction can be characterised in terms of *mimesis*, or representation. More particularly, in the context of identity law, mimesis can be analysed in terms of the organisation and evaluation of identifications and perceived resemblance among people and between people and identity categories.

Mimesis

Mimesis always concerns a relationship of likeness – a relationship which can run the gamut from identicality to radical alterity – between one thing and another. As a categorical term, then, mimesis refers to the nature and qualities of such relationships. The concept of *jus mimesis* addresses social incorporation and excorporation as a juridical field of culturally specific practices for producing and determining likeness and unlikeness.

Historically, the term mimesis has taken two central forms; in its pre-Platonic or 'sensuous' configuration, *mimeisthai* referred to the manifestation of spirit in music and dance, that is, to ecstatic or 'dionysian' expression (Koller 1954). Sensuous mimesis locates agency, the impulse driving representation, to forces beyond the control of the individual; the person is merely a vehicle for the mimesis of spirit, god or nature. By contrast, in its Platonic or imitative form, mimesis refers to parody and mimicry; for Plato the laws of the state imitate the laws of the divine, and the mimetic work of poets is seen as simply a poor and ultimately destructive copy of reality.

The mimetic fissure opened by Plato between object and representation was bridged most famously by Aristotle in the *Poetics*. Aristotle stressed the importance of cultural norms in determining mimetic practice; poetry was to represent the world not as it is, but as it is most plausible. From this perspective, to analyse mimesis would be to investigate the internal logic of representation, to seek the cultural reality of the 'true'.

In his famous study *Mimesis: The Representation of Reality in Western Literature*, Erich Auerbach took up just such a project, asking how literary works represent the 'reality' of particular historical periods (1953). What strategies, what artifice, and what assumptions allow narrative to 'represent' reality?

Mimesis, in this sense, is guided by the culturally defined realm of possibility that defines the 'we' of the readership. It invokes and creates the social group, even as it depends upon it for its substance. Mimesis is also, then, as Derrida has written, a form of control, a 'matter for the police':

> The narratorial voice is the voice of a subject recounting, knowing who he is, where he is, what he is and what he is talking about ... In this sense, all organised narration is a 'matter for the police.' (Cited in Prendergast 1986: 219)

Nowhere, perhaps, is this more clearly exemplified than in the case of ethnic German repatriation. Ethnic Germans are required to bring their life stories into conformation with prototypic plots; they must claim to have had the proper kinds of relationships, to have felt the appropriate pain, and to have experienced their own being in specific and predetermined forms.[4]

Mimesis and Legal Discourse

All identity law is fundamentally mimetic. To be 'a German', for example, is to assert in narrative form a particular relationship to a prototypic identity category. The category is, to quote Judith Butler (who was talking about gender), 'a "normative" one, a "regulatory ideal" that is part of an iterative regime of practice which produces the very bodies it projects and controls' (1993: 1). Citizens, in other words, are produced, not born, and they are produced in relation to models both ideal and abject. The project of producing citizens, and identities generally, entails what we couldcall 'mimetic identification', the reproduction of conceptual categories in human self-consciousness.

In most cases mimetic identifications are seemingly transparent; for example, people born in Germany to German parents grow up feeling themselves to be unquestionably German. Such identifications are fundamentally doxic, in that they are fully naturalised, and thus resist investigation (Bourdieu 1977: 164–7). Inevitably, however, there are cases that challenge normative and regulatory ideals, exposing the categories that underlie them. Ethnic German repatriation is one such case. The ambiguity of repatriate claims to German identity has led to the establishment of bureaucratic procedures designed to test ethnic Germans, to investigate their identities and probe their stories.[5]

The Legal Discourse of Identity

At the end of the Second World War, Germany took on the task of integrating the millions of 'German' refugees and expellees who had fled the Russian advance or who had been forcibly resettled as a result of the Potsdam Accords. These refugees and expellees were given official status in the 1949 Basic Law, which in Article §116 distinguished between German 'citizens' (*Staatsangehörige*) and those of ethnic Germans (*Volksangehörige*).[6] The category of 'ethnic German' is defined in the Federal Refugee Law. The key paragraph, §6, reads as follows:

> Members of the German *ethnie*, within the meaning of this law, are those who in their homeland have maintained and acknowledged German belonging and can confirm it through such evidence as descent, language, upbringing or culture.[7]

The wording is extraordinarily vague; what form of 'culture' might be sufficient evidence for German identity? What is meant by the requirements to have 'maintained' and 'acknowledged' German belonging, and what kind of procedures might determine its presence?

The legal concept of German identity is fundamentally romantic – it assumes an inner core of true identification – and it is primarily narrative–based. To be German, individuals are called on to demonstrate the 'truth' of their identifications by presenting and representing their stories to bureaucrats; they must tell, perform and argue their identities.

Despite the romantic ideology driving identity law, the bureaucracy that enacts it is structured around irony; it is founded on the assumption that applicants will lie, that they will merely imitate Germans. In this context 'internal' feeling and 'external' representation are defined legally as key to Ethnic German identity claims.[8] But how are ambiguous cases decided? What kinds of arguments are used to sustain or undermine claims to German identity?

Case Report

In July of 1990, Elisabeth Spengler arrived in Germany with her grandparents, parents, brother and daughter.[9] They had come with provisional acceptance as 'ethnic Germans', and they expected to be welcomed into Germany as Germans. Upon arrival the members of Elisabeth's family were granted Ethnic German status. Elisabeth, however, was refused. She was judged to be 'not permeated' with Germanness.[10] Elisabeth appealed against the ruling, and the court of appeal, after personal hearings with Elisabeth and her grandparents, overturned the first decision and granted her ethnic German status.

In writing up the case the court of appeal began with Elisabeth's genealogy. For the court the narrative of genealogical descent is not a sufficient basis for her bid for German citizenship. It merely sets the stage for a more subtle and conditional interpretation of belonging. The descent narrative was then combined with one of suffering and deportation.

> In 1941 the grandfather, K_ A_, was deported from his home to Solikamsk in the Urals, and the Grandmother K_ K_ was then deported first to Kazakhstan and then to Solikamsk, where she was interned in a forced-labour camp of the so-called 'labour-army'. From 1946 to 1956 both lived in a labour-camp in Perm, which was at that time called 'Molotov'. It was here that they were married on the 7th of January, 1949. The plaintiff's mother, E_ A_, was born in Perm on the 15th of January, 1949. In 1956 the grandparents, and the then seven-year-old mother of the plaintiff, moved to Kazakhstan to the village of Wladimirovka, in the area Balkaschinsk, Zelinograd region. Here the mother married the Russian (*Volkszugehöriger*) V. D. on the 4th of June, 1968.[11]

Only after the court has recited the plaintiff's lineage back three generations, and only after the history of suffering has been introduced, does Elisabeth herself enter the story.

Elisabeth was born in 1969, and in 1977 she moved with her extended family to the Caucasus. There she attended school taught in Russian until 1988, when she took a job as a cook in a dairy-processing-plant. In November 1987 she married A_ S_, a Russian, with whom she had a daughter in the spring of 1986. The marriage was dissolved in the winter of 1989.

The court had argued that Elisabeth, who came in any case from a 'mixed-nationality marriage',[12] had become a Russian like her father and ex-husband. She had even gone so far as to register herself in her first domestic passport as a Russian. Even more important, perhaps, was that in her daughter's birth certificate Elisabeth's nationality was given as 'Russian.' As far as the court was concerned, she had 'acknowledged herself' as a Russian[13] and thus given up her German identity.

Elisabeth agreed that she had indeed been listed in her daughter's birth certificate as a Russian. But, she said, her former husband was to blame for that; he had had the certificate issued. To further support her claim to German identity, Elisabeth argued that she had possessed three passports while in the Soviet Union – one before the marriage, one during the marriage and one after the separation. In all three cases, she said, she had registered *herself* as 'German'. The court, however, argued that in her first (adult) Soviet passport she had identified herself as a Russian, the same nationality as her father.

The court, finally, could neither confirm nor deny that Elisabeth had thought of herself as German during her marriage. They found it conceivable, however, that any shift in her self-identification was indicative not of internal change, but of the influence of her husband. 'One cannot exclude … that the plaintiff, under the influence of her then husband between 1987 and 1989, was registered as "Russian".'[14] Elisabeth's identification, then, was seen as a function of power and intimacy: the mimetic impulse is always open to influence and transformation. But the court was stymied. How could they determine whether Elisabeth had actually changed her self-identification? Had she simply let her husband write what he wished? Or had she actually submitted to his power and become, even temporarily, Russian? Just as important are the consequences of representation; to be a German one must be seen as German:

> If the applicant was continuously listed as 'German' in her domestic passport during the period from the issue of her passport until the time of her leaving the Soviet Union, if she therefore was regarded as having continuously counted as a German and as having suffered consequential disadvantagement, then she could be considered as having a 'connection of acknowledgement' with the German ethnie, even without mastery of the German language. The official expression of German nationality in the passport would have led to stigmatisation which would constitute a 'key experience of duration'.[15]

Elizabeth, it was argued, had spent enough time with her grandparents, who had been deported from the Volga region, for her to establish a psychological identification with them resulting in 'deep experiences'[16] leading to 'identification with [their] ethnic consciousness.'[17] That is, she had 'internalised'[18] their experiences as her own. Moreover, the time spent with her grandparents constituted a 'key experience of duration'[19] that cemented her connection to the German 'community of fate'.[20] She had been 'drawn into the current of fate'[21] and she had 'paid the collective price'[22] for it. Elisabeth's mother is quoted as saying,

> I told Elisabeth about my parents' fate – the deportation and the labour-army. And I've told her about how it was for us in school. As a child I was always insulted as a German, and even today that's still a wound in my heart. At that time I asked my mother: 'Why

do they say that to us?' And it was just the same then as it was when Elisabeth asked me. I explained: 'We have to accept that because Germany and Russia had a war, and we, as Germans, must now pay the price for it.[23]

Social Practice

The court of appeal then turned to practice and custom to determine Elisabeth's German identity. They looked, in particular, for such practices as the 'celebration of German holidays, maintenance of German customs and culture, participation in the life of a German *ethnie*, and membership in a predominantly German religious community'.[24]

Membership of one of the 'traditional religious confessions'[25] of the ethnic Germans, and participation in services of the church communities or special religious communities, which were permitted again from the end of the 1950s, would, on account of the historical meaning of such communities for the ethnic Germans from Russia, also serve the function of augmenting German identity and could therefore be counted as 'a German custom'.[26]

Along with church attendance, the maintenance of religious practices, especially the celebration of Christmas, were to be considered important evidence of identification – all the more so if they had been celebrated according to the Gregorian calendar. In hearings Elisabeth and her family made specific reference to their family celebrations:

> [Her] family-life, under the influence of her German grandparents who lived nearby, was acted out in accordance with German ways of life, and [her] Russian father accepted it and went along with it. The Christian holidays, above all Christmas, were celebrated in accordance with German traditions and the Gregorian calendar. The grandparents saw to the keeping of German traditions: they said grace in German at table, and they sang German songs, which they had preserved by writing them down in books.[27]

The court of appeal wrote that in Elisabeth's family such 'German' practices had been passed down from grandmother to mother, and finally to Elisabeth herself. Tradition, here in the form of social practice, takes a form analogous to matrilineal 'descent'; it is passed down along maternal lines. But unlike any strict notion of descent, the concept of influence and power plays an important role. It is 'under the influence' of the mother and grandmother that such practices survive, and it is to such influence that the 'Russian' males in the family submit. Finally, it is maternal influence that leads the plaintiff to 'internalise'[28] and 'take on'[29] German ways of life.

History

The court then addressed Elisabeth's subjective sense of belonging. In particular, they sought a sense of 'group-consciousness',[30] a 'consciousness of belonging to a community of fate possessing a communal past and a communal experience'.[31] Part of that consciousness, they argued, takes the form of knowledge of family history, especially knowledge of the history of the 'experience-generation'.[32]

Elisabeth's mother had been traumatised in childhood by insults and exclusion because of her German identity. Elisabeth, argued the court, was aware of her mother's trauma, and she had experienced exclusion herself, despite which she had not renounced her 'ethnic German identity-consciousness'.[33] Her German grandparents, moreover, with whom she maintained close contact, had experienced directly the deportation and dispossession that was the specific lot of the *Russlanddeutsche*.[34] The court found it believable that Elisabeth had been 'drawn into this line-of-fate'[35] through discussion and through listening, despite the fact that she had never had a 'special key experience'[36] herself.

Again, the notion of the 'key experience' is antithetical to any concept of essential or descent-based identity. People are seen as open to influence and capable of transformation.

Language

The court of appeal argued that Elisabeth had already demonstrated a high degree of 'Germanness'.[37] To test the claim the court paid special attention to her psychological self-inclusion in the Russia German narrative of suffering. To what extent, they wondered, had she shared in the 'group-fate'[38] of the Russian-Germans, and how might that account for the second key point in the case – her inability to speak German?

In such cases the ability to speak German is critical. To speak German is seen as a sign of an inner German identity; it affirms the belonging of the speaker. At the same time, language is taken to be a primary *source* of group identification; to speak a language as a mother tongue is to come into being in a social world determined by that language. Elisabeth's lack of fluency had been taken as a sign of an internal absence, a lack of German identification. It had also been seen as evidence that she had no plausible internal connection to the German *ethnie*.

The court of appeal countered, arguing that an applicant's linguistic ability could not be interpreted as a simple sign of identity; the social and historical context of speech was also important. In particular, they argued, Germans in the Soviet Union had been prohibited from speaking German in public, and they had been ridiculed, punished or ostracised when they tried.

> If an applicant is unable to speak High- or Standard-German well or at all, the speaking, or even the understanding, of a Russian-German dialect – or passive knowledge of German picked up within the family – can be important evidence of the existence within the family of a context conducive to the maintenance of ethnic German traditions.[39]

'In judging the nationality of the plaintiff', they argued,

> the especially severe fate of the ethnic Germans in the former Soviet Union must not be excluded from consideration. It is marked by deportations, beginning with the start of

the German-Soviet war on the 22nd of June, 1941, in which Germans were deported to special settlements where they did forced labour as 'fascist enemies ... This led to a pariah situation for the ethnic Germans, which they continued to endure in many forms of discrimination even after the special settlements had been dissolved.[40]

Ironically, Elisabeth's inability to speak German was taken as a sign that she had suffered repression, which in turn was read as a sign of her German identity; the absence of German language confirmed the presence of German identity. Moreover, the court of appeal argued that independent facts confirmed Elisabeth's 'German belonging'.[41] With the combined evidence, she had convincingly demonstrated 'fundamental ethnic German consciousness'.[42] The appeal was successful, and Elisabeth was granted *Aussiedler* status.

The court of appeal went so far as to argue that for applicants from the former Soviet Union the language requirement should be dropped entirely. In future cases, they suggested, it should simply be assumed that applicants had been unable to learn and speak German. While Elisabeth's status was no longer in question, the legality of the court of appeal's decision was. In a review of the appeal, an administrative court rejected the suggested statutory revisions, arguing that the

opinion of the appeal court that a declaration of German nationality as well as the passing on of the German language had been unreasonable requirements. [To do so] would, in effect, reduce the requirements for belonging to the German ethnie to descent, which is, however, not the law ... Ethnic German identity is a legal concept, and moreover, primarily an acknowledgement concept. The acknowledgement of German *Volkstum*, ... is composed of an inner fact, namely that of a determined desire, carried in the consciousness, to belong to the German *ethnie* as a national cultural community – and an external fact, namely the external display of that consciousness-situation.[43]

Conclusions

Elisabeth's case demonstrates the complex configuration of mimetic modes and practices that define terms of belonging in ethnic German repatriation. It should be clear that German identification can be created through a wide variety of practices including discussion, memory, identification and suffering, in addition to descent claims. It should also be clear that many of the criteria used to determine a German identity are subsumed under the category of descent. That is, once one has been identified as German on any basis, German genealogical descent is assumed.

German identity law is founded on *recovery* rather than transformation; it is fundamentally narcissistic, marking any divergence from the self as an aberration, a temporary lapse. Ideologies of recovery are always troublesome. In their extreme forms they have proved an ideal foundation for despotism and totalitarianism. In their lesser forms they undermine democratic principles. Germany's narcissistic approach to national reproduction leads to the occupation of what Claude Lefort has called the 'empty place' of power that is fundamental to democracy (1986: 279); in place of 'the people', we find 'Germans'. Democracy, argues Lefort, depends on the tension between the notion of 'the people' as a source of popular sovereignty, and 'the people' as 'an empty place, a place impossible to occupy.' Democracy, he continues, 'combines these two apparently contradictory principles: on the one hand, power emanates from the people; on the other, it is the power of nobody ... Whenever the latter risks being resolved or is resolved, democracy is either close to destruction or already destroyed' (1986: 279). It is this critical emptiness of 'the people' that 'ethnic German' repatriation puts at risk; repatriation fills-in the space of political identification, excluding possibilities of difference.

In the future Germany will have to come to terms with its manifest status as a 'country of immigration',[44] and this will entail the adoption of a more inclusive, forward-looking citizenship law. A close examination of repatriation law can assist in this process. Law-makers must recognise that mimetic identification is a dynamic and reciprocal process, one that undermines any fantasy of recovering a 'true' German identity. The seeds for such a revision can be found in current repatriation law. The law already recognises that descent alone does not define identity, that human beings are in a constant process of transformation, and that identities are not given by nature but made, mimetically, in human interaction.

Notes

1. Brubaker, it should be said, takes pains to examine the role of ethnic German repatriation in relation to German citizenship law more broadly, and he points out the transitional and 'ethno-cultural' basis of the repatriation – that it is more than just blood (1992: 168–71). Unfortunately, the subtlety of Brubaker's argument is often obscured by his strongly-worded summations, such as that cited.

2. See Bohannan 1963: 59; Borneman 1992.

3. *Flüchtlinge und Vertriebene.* The most recent of the expellee laws is the 'Law taking care of the consequences of the War', the *Kriegsfolgenbereinigungsgesetz* (KfbG) of 1993. It is a modification of the Federal Expellee and Refugee Law (*Bundesvertriebenen- und Flüchtlingsgesetz*) of 1953, and it increases restrictions on *Aussiedler* repatriation; the KfbG, despite politicians' claims to the contrary, represents a 'closing of the door' to repatriation.

4. For more on narrative and experience, see Borneman 1992.

5. For more on the testing process, see Senders 1997, 1998.

6. This was not the *earliest* introduction of the distinction, just the most important for the purposes of this chapter. For more detailed historical studies see Haberland 1991; Brubaker 1992; Gosewinkel 1995.

7. Deutscher Volkszugehöriger im Sinne dieses Gesetzes ist, wer sich in seiner Heimat zum deutschen Volkstum bekannt hat, sofern dieses Bekenntnis durch bestimmte Merkmale wie Abstammung, Sprache, Erziehung, Kultur bestätigt wird.

8. The tension between the two forms of mimesis is played out explicitly in the public sphere, in which *Aussiedler* are portrayed simultaneously as impostors and as exemplars. Social service organisations such as the German Red Cross and the Evangelical Church have taken strong positions on the issue. Posters declaring that '*Aussiedler* are German!' (*Aussiedler sind Deutsche!*) can be seen all over the Marienfelde refugee camp, standing both as declaration and as injunction. In situ, however, the poster only reasserts the omnipresence of suspicion and deceit; a copy of the poster hung outside a bureaucrat's door had pencilled in beside the title line '*manche*' thus rewriting the poster as '*manche Aussiedler sind Deutsche!*' or '*some Aussiedler* are German!' That there is disagreement over the reality of *Aussiedler* identity claims will come as no surprise. Certainly most English-language publications that refer to *Aussiedler* repatriation do so in a heavily and strictly ironic tone; taken in the context of Germany's exclusionary policies, *Aussiedler* claims to German identity are assumed prima facie to be bogus. The public debate in Germany has been well documented by Gugel 1990; Otto 1990; Bade 1992, among others. The debate has been less well covered in the Anglo-American literature, although summaries will be found in Shlaes 1991; Brubaker 1992; Klusemeyer 1993; Bade 1994; Senders 1996, and others.

9. The name used here is not the plaintiff's real name. The case presented is: Judgement of 13 June 1995 - BVerWG 9C 392.94. See also Ministry of the Interior: Vt l 1 - 902 000-1/242 V. For related cases, see the Judgment of 28 September 1994 - 16 S 1170/93 (Reported in Informationsbrief Ausländerrecht 3/95, pp. 119-25.); Der Bucholz, BVerwG, 685, Lieferung des Gesamtwerks – December 1985–41 2.3 §6 BVFG: Nr. 44-5; also Makarov 1993; Ruhrmann 1994.

10. ... nicht im Sinne deutschen Volkstums geprägt

11. 1941 wurde der Großvater K.A. aus seiner Heimat nach Solikamsk im Ural, die Großmutter K.K. zunächst nach Kasachstan und sodann ebenfalls nach Solikamsk in Zwangsarbeitslager der sog. Arbeitsarmee deportiert. Von 1946 bis 1956 lebten beide – zunächst wiederum in Arbeitslagern – in Perm, das damals Molotow hieß. Hier schlossen sie am 7. Januar 1949 die Ehe. In Perm wurde am 15. Januar 1949 auch die Mutter der Klägerin, E. A. geboren. Im Jahre 1956 zogen die Großeltern und die damals siebenjährige Mutter der Klägerin nach Kasachstan in das Dorf Wladimirowka, Rayon Balkaschinsk, Gebiet Zelinograd. Hier heiratete die Mutter am 4. Juni 1968 den russischen volkszugehörigen V. D.

12. gemischt-nationalen Ehe

13. damit habe sie sich zum russischen Volkstum bekannt

14. Es sei nicht ganz auszuschließen, daß die Klägerin von 1987 bis 1989 unter dem Einfluß ihres damaligen Ehemanns auf allen ihren Personenstandsurkunden als 'Russin' geführt worden sei.

15. Sie der Ausweisbewerber ununterbrochen von der Ausstellung des Passes bis zu seiner Ausreise in seinem sowjetischen Inlandspaß als 'Deutscher' eingetragen gewesen, habe er also nach außen hin kontinuierlich als Deutscher gegolten und die daraus folgenden Benachteiligungen ertragen müssen, so könne auch ohne Beherrschung der deutschen Sprache vom Bestehen eines Bekenntniszusammenhanges ausgegangen werden. Die amtliche Verlautbarung der deutsche Volkszugehörigkeit im Paß habe nämlich mit stigmatisierenden Folgen die Bedeutung eines 'Schlüsselerlebnisses auf Dauer'.

16. tiefgehenden Erlebnisse

17. Identifizierung mit dem Volkstumsbewußtsein

18. verinnerlichen

19. Schlüsselerlebnis auf Dauer

20. Schicksalsgemeinschaft

21. in eine Schicksalslinie einbezogen worden

22. mitbüßen

23. Vom Schicksal meiner Eltern mit der Verschleppung und der Arbeitsarmee habe ich auch der Elisabeth erzählt. Auch davon, wie es uns schon in der Schule ergangen ist. Ich selbst bin als Schulkind auch immer als Deutsche beschimpft worden und das ist heute noch eine Wunde in meinem Herzen. Ich habe schon damals meine Mutter gefragt, 'Warum tun sie uns so was sagen?' Und genau so ist es dann gewesen, als mich die [Elisabeth] gefragt hat. Ich habe dann erklärt: 'Wir müssen das mitnehmen, weil Deutschland und Rußland einen Krireg hatten und wir als Deutsche jetzt für diesen Krieg mitbüßen müssen.'

24. ... das Feiern deutscher Feste, das Pflegen deutscher Sitten und Gebräuuche, eine Teilnahme am Leben der deutschen Volksgruppe und die Zugehörigkeit zu einer überwiegend aus Deutschen bestehenden Religionsgemeinschaft.

25. überlieferten religiösen Bekenntnissen

26. deutsches Brauchtum

27. Das Familienleben habe sich unter dem Einfluß der nahe wohnenden deutschen Großeltern im Alltag und an den Festtagen nach deutschem Brauch und deutscher Lebensweise abgespielt. Auch der russische Vater der Kläger habe das akzeptiert und sich darin eingeordnet. So seien die christlichen Feste, vor allem Weihnachten, an den gregorianischen Kalendertagen und auf deutsche Weise gefeiert worden. Die Großeltern hätten auf die Einhaltung deutschen Brauchtums geachtet. Sie hätten deutsche Tischgebete gesprochen. Es seien auch deutsche Lieder gesungen worden, die sich die Familie durch Aufschreiben in Hefte bewahrt habe.

28. verinnerlichen

29. übernehmen

30. Gruppenbewußtsein

31. ... das Bewußtsein, einer Schicksalsgemeinschaft mit gemeinsamer Vergangenheit und gemeinsamen Erfahrungen anzugehören.

32. Erlebnisgeneration

33. Volkdeutsches Identitätsbewußtsein

34. ... das spezifisch rußlanddeutsche Vertreibungs- und Entrechtungsschicksal noch am eigenen Leib erlebt.

35. ...in diese Schicksalslinie einbezogen worden

36. spezielles Schlüsselerlebnis

37. deutsche Prägung

38. Gruppenschicksal

39. Sei der Ausweisbewerber der deutschen Hoch- und Standard-sprache nicht oder nicht in vollem Umfang mächtig, könnten doch das Sprechen oder zumindest Verstehen eines rußland-deutschen Dialekts sowie im familiären Umgang erworbene passive deutsche Sprachkenntnisse ein wichtiges Indiz für einen in der Familie vorhandenen volksdeutschen Überlieferungszusammenhang bilden.

40. Dürfe das besonders schwere Schicksal der Volksdeutschen in der früheren Sowjetunion ... nicht außer Betracht bleiben. Es sei gekennzeichnet durch ihre bei Beginn des deutsch–sowjetischen Kriegs am 22. Juni 1941 durchgeführte Deportation in Sondersiedlungen, wo sie ebenso wie in der sog. Arbeitsarmee als faschistische Feinde hätten Zwangsarbeit leisten müssen. Das habe zu einer Paria-Situation der Volksdeutschen geführt, die infolge vielfacher Diskriminierungen auch nach Aufhebung der Sondersiedlungen fortbestanden hätte.

41. deutsche Volkszugehörigkeit

42. volksdeutsche Bewußtseinslage

43. Der Auffassung des Berufungsgerichts, eine Erklärung zur deutschen Nationalität sowie eine Vermittlung deutscher Sprachkenntnisse sei generell nicht zumutbar gewesen, könne nicht gefolgt werden, weil sich dann die Voraussetzungen der deutschen Volkszugehörigkeit im wesentlichen auf die Abstammung reduzierten. Dies entspreche jedoch nicht dem Gesetz. ...Der Begriff des deutschen Volkszugehörigen...ist ein Rechtsbegriff, und zwar in erster Linie ein Bekenntnisbegriff. Das Bekenntnis zum deutschen Volkstum...setzt sich zusammen aus einer inneren Tatsache, nämlich dem von einem entsprechenden Bewußtsein getragenen Willen, ausschließlich dem deutschen Volk als einer national geprägten Kulturgemeinschaft anzugehören, und einer äußeren Tatsache, nämlich der Verlautbarung dieser Bewußtseinslage nach außen.

44. Einwanderungsland

References

Auerbach, E., *Mimesis: The Representation of Reality in Western Literature*. Princeton: 1953.

Bade, Klaus J., 'Immigration and Social Peace in United Germany', in *Daedalus*, Winter 1994, pp. 85–105.

——, ed., *Ausländer, Aussiedler, Asyl in der Bundesrepublik Deutschland*. 3rd ed. Hannover, Niedersächsische Landeszentrale für politische Bildung, 1992.

Bade, Klaus J. and Myron Weiner, eds., *Migration Past, Migration Future*. Providence, Berghahn Books, 1997.

Bohannan, Paul, *Social Anthropology*. New York, Holv, Rinehart and Winston, 1963.

Bourdieu, Pierre, *Outline of a Theory of Practice*. Cambridge, Cambridge University Press, 1977.

Borneman, John, *Belonging in the Two Berlins: Kin, State, Nation*. Cambridge, Cambridge University Press, 1992.

Brubaker, Rogers, *Citizenship and Nationhood in France and Germany*. Cambridge, MA, Harvard University Press, 1992.

Butler, Judith, *Bodies that Matter*. London, Routledge, 1993.

Falk Moore, Sally, 'Descent and Legal Position', in *Law in Culture and Society*, ed. Laura Nader, Chicago, Aldine, 1974.

Früchtl, Joseph, *Mimesis–Konstellation eines Zentralbegriffs bei Adorno*. Würzburg, Königshausen & Neumann, 1986.

Giordano, Christian, 'Affiliation, Exclusion and the National State: 'Ethnic Discourses' and Minorities in Est Central Europe', in *Rethinking Nationalism & Ethnicity: the Struggle for Meaning and Order in Europe*, ed. Hans-Rudolf Wicker. Oxford, Berg, 1997.

Gosewinkel, Dieter, 'Die Staatsangehörigkeit als Institution des Nationalstaats. Zur Entstehung des Reichs- und Staatsangehörigkeitsgesetzes von 1913', in *Offene Staatlichkeit: Festschrift für Ernst-Wolfgang Böckenförde zum 65. Geburtstag*, ed. Rolf Grawert et al. Berlin, Duncker & Humblot, 1995, pp. 359–79.

Gugel, Günther, *Ausländer, Aussiedler, Übersiedler: Fremdenfdeindlichkeit in der Bundsrepublik Deutschland*. Tübingen, Verein für Friedenspädagogik, 1990.

Haberland, Jürgen, *Eingliederung von Aussiedlern: Sammlung von Texten, die für Eingliederung von Aussiedlern aus den osteuropäischen Staaten von Bedeutung sind*. Leverkusen, Heggen-Verlag, 1991.

Herzfeld, Michael, *Cultural Intimacy: Social Poetics in the Nation-State*. New York, Routledge, 1997.

Klusemeyer, Douglas B., 'Aliens, Immigrants, and Citizens: The Politics of Inclusion in the Federal Republic of Germany', in *Daedalus*, vol. 3, no. 122, 1993, pp. 81–114.

Kohli, Martin, 'Die Institutionalisierung des Lebenslaufs', in *Kölner Zeitschrift für Soziologie und Sozialpsychologie*, vol. 37, no. 1, 1985, pp. 1–29.

Koller, H., *Die Mimesis in der Antike: Nachahmung, Darstellung, Ausdruck*. Bern, Lang, 1954.

Kramer, Jane, *The Politics of Memory: Looking for Germany in the New Germany*. New York, Random House, 1996.

Lefort, Claude, *The Political Forms of Modern Society: Bureaucracy, Democracy, Totalitarianism*, ed. John B. Thompson. Cambridge, MA, MIT Press, 1986.

——*Erzählstruktur und Lebenslauf: autobiographische Untersuchungen*. Frankfurt am Main, Campus, 1983.

Lehmann, Albrecht, *Im Fremden ungewollt zuhaus: Flüchtlinge und Vertriebene in Westdeutschland, 1945-1990*. Munich, Beck, 1991.

Makarov, Alexander N., *Deutsches Staatsangehörigkeitsrecht: Kommentar*. Neufeld, Alfred Metzner Verlag, 1993.

Morrison, Karl F., *The Mimetic Tradition of Reform in the West*. Princeton, Princeton University Press, 1982.

Münz, Rainer and Weiner, Myron, eds., *Migrants, Refugees, and Foreign Policy*. Providence, Berghahn Books, 1997.

Murdoch, Iris, 'Metaphysics and Ethics', in *The Nature of Metaphysics*, ed. D. F. Pears. London, Macmillan, New York, St. Martin's Press, 1957, pp. 99–123.

Otto, Karl A., '*Aussiedler* und *Aussiedler-Politik* im Spannungsfeld von Menschenrechten und Kaltem Krieg: Historische, politisch-moralische und rechtliche Aspekte der Aussiedler-Politik', in *Westwärts–Heimwärts? Aussiedlerpolitik zwischen 'Deutschtümelei' und 'Verfassungsauftrag'*, ed. Karl A. Otto. Bielefeld, AJZ, 1990.

Peck, Jeffery et al., 'Natives, Strangers, and Foreigners: Constituting Germans by Constructing Others', in *After Unity: Reconfiguring German Identities*, ed. Konrad H. Jarausch. Providence, Berghahn Books, 1997, pp. 61–103.

Prendergast, Christopher, *The Order of Mimesis: Balzac, Stendhal, Nerval, Flaubert*. Cambridge, Cambridge University Press, 1986.

Räthzel, Nora, 'Germany: one race, one nation?', in *Race & Class: A Journal for Black and Third World Liberation*, vol. 32, no. 3, 1990, pp. 31–49.

Ricoeur, Paul, *Time and Narrative*. Chicago, University of Chicago Press, 1984.

Ruhrmann, Ulrike, *Reformen zum Recht des Aussiedlerzuzugs*. Berlin, Duncker & Humblot, 1994.

Schwenker, William, *Mimetic Reflections: A Study in Hermeneutics, Theology, and Ethics*. New York, Fordham University Press, 1990.

Senders, Stefan, 'Laws of Belonging: Legal Dimensions of National Inclusion in Germany', in *New German Critique*. no. 67, 1996, pp. 147–77.

——'Time and Identification in Post-Cold War *Aussiedler* Repatriation.' Unpublished paper presented at the Graduate Student Workshop on Politics and Identity Formation in Contemporary Europe, Harvard University, Cambridge, MA, April 1997.

——'Language Policy, *Muttersprache*, and Mimesis: Language and Identity in *Aussiedler* Repatriation.' Unpublished paper presented at the Cornell University Anthropology Department Colloquium, February 1998.

Shlaes, Amity, *Germany: The Empire Within*. New York, Farrar, Straus & Giroux, 1991.

Spariosu, Mihai, ed., *Mimesis in Contemporary Theory: An Interdisciplinary approach. Volume I: The Literary and Philosophical Debate*. Philadelphia, John Benjamins Publishing Company, 1984.

Chapter 6

The Decline of Privilege: The Legal Background to the Migration of Ethnic Germans[1]

Amanda Klekowski von Koppenfels

Since the early 1990s, German government policy permitting ethnic Germans from East Central Europe to migrate to Germany has undergone a shift in two discrete areas: acceptance policy and integration policy. Before 1990, ethnic Germans from the Communist Bloc on tourist visas to Germany could present themselves at the German border and claim *Aussiedler* status. As of 1990, potential *Aussiedler* must undergo a lengthy application procedure starting in their country of origin. Before 1990, *Aussiedler* were virtually guaranteed a one-year intensive German language course, job retraining and other privileges and benefits. Such benefits have been steadily reduced since 1990. The legal changes in these two areas reflect a decline in Germany's previously generous policy towards ethnic German migrants.

This chapter will examine the evolution of the laws affecting *Aussiedler*. The development of these laws is best understood by examining the political constellations in post-war and Cold War Europe which, rather than ethnicity, played the decisive role in determining *Aussiedler* acceptance. Finally, this chapter will pose questions as to the impact the new laws have had on *Aussiedler* integration.

The Ethnicisation of German Citizenship

Until the Second World War, German citizenship was based purely on the 1913 German citizenship act, the *Reichs- und Staatsangehörigkeitsgesetz* (Imperial and State Citizenship Act, or RuStaG). The RuStaG is a law of descent, or *jus sanguinis*, but does not draw upon a specific ethnically based status.

Nonetheless, the RuStaG is often mistakenly seen as creating a highly exclusive and ethnically based German citizenship. While the RuStaG cannot be said to play this role, two key events during the Second World War, however, did have the effect of ethnicising German citizenship. When Hitler invaded Russia in 1941, Stalin, fearing that the ethnic Germans resident in Russia since the eighteenth century might be loyal to Hitler, deported 500,000 ethnic Germans eastward to Kazakhstan and Siberia, on the basis of their German ethnicity, where they remained in internment camps until 1956. After the end of the Second World War, a decision to expel Germans, westward this time, was again made on the basis of ethnicity.[2] In both cases, the Germans were expelled purely on the basis of their German ethnicity.

Deportation and expulsion played a large part in the inclusion of ethnicity per se in laws affecting West German citizenship. The new role[3] of ethnicity and its connection to the 1941 deportations and the 1945 expulsions becomes clear when we examine three post-war legal texts: Article 116, Paragraph 1 of the Basic Law (*Grundgesetz*, 1949); the Expellee and Refugee Law (*Bundesvertriebenen und Flüchtlingsgesetz*, or BVFG, 1953); and the Act for the Regulation of Questions of Citizenship (*Gesetz zur Regelung von Fragen der Staatsangehörigkeit*, or StaReG, 1955). These laws were drafted to include the expellees in postwar Germany and to provide options for the estimated three to four million ethnic Germans remaining in the Eastern bloc.

Table 6.1: Privileging Laws

1949	Basic Law, Article 116, Paragraph 1	'A German in the sense of this Basic Law is – pending other regulation – a person who possesses German citizenship or, as an ethnically German refugee or expellee, spouse or child who found refuge in the area of the German Empire in its borders of 31 December 1937.'[4]
1953	Article 1 BVFG	'An Expellee is someone who, as a German citizen or ethnic German...'[5] left the Eastern bloc.
1953	Article 6 BVFG	'An ethnic German is, in the sense of this act, someone who acknowledged himself to belong to the German people, in so far as this acknowledgement can be confirmed through such specific characteristics as descent, language, upbringing or culture.'[6]
1955	Article 1, Paragraph 6 StaReg	'Whoever is a German on the basis of Article 116 of the Basic Law without possessing German citizenship, must be naturalised upon his application, unless it can be assumed, based on facts, that his naturalisation would compromise the domestic or external security of the Federal Republic or a German *Land*.'[7]

Article 116

In the wake of the 1945–9 expulsions, the citizenship status of the eight million German expellees residing in West Germany was legally unclear. Some were German citizens, others were Polish or Czech citizens. Article 116, paragraph 1 of the Basic Law clearly included expellees as full members in the German polity (see Table 6.1), making expellees equal to native Germans with no differentiation between them. To assure the legal equality of the expellees, the phrase *deutsche Volkszugehörigkeit*, roughly translated as '(German) ethnicity', but literally meaning 'belonging to the German people', was explicitly introduced into the text of Article 116.[8] This phrase is a direct result of Stalin's and the Allies' use of German ethnicity as the determining factor for deportation and expulsion.

The growing ideological conflict of the Cold War also played a key role in Germany's policy towards ethnic Germans in the Eastern bloc, as reflected in these legal texts. Some three to four million ethnic Germans remained in East Central Europe after the expulsions. An additional four million expellees also resided in the Communist Bloc, in East Germany.[9] West German parliamentarians felt that both these groups of Germans were owed a special debt, particularly as they continued to suffer ethnically based discrimination within the Eastern bloc. Consequently, West Germany welcomed all of these ethnic Germans as a means of registering political protest against the Eastern bloc. Similarly, West Germany chose not to acknowledge the East German state out of purely political considerations. To underscore this decision, the 1913 RuStaG was never altered: as long as the Federal Republic never created its own citizenship law, even after the Federal Republic recognised the existence of a second state in Germany, the 1913 law was regarded as the legal basis for a single German citizenship. Because East Germans were always regarded as having a West German passport, they were always welcome in West Germany as full citizens. The status of ethnic Germans in the Eastern bloc is codified in Article 116 as well as in the second, more extensive legal text relevant for postwar citizenship developments, the BVFG.

The Expellee and Refugee Law (BVFG)

While the 1949 Basic Law (Article 116) had established the fact that expellees were full German citizens and, as such, subject to all rights, obligations and privileges of German citizenship, the Basic Law did not address the issue of integration. Article 119 of the Basic Law clearly provides the basis for additional legislation, stating that 'In the matter of the refugees and expellees, in particular with reference to their distribution among the *Länder*, the Federal Government may, with the consent of the Bundesrat, issue regulations having the force of law, pending the settlement of the matter by federal legislation.'[10] The BVFG served many purposes in one, providing for the integration of the expellees as well as the continued acceptance of (including the granting of West German citizenship to) ethnic Germans remaining in Central and Eastern Europe and refugees from East Germany. The BVFG fulfilled this role and was in force until 1993, when it was replaced by the War Consequences Consolidation Act (*Kriegsfolgenbereinigungsgesetz*, or KfbG).

The BVFG established a legal basis for the integration and equality of the expellees in all spheres – economic, professional, social, educational and residential. Their integration was to be aided where necessary, even if it appeared that expellees were privileged over native Germans.[11] One of the means of aiding the expellees was to distribute them more evenly throughout Germany. This distribution would be fully voluntary (§27) and was intended to help them find housing and jobs in the war-torn Federal Republic. Expellees were explicitly made equal to native Germans in all *Sozialversicherung* (social security) issues; pensions, unemployment and health insurance were to be paid as if the expellees had been born and had worked in the Federal Republic. Explicit means of integration, such as language courses or job retraining programmes, were not emphasised. Rather, emphasis was placed on equal representation of expellees in all spheres of German society. Ultimately successful in promoting integration, the BVFG provided a legal framework which enabled the expellees to take control of their own future.

Provisions for the continued acceptance of *Aussiedler* and refugees from East Germany, again reflecting West Germany's political positioning during the Cold War, were contained in the BVFG. It is worth noting that the BVFG was not a proactive law. It was, rather, the West German reaction to expulsion and discrimination. As the expulsions were based upon ethnicity, it seemed only logical that the reacting German law should be based upon ethnicity as well. The term *Volkszugehörigkeit* figures more prominently in the BVFG than it did in the Basic Law, even being explicitly defined. This definition of German ethnicity which, it is important to note, is a purely legal definition and is not an ethnological concept, provides a clear legal basis for the acceptance of ethnic Germans. The Basic Law merely provided the basis for a new clause of citizenship in the Federal Republic, whereas the BVFG specifically addressed the integration of the expellees and acceptance of ethnic Germans.

The 1955 *Gesetz zur Regelung von Fragen der Staatsangehörigkeit* (StaReG) explicitly draws on Article 116 of the Basic Law, stating that 'whoever is a German in the sense of Article 116 without being a German citizen must be naturalised upon application',[12] ... unless his or her naturalisation would compromise the domestic or external security of the Federal Republic (§6). German law distinguishes between two types of naturalisation: *Ermessenseinbürgerung* (discretionary naturalisation) and

Anspruchseinbürgerung (the legal right to naturalisation). The 1955 StaReG indicates that Germans in the sense of Article 116 have a right to naturalisation with the use of the phrase 'must be naturalised.'[13] Together with two later amendments, the StaReG is the last of the postwar regulations that explicitly include the postwar expellees and ethnic Germans remaining in the Eastern bloc.

Aussiedler **Acceptance**

The conclusion of the expulsion measures in 1949 was accompanied by a change in terminology: ethnic Germans coming to Germany after 1950 were no longer referred to as *Vertriebene* (expellees) but rather '*Aussiedler*'. It is important to note here that '*Aussiedler*' indicates a special legal status rather than being a collective term for ethnic German migrants. The continued acceptance of *Aussiedler* after 1950 can be seen as arising from two causes: first, it was an after-effect of the expulsions – it provided an option for those left behind – and, secondly, as discussed above, it was an ideologically determined provision. The BVFG regulations for *Aussiedler* were largely instituted to ensure that any Germans remaining under communist governments would have the legal right to be accepted in the Federal Republic as German citizens. The more political, rather than ethnic, nature of the policy is supported by the inclusion of the small number of ethnic Germans in China in the BVFG after 1957 and the exclusion of, for instance, South American Germans. Although the term 'expellee' was no longer used, the assumption continued to be that *Aussiedler* were leaving their homes in Central and Eastern Europe involuntarily, as a result of ethnically based pressure to immigrate, or *Vertreibungsdruck*.[14] Averaging no more than 40,000 per year from 1950 to 1986 (see Table 6.2), it is clear that, numerically, the immediate postwar *Aussiedler* migration flow was secondary to the eight million expellees who settled in West Germany within the four immediate postwar years, yet, as long as the Cold War continued, the *Aussiedler* were welcomed. The legal framework accepting and incorporating *Aussiedler* into Germany was seen as an important tool in regulating treatment of ethnic German minorities in Central and Eastern Europe and shifted accordingly over the decades following the Second World War.

Table 6.2: Numbers of *Aussiedler* entering Germany

Year	(Average) Number	Year	(Average) Number
1950–4	23,293	1990	397,073
1955–9	64,351	1991	221,995
1960–4	17,814	1992	230,565
1965–9	26,489	1993	218,888
1970–4	24,909	1994	222,591
1975–9	46,264	1995	217,898
1980–4	48,816	1996	177,751
1985	38,968	1997	134,419
1986	42,788	1998	103,080
1987	78,523	1999	104,916
1988	202,673	2000	95,615
1989	377,055		

Contrary to popular opinion, the basis for acceptance as an *Aussiedler* in Germany is not German ethnicity per se, but is rather *Vertreibungsdruck* arising as a result of German ethnicity. Thus, the potential *Aussiedler* must have seen himself in his home as a German, represented himself as a German to others and, as a direct result, have suffered ethnically based discrimination. The distinction between ethnicity and ethnically based discrimination is a crucial one.

Until the late 1970s, ethnically based discrimination was generally taken for granted by the German authorities. Thus, at the height of the Cold War, ethnicity and ethnically based discrimination were essentially synonymous; any ethnic German from the Eastern bloc could be virtually guaranteed admission as an *Aussiedler*. As we will see, however, this equation did not persist in post-Cold War Germany. The necessary 'subjective acknowledgement of belonging to the German *Volk*', (*Bekenntnis zum deutschen Volkstum*) required certain 'objective characteristics', (*objektive*

Merkmale) such as the following: German descent, language, upbringing or culture (as expressed in the retention of certain German dishes, songs, fairy tales or religious practices).[15] Until the late 1970s, this requirement was interpreted rather loosely. Ethnically based discrimination was taken for granted. In general, documents showing German descent were regarded as sufficient, while knowledge of the German language was not required (Ruhrmann 1994: 108). The courts and other relevant authorities saw the situation in the following light: one of the distinguishing characteristics of the ethnically based discrimination in Central and Eastern Europe was that Germans, as part of the enforced assimilation policy of the Central and Eastern European governments, were not permitted to speak German. Consequently, therefore, it was not reasonable to ask them to be conversant in German (Ruhrmann 1994: 108).

Starting in the late 1970s, however, the situation shifted somewhat, not owing to any change in the laws, but rather to court decisions altering the interpretation of the relevant laws in reaction to changes in the political landscape (Ruhrmann 1994: 108). Rather than *Vertreibungsdruck* being taken for granted in all situations, certain factors were now regarded as a refutation of *Vertreibungsdruck*. These included an active turning away from German *Volkstum*, a high-level political or professional employment which implied supporting the (communist) political system, and an application for asylum in Germany that would imply a reason for migrating to Germany, such as economic, other than ethnically based discrimination (Ruhrmann 1994: 111).

When Gorbachev came to power in the Soviet Union in 1985, the political landscape of East Central Europe was set to change even more. In recognition of this shift in the poles of the Cold War, the German Federal Administrative Court decided in 1986 that there could be exceptions to the rule: the legislature should develop new regulations to adapt to the new political developments (Ruhrmann 1994: 111). However, in practice, the policy was the following: if the investigating authorities could not explicitly disprove the assumed *Vertreibungsdruck*, then the potential *Aussiedler* had to be accepted into Germany. This generous admission policy continued along roughly these lines until the end of 1992 and the passage of the KfbG.

Aussiedler **Benefits**

The various benefits (Table 6.3) to which *Aussiedler* were entitled in the Cold War era fell into two categories: first, the acquisition of German citizenship and the accompanying rights, primarily the right to social insurance coverage. The second category was the right to specific integration-related benefits. In the first category, *Aussiedler* received pensions at the same level as native Germans (as regulated by the FRG; *Frem-*

drentengesetz [Foreign Pensions Act]), health insurance (Article 90 BVFG) and unemployment benefits (Article 62a AFG; *Arbeitsförderungsgesetz* [Work Promotion Act]). Second category benefits consisted of two sub-categories: those which were professional, and those which were specifically related to the move to Germany. These benefits provided *Aussiedler* with the necessary means of integrating into German society. Participation in a job retraining programme (Articles 44, 59 AFG) entitled the participant to Integration Benefit as a means of support. Language training and support during language training and job retraining were both of limited duration, with a maximum upper limit on Integration Benefit of eleven months. *Aussiedler* took advantage of the retraining programmes available and became full and active members of society. *Aussiedler* were generally seen as valued members of society and were welcomed as refugees from communism and as Germans.

Table 6.3: Summary of Benefits Received by *Aussiedler* until 1992

Social Insurance	Integration-Related Benefits	
	Professional	**Move-Related**
Pension – at same rate as native Germans for equivalent work (FRG).	Integration Benefit – paid during job retraining or further education (Articles 44, 59 AFG). Limited duration.	Subsidised Loans for building and furniture up to 10,000 DM (Interior Ministry Guideline).
Health Insurance – at same level as native Germans (Article 90 BVFG).	Language Training – Cost of course and support in the form of Integration Help (Articles 62ff. AFG). Limited duration.	Lump Sum Payments – in some cases, *Aussiedler* are entitled to a lump sum payment to compensate for suffering (various laws).
Unemployment Benefits – replaced by Integration Help, which is set at the level of welfare payments (dropped to 70% of welfare payments in 1989) (Article 62 AFG).	Wide-ranging benefits to aid *Aussiedler* in integration in schooling and various professions.	

Source: Ruhrmann (1994: 111)

Benefits related directly to the move to Germany included building loans and subsidised loans for furniture and other household items. Finally, various *Aussiedler* were entitled to a lump sum payment, either as compensation for internment in a labour camp or other issues related to ethnically based discrimination (*Infodienst* 1991: 2–8).

Decline of Privilege

As emigration restrictions were eased in Central and Eastern Europe in the late 1980s, the *Aussiedler* migration flow rose correspondingly steeply (see Table 6.2). On a purely practical level, West Germany was simply not equipped to accept the nearly 380,000 *Aussiedler* who arrived in 1989 and the 400,000 *Aussiedler* who arrived in 1990. In addition, as the Eastern bloc opened up, the situation for ethnic minorities improved and opportunities for ethnic Germans to remain in their homes increased. Germany and the Soviet Union signed a bilateral agreement which also provided for the protection of ethnic minorities in 1990, Germany and Poland signed a similar agreement in 1991, and Germany and Romania, Hungary and the Czech and Slovak Republics did so in 1992 (*Infodienst* 1991: 2–8). However, *Aussiedler* policy could not be abolished completely. Domestic considerations played a large part in maintaining the *Aussiedler* regulations: not only did conservative factions still believe in the concept of protecting ethnic Germans abroad, but the postwar expellees, who supported the maintenance of the *Aussiedler* policy, still exercised a certain amount of power within Germany (Haberland 1994: 21).

Thus, starting in 1989, a series of laws were passed which began to control and restrict the acceptance and integration of *Aussiedler* without wholly abolishing the practice.

The Wohnortzuweisungsgesetz (Residence Assignment Act, WoZuG) of 1989 called for the even distribution of *Aussiedler* within West Germany according to a quota system; each *Land* receives a percentage based upon area and population. The *Länder* are then responsible for distributing the *Aussiedler* evenly within each *Land*. Unlike the distribution of expellees (Article 27, BVFG), this distribution was not voluntary. Initially valid for three years and, as of 15 December 1999, extended until 2009 – fully twenty years since its initial passage – this act was intended to lessen the impact of *Aussiedler* migration on any particular *Bundesland*. *Aussiedler* migration had been concentrated primarily in Lower Saxony, Northrhine-Westphalia, Baden Württemberg and Bavaria, due to family-determined network migration. The *Aussiedleraufnahmegesetz* (AAG, *Aussiedler* Acceptance Act) of 1990 shifted part of the burden of determining *Aussiedler* status outside the borders of Germany. As of 1990, potential *Aussiedler* were

Table 6.4: Laws Affecting Acceptance and Distribution

1989 *Wohnortzuweisungsgesetz* (WoZuG): Article 1 'In the interests of achieving a sufficient standard of living for *Aussiedler* ... ', Article 2 '*Aussiedler* and *Übersiedler* ... can
be assigned to a temporary residence.' Intended to remain in effect for three years,
until 5 July 1992.

1990 *Aussiedleraufnahmegesetz*: Requires potential *Aussiedler* to apply for
admission from their countries of origin. In conjunction with WoZuG,
Aussiedler are assigned to a particular Land. This Land must also agree that potential *Aussiedler* fulfil all admission requirements.

1992 *Kriegsfolgenbereinigungsgesetz*:
Article 4: Creates new legal category: '*SpätAussiedler*' (late *Aussiedler*);
not all spouses or children are included in this category. Article 5: Lists   grounds
for exclusion from *Spätaussiedler* category. Article 6: Creates new 'definition' of
German ethnicity:
'(2) Anyone born after 31 December 1923 is an ethnic German if:
1. he is descended from a German citizen or an ethnic German,
2. his parents, one parent or other relatives have passed confirming characteristics,
such as language, upbringing, on to him, and
3. he declared himself, up until he left the area of German settlement, to be of German nationality, or recognised himself as German in some other manner or
belonged to German nationality according to the law of his country of origin.
The requirements according to Number 2 are seen as fulfilled if the passing on of
such confirming characteristics was not possible, or cannot be seen as reasonable
because of the conditions in the country of origin.
The requirements of Number 3 are seen as fulfilled if the recognition as a German
would have endangered life and limb, or would have been connected with grave
professional or economic disadvantages ... '[16]
Article 27: Sets limit at an average of the numbers of *Aussiedler* migration of 1991
and 1992 ± 10% (c. 220,000).

1992 WoZuG extended to 5 July 1995.

1995 WoZuG extended to 5 July 2000.

1996 WoZuG altered: Non-residence in assigned Bundesland for the first two   years of
residence in Germany now results in non-payment of all benefits from Work Promotion Act, Federal Welfare Act for that time.

1996 Language test introduced as fully institutionalised method of checking
'objective characteristics'; nearly one-third of those taking the test fail.

1999 WoZuG extended until 31 December 2009.

2000 On 1 January 2000, the number of *Aussiedler* permitted to enter annually is reduced
to 100,000.

required to fill out a form establishing information about the applicant and their family. For families, information was collected on birthdates, places of birth, place of residence later in life, 'nationality', including the nationality entered in the domestic Soviet passport, and maintenance of German language and customs. Applicants were also asked to provide information on German language knowledge. Which languages were spoken at home: German, Russian, other? At what age did the applicant start speaking German? From whom did the applicant learn German: the mother, father, grandmother, grandfather or other relative? How often (never, seldom, often, exclusively) were the following languages currently spoken by the applicant: German, Russian, other? How well did the applicant understand German (not at all, little, almost everything, everything)? How well did the applicant speak German (not at all, only single words, enough for a simple conversation, fluently)? Did the applicant write German (yes, no)?[17] The application was handed in at a German consulate in the country of origin, then forwarded on to Germany for the decision-making process, which could take three or more years. Upon arrival in Germany, the statement of language ability was tested in a brief oral exam consisting of a simple conversation. If it appeared that the potential *Aussiedler* had misrepresented his German abilities in the application form, he could be denied entry and returned to his country of origin.[18] This application proved effective immediately; the numbers of *Aussiedler* dropped from nearly 400,000 in 1990 to around 222,000 in 1991. From 1990 on, ethnic Germans who migrated to Germany on tourist visas, rather than following the prescribed path, forfeited their *Aussiedler* status.

The passage of the KfbG in 1992 as part of the so-called asylum compromise marks the end of the era of loose regulations on *Aussiedler* admission. The asylum compromise of 1992 refers to the concession of the political left to restrict the right to asylum (amendment of Article 16 of Basic Law) and the concession of the political right to restrict *Aussiedler* migration (passage of KfbG). Only ethnic Germans from the former Soviet Union are said to be suffering under *Vertreibungsdruck*; all others must prove explicitly that they still suffer ethnically based discrimination or the after-effects of such earlier discrimination. Ethnically based discrimination is no longer taken for granted, and certainly no longer synonymous with ethnicity; since 1992, only some ethnic Germans from the former Soviet Union have been eligible for *Aussiedler* status. In a significant procedural change, the KfbG now specifically lists bases for exclusion from *Aussiedler* status (Article 5). The KfbG has also set out an end to *Aussiedler* migration, stating that those who were born after 1992 may not enter as *Aussiedler* after 2010.

In June 1996, language tests, administered before the submission of the application, were formally introduced as a means of testing German abilities, thus shifting yet another part of the application process outside Germany. The language test is administered by a civil servant who starts with a relaxed conversation and then moves to the actual test. According to the *Bundesverwaltungsamt*, 'the applicant must be capable of carrying on a conversation about the simple facts of daily life'.[19] The conversation could be about professional life in Kazakhstan or the life of a German in the former Soviet Union and may be either in High German or in dialect. The questions are not rote questions, but are improvised by the examiner for each case. The examiner writes down what questions were asked, whether the applicant understood the question, and whether the question was answered in High German, dialect or in Russian. While passing the language test does not guarantee admission as an *Aussiedler*, passing the test is required for entry. Partially explained by the increase in mixed German–Russian marriages, the German language competence of the post-Cold War *Aussiedler* is at a much lower level than that of their predecessors. Thus, these tests are a means of ensuring that ethnic Germans have the linguistic tools to ease their integration into contemporary German society; almost 65 percent have passed. A Federal Administrative Court decision in November 1996 lent extra support to this decision, declaring that ethnicity or descent alone does not suffice for claiming *Aussiedler* status; some basic grasp of the German language must also be in evidence. The institution of language tests can be interpreted as testing for integration capacity. The emphasis once placed on language as a carrier of identity has shifted to an emphasis on the significance of language for integration and communication.

By the late 1990s, it became apparent that the 1989 *Wohnortzuweisungsgesetz* (extended in 1992 until 1995) was not working according to plan; *Aussiedler* would be assigned to a *Land*, but promptly move to, for instance, Lower Saxony to be near family or friends. Accordingly, a new version of the WoZuG was passed in 1996 which linked social services to place of residence. For two years after entry to Germany, the *Aussiedler* must remain in the Land of assignment, or must forfeit all social services such as language courses, welfare, unemployment benefits, job retraining programmes, etc. Since the majority of *Aussiedler* are on some form of public assistance during their first two years, this law has been successful in ensuring that *Aussiedler* remain in the assigned *Land*, thus evening out the burden on the *Länder*. This law raises questions about restrictions of the basic rights of *Aussiedler* since their freedom of movement is no longer guaranteed within the German border. Most recently, the WoZuG has been extended until 2009, restricting some *Aussiedler* for up to four years, depending upon their year of migration to Germany.

Changes in Benefits to *Aussiedler*

Aussiedler benefits have changed dramatically since the early 1990s (see Table 6.5). Monetary benefits have largely been cut back, while social programmes have been added. *Aussiedler* now draw pensions at levels that are

60 percent of the native German level rather than corresponding to the normal level. Additionally, if both husband and wife draw pensions, their combined income may not exceed 1.6 times the amount of 'Integration Help' (*Eingliederungshilfe*), which is calculated at 60 percent of the average pension. In 1994, 1.6 times the Integration Help varied between 1,060 DM and 1,536 DM per month, thus setting the upper limit for a dual pension-receiving couple. Integration help itself has been limited to six months, as have German language courses (*Info-Dienst* 1998: 32–7).

Benefits are also now linked to specific groups, emphasising assistance to young *Aussiedler* and the long-term unemployed (more than one year). Job retraining and further education has now been re-orientated towards young adults while a number of programmes such as 'Sports with *Aussiedler*' have been instituted to address general cultural and social integration. Other job retraining programmes remain, but participation is no longer guaranteed; an application must be made and costs of the course may or may not be covered.

Table 6.5: Summary of Benefits Received by *Aussiedler* after 1992

Social Insurance	Integration-Related Benefits	
	Professional	**Move-**
Pension – at 60% of native German rate for equivalent work. Non-German spouses may not be eligible. Upper limit on payment (FRG).	Integration Help – paid during job retraining or further education. Six-month limit; may be then taken up by welfare (Article 62 AFG).	**Related** Lump Sum Payments – in some cases, *Aussiedler* are entitled to a lump sum pay-
Health Insurance – at same level as native Germans (Article 11 BVFG, 1993 version).	Language Training - Cost of course and support in the form of Integration Help. Six-month limit (may not be added to six months of re-training) (Articles 62ff. AFG).	ment to compensate for suffering (various laws).
Unemployment Benefits – replaced by Integration Help, which is set at the level of 60 percent of welfare payments. Six-month limit (Article 62 AFG).	Fewer benefits to aid *Aussiedler* in integration in schooling and various professions, but more local programmes (also EU-funded) to aid social and cultural integra-	Subsidised loans for building and house-furnishing remain.

Source: Info-Dienst 1997: 25; Haberland 1991: 260-261

Conclusion

Unlike the laws designed to help the integration of the expellees and Cold War *Aussiedler*, the changes in the laws concerning post-Cold War *Aussiedler* have complicated their integration. The reduction of language courses to six months and the reduction in eligibility for job training programmes are likely to be the most serious objective hindrances to integration. Post-Cold War integration programmes are designed to cover – at low cost – the failure of the reduced job training programmes. Rather than increasing language programmes to compensate for the lower proficiency in German of the post-Cold War *Aussiedler*, language testing now takes places outside the German borders. *Aussiedler* are tested for their ability to integrate and contribute to society, rather than being offered a retreat from communism.

On a subjective level, the *Aussiedler* have had a very different experience from their predecessors, the expellees. Rather than being included in the policy process as co-decision makers, the post-Cold War *Aussiedler* have been the recipients of a federal decision-making process every step of the way. The introduction of the language test was a step which gave the government the final say: questions on the language test are not prescribed, but may be improvised by the examiner. Hence, the government has the power to stop *Aussiedler* immigration at its will.

The laws designed to protect ethnic Germans under communism and offer them the possibility of migration to Germany were passed at the beginning of the Cold War, as seen in Article 116 of the Basic Law (1949), the BVFG (1953) and the StaReG (1955). In court cases, it is clear that, while in the 1970s, ethnically based discrimination was taken for granted, by the late 1980s, this was no longer the case. Indeed, ethnically based discrimination had declined by the 1980s. The inclusion of minority rights in various bilateral treaties hastened the end of ethnic discrimination. Thus, as the Cold War drew to an end, the necessity of protecting ethnic Germans abroad declined. Concurrently, however, large waves of *Aussiedler* migrated to Germany. In the face of conservative groups' support for the *Aussiedler* policy, including expellee support, the German government could not abolish the *Aussiedler* policy completely, but instituted significant changes as part of the asylum compromise of 1992, as well as subsequent policy decisions.

The 1992 KfbG essentially restricted *Aussiedler* migration to the former Soviet Union, but was also accompanied by a substantial policy to provide other options to ethnic Germans in the former Soviet Union. The German government hopes to convince ethnic Germans that they have a future in the former Soviet Union. Entry to Germany has been made more difficult, while so-called 'islands of hope', or German communities, have been developed in the former Soviet Union, although under the *Aussiedler* Commissioner appointed by the red–green government in 1998, Jochen Welt, more emphasis has been placed on the integration of *Aussiedler* in Germany instead. As the Cold War has ended, protection of ethnic minorities has become more widespread, ending Germany's previously necessary role of protecting ethnic Germans abroad. From this perspective, this policy was never wholly dominated by ethnonational criteria but far more by ideological and political considerations now defunct.

Notes

1. My thanks to Samuel Barnes for his guidance, and to Barbara Schmitter Heisler, Ulrich von Koppenfels and Rainer Ohliger for their helpful comments and criticisms. The views and opinions expressed in this article are the author´s alone and in no way represent the views of the International Organisation for Migration.

2. The Allies, fearing instability and ethnic conflict in Central and Eastern Europe, determined at the Potsdam Conference in July 1945 that the estimated several million ethnic Germans remaining to the east of the four occupied zones of Germany, in Poland, East Prussia and Czechoslovakia, were to be expelled in an 'orderly and humane fashion' to Germany between 1945 and 1949. The number was underestimated; twelve million ethnic Germans were expelled, eight million to West Germany and four million to East Germany.

3. In laws from the period of Nazi dictatorship, the words 'Volkszugehörigkeit' (ethnicity) and 'Volkstum' (nationhood) are used, but I am of the opinion that the twelve-year period of the Nazi dictatorship should be viewed as an exception and not as part of the continuous development of German citizenship. Hence my statement of ethnicity's 'new role' after the Second World War.

4. Deutscher im Sinne dieses Grundgesetzes ist vorbehaltlich anderweitiger gesetzlicher Regelung, wer die deutsche Staatsangehörigkeit besitzt oder als Flüchtling oder Vertriebener deutscher Volkszugehörigkeit oder als dessen Ehegatte oder Abkömmling in dem Gebiete des Deutschen Reiches nach dem Stande vom 31. Dezember 1937 Aufnahme gefunden hat.

5. Vertriebener ist, wer als deutscher Staatsangehöriger oder deutscher Volkszugehöriger seinen Wohnsitz...

6. Deutscher Volkszugehöriger im Sinne dieses Gesetzes ist, wer sich in seiner Heimat zum deutschen Volkstum bekannt hat, sofern dieses Bekenntnis durch bestimmte Merkmale wie Abstammung, Sprache, Erziehung, Kultur bestätigt wird.

7. Wer auf Grund des Artikels 116 Abs. 1 des Grundgesetzes Deutscher ist, ohne die deutsche Staatsangehörigkeit zu besitzen, muß auf seinen Antrag eingebürgert werden, es sei denn, daß Tatsachen die Annahme rechtfertigen, daß er die innere oder äußere Sicherheit der Bundesrepublik oder eines deutschen Landes gefährdet.

8. Parlamentarischer Rat, Hauptausschuß, 45th Session, 19 January 1949, p. 596.

9. Some areas (Romania, Hungary, Soviet Union) were not subject to the widespread expulsions. In addition, a number of ethnic Germans were able to escape expulsion in Poland and Czechoslovakia; those who were of use to the Communist governments, such as miners or skilled craftsmen, were not permitted to leave, and those who were married to Polish or Czech spouses could often avoid expulsion.

10. In Angelegenheiten der Flüchtlinge und Vertriebenen, insbesondere zu ihrer Verteilung auf die Länder, kann bis zu einer bundesgesetzlichen Regelung die Bundesregierung mit Zustimmung des Bundesrates Verordnungen mit Gesetzeskraft erlassen.

11. Among the Bundestag members, great concern was exhibited that the expellees should not be treated as second-class citizens in any way. See, e.g. Stenographische Berichte, 12th Session, 20 October 1949, p. 285ff; 250th Session, 25 February 1953, p. 11971ff.

12. Wer auf Grund des Artikels 116 Abs. 1 des Grundgesetzes Deutscher ist, ohne die deutsche Staatsangehörigkeit zu besitzen, muß auf seinen Antrag eingebürgert werden.

13. muß ... eingebürgert werden

14. Literally, 'expulsion pressure.' This term is widely used to mean the ethnically based discrimination which theoretically made conditions in the country of origin impossible and caused ethnic Germans to return to Germany. Any other reasons for migration were not compatible with Aussiedler status.

15. 'Aussiedler/SpätAussiedler', 1996: 2-5; Info-Dienst Deutsche Aussiedler, 1998: 5-6; Info-Dienst Deutsche Aussiedler, 1998: 26-8.

16. (2) Wer nach dem 31. Dezember 1923 geboren ist, ist deutscher Volkszugehöriger, wenn

1. er von einem deutschen Staatsangehörigen oder deutschen Volkszugehörigen abstammt,

2. ihm die Eltern, ein Elternteil oder andere Verwandte bestätigende Merkmale, wie Sprache, Erziehung, Kultur vermittelt haben und,

3. er sich bis zum Verlassen der Aussiedlungsgebiete zur deutschen Nationalität erklärt, sich bis dahin auf andere Weise zum deutschen Volkstum bekannt hat oder nach dem Recht des Herkunftsstaates zur deutschen Nationalität gehörte.

Die Voraussetzungen nach Nummer 2 gelten als erfüllt, wenn die Vermittlung bestätigender Merkmale wegen der Verhältnisse im Herkunfsgebiet nicht möglich oder nicht zumutbar war; die Voraussetzungen nach Nummer 3 gelten als erfüllt, wenn das Bekenntnis zum deutschen Volkstum mit Gefahr für Leib und Leben oder schwerwiegenden beruflichen oder wirtschaftlichen Nachteilen verbunden gewesen wäre, jedoch auf Grund der Gesamtumstände der Wille, der deutschen Volksgruppe und keiner anderen anzugehören, unzweifelhaft ist.

17. 'Antrag auf Aufnahme nach dem Bundesvertriebenengesetz (BVFG) aus den Republiken der ehemaligen Sowjetunion, Estland, Lettland oder Litauen.' Publication of the *Bundesverwaltungsamt*.

18. The applicant is, in fact, warned of this on the application form as well as that permission to settle in Germany can be rescinded if it is determined that the information given is untrue or incomplete.

19. Der Antragsteller muss in der Lage sein, ein Gespräch zu einfachen Dingen des täglichen Lebens zu führen.

References

Federal Republic of Germany, *Arbeitsförderungsgesetz*. Bonn, 1969.
Federal Republic of Germany, *Aussiedleraufnahmegesetz*. Bonn, 1990.
Federal Republic of Germany, *Bundesvertriebenen und –Flüchtlingsgesetz*. Bonn, 1953.
Federal Republic of Germany, *Deutscher Bundestag Plenarprotokoll*; 1. Wahlperiode, 12. Sitzung, 20 October 1949, pp. 285ff.
Federal Republic of Germany, *Deutscher Bundestag Plenarprotokoll*; 1. Wahlperiode, 250. Sitzung, 25 February 1953, pp. 11971ff.
Federal Republic of Germany, *Fremdrenten- und Auslandsrentengesetz*. Bonn, 1953.
Federal Republic of Germany, *Gesetz zur Regelung der Staatsangehörigkeit*. Bonn, 1955.
Federal Republic of Germany, *Grundgesetz*. Bonn, 1949.
Federal Republic of Germany, *Kriegsfolgenbereinigungsgesetz*. Bonn, 1992.

Federal Republic of Germany, *Parlamentarischer Rat, Hauptausschuß*, 45. Sitzung, 19 January 1949, p. 596.

Federal Republic of Germany, *Wohnortzuweisungsgesetz*. Bonn, 1989; 1992; 1996; 1997.

German Empire, *Reichs- und Staatsangehörigkeitsgesetz*. Berlin, 1913.

Haberland, Jürgen, *Eingliederung von Aussiedlern*, 5th edn. Leverkusen, Heggen, 1991.

Haberland, Jürgen, *Eingliederung von Aussiedlern*, 6th edn, Leverkusen, Heggen, 1994.

Info-Dienst Deutsche Aussiedler, no. 24 (1991).

Info-Dienst Deutsche Aussiedler, no. 82 (1996).

Info-Dienst Deutsche Aussiedler, no. 93 (1997).

Info-Dienst Deutsche Aussiedler, no. 95 (1998).

Info-Dienst Deutsche Aussiedler, no. 97 (1998).

Ruhrmann, Ulrike, *Reformen zum Recht des Aussiedlerzuzugs*. Berlin, Duncker und Humblot, 1994.

Part II

The Transition from German Minority
Culture to the National Culture of Germany:
Art as a Medium to Address and Express
the Challenges of Migration and Integration

Chapter 7

'From the periphery to the centre and back again': An Introduction to the Life and Works of Richard Wagner

David Rock

'My life had become pointless and my writing had too' (Broos 1993: 18; hereafter referred to as 'B' plus page reference).[1] These words of the Romanian-German writer Richard Wagner were uttered in 1993, looking back to the year 1987 when he was 35 years old and had been a writer for some eighteen years. In March of that year, he had emigrated to West Berlin with his then wife, the writer Herta Müller. Born on 10 April 1952 in Lovrin in the Banat region of Romania, he had started writing whilst he was still at the grammar school and at the age of seventeen he published his first poems in local German newspapers. He went to study German at the university in Timisoara where in 1972 he joined the Communist Party of Romania and also became a member of the 'Aktionsgruppe Banat' (the Banat Action Group), which included Herta Müller. He remained a member of the group until it was broken up by the authorities in 1975. His first collection of poems *Klartext* (Uncoded Text) appeared in 1973. He worked from 1975 to 1978 as a teacher of German (in Hunedoara), and from 1979 to 1984 as a journalist for the weekly newspaper in Brasov (Kronstadt), the *Karpaten-Rundschau* (Carpathian Review). Seven volumes of poetry and prose appeared in Romania and he received several prizes. In view of his critical stance, though, his situation was becoming increasingly difficult: in 1984, an open letter to the Party and the Writers' Union led to *Berufs- und Publikationsverbot* (debarment from writing and publishing) for Wagner and other Romanian German writers, many of whom as a result applied to leave for the German Federal Republic.

Life at the Periphery: a German in Romania

Taking stock of his life hitherto, then, Wagner made the bitter decision to leave Romania for the West after being forced to admit that in the pre-ceding years, all his hopes had proved illusory: 'Basically, all the things that I did in Romania foundered' (B, 18).[2] The most famous of the 'things' he was involved in was the 'Aktionsgruppe Banat' which he had helped to found. This group consisted of young intellectuals from German-speaking Banat families. Inspired by the Prague Spring and by the idealism of the 1968 student movements in Paris and West Germany, they had both polit-ical and literary aims: their utopian socio-political model inspired both their hopes for *Reformsozialismus* (reform socialism) and their efforts to pro-duce literature which was modern and up-to-date, not only in terms of its form but also its desire for political and social influence: it was to be 'bewußtseinserweiternd' ('expanding people's consciousness') (Csejka 1991: 3).[3] Unfortunately, yet predictably, they also managed to attract the attention of the Securitate, and although early on the Secret Police were disconcerted by the Group's policy of 'kritische Offenheit' ('critical open-ness' – they made no attempt to keep their activities secret), several mem-bers of the group were eventually imprisoned.

For Richard Wagner, this group was the expression of a way of life: 'We tried to live our lives the way we wanted to, using our imagination, and not submitting to the regimented world around us' (B, 18).[4] The concerns of this group of young intellectuals in Communist Romania were actually not so far removed from those of their Western counterparts at the time. Richard Wagner himself, for instance, seems to have been something of a village hippie, with long hair, flower-power shirts and songs by the Rolling Stones constantly on his lips, writing protest songs about Vietnam. This is how he describes the period in his Frankfurt lecture of 1993:

> In the sixties, music conveyed, across walls and fences and barbed-wire, a feeling of being alive which affected young people world-wide ... My affinity for popular culture and its forms probably stems from this time and from this context. I didn't give a damn about the Eternal. Aesthetics were fun and provocation and fun.[5] ('Die Bedeutung der Ränder oder vom Inneren zum Äußersten und wieder zurück, 44; hereafter referred to as 'F')

For many intellectuals in the Communist Bloc, the year 1968 was a water-shed, and Richard Wagner was no exception. In an interview in 1993, he commented that 1968 was 'the year in which, poetically speaking, my world-view was established' (B, 19).[6] For Romanian-Germans, 1968 meant not only the 'Prague Spring', with its attempts to reform communism, and 'Paris in May', but more importantly, also the German student movements and the Frankfurt School, for as Richard Wagner pointed out, first and foremost 'the Germans in Romania always related to what was going on in the Federal Republic' (B, 19).[7]

As far as the immediate situation in Romania was concerned, 1968 meant the notion of a more open Romania where new ideas for a reformed communism could be discussed more openly. The relaxed atmosphere prevailing at the time meant that Romanian-German writers were much less restricted than, for instance, their GDR counterparts, as Wagner explained: 'When I started writing, you could write what you wanted to' (B, 19).[8] Given Ceauçesu's differences with Moscow, Socialist Realism was not the all-controlling canon in Romania that it sought to be elsewhere in the Soviet Bloc. The young Richard Wagner was therefore prepared to give socialism a chance for, as he commented in a recent interview: 'You see, I was born into Socialism and I didn't know anything else' (B, 19).[9] So as a young man, Wagner's attitude was: 'We've got this society, let's accept it and try to make the best of it' (B, 19).[10]

Richard Wagner, then, like many other authors in Eastern Europe, was in fact only subsequently turned into an opponent of the system by the system itself. When he started out as a writer, he was less an opponent of the system, more an oppositional voice against something which was much more tangibly in the foreground of his life, namely the sinister nationalistic tendencies of the small German village communities in Romania. He describes the people he was frequently confronted by during his childhood and youth as follows: 'When they were drunk, they sang soldiers' songs; 90 percent of my father's generation were in the Waffen-SS; and the pseudo-intellectual class was made up of reactionary village schoolteachers. ... My writing was directed against these people, this milieu' (B, 20).[11] The young members of the 'Aktionsgruppe' therefore took every opportunity to parody the German 'Heimatliteratur' (literature about the homeland) of the region, and as a result of their provocative public performances, they were denounced as 'Nestbeschmutzer' (people fouling their own nest) by many of their fellow Germans.

Wagner later adopted 'eine kritische Grundhaltung' (a critical position) towards the political system, but early on, these young, mostly twenty-year-old intellectuals in the Banat Action Group were not so much interested in political tactics and manoeuvring, as in simply adopting an insolent and impudent stance. Impromptu events were organised, such as the one for Chile after the fall of Allende. The literary circle, held in the students' cultural centre in Timisoara, was run by Richard Wagner and discussed not only contemporary writers such as Handke and Heißenbüttel, but also political radicals in the West such as Rudi Dutschke and the Baader–Meinhof terrorists.

As far as their writing was concerned, they tried to produce their own distinctive voices: they 'wrote in a completely different language' (B, 19),[12] knowing full well that the Romanian secret service, the hated *Securitate*, would always be listening in to what they said and reading what they wrote. Their sense of solidarity in discussing and publishing their experimental texts and debating controversial new literary and political developments led to the forging of lasting friendship: 'We sat in pubs and told novels to one another' (B, 19).[13] Wagner sees a lot of similarities between the Banat Action Group and the Prenzlauer Berg Poets in the GDR, but with one important distinction: the Romanian-German writers were always politically aware in what they were doing.

When he was in Romania, Richard Wagner wrote primarily poetry. In his recent essay (Csejka 1991: 1–5), Gerhardt Csejka explains how Wagner's first lyric poems at the end of the 1960s demonstrated his ability to exploit the poetic potential of concrete language. With this he was very much going against the prevalent tendency at that time when young Romanian poets, struggling to rehabilitate aesthetic values from the formal tyranny of Socialist Realism, were seeking to produce 'higher' forms of poetry, remote from real life. The twenty-one-year-old Richard Wagner's first volume of poetry, *Klartext*, published in 1973, contains programmatic poems which point clearly in the direction in which the author was going but also back to the big early influence on him, namely Bertolt Brecht. The words 'Lakonie' (laconic style), 'Sachlichkeit' (objectivity), 'Understatement' and 'Ironie' are the ones most frequently used by Richard Wagner to describe Brecht's lyric poetry, but they are also words applicable not only to Wagner's own poetry written in Romania but also his later prose works. In *Klartext*, though, as he has commented in a conversation in Keele, he 'was looking for a tone to oppose the false pathos of the literature written about the homeland but also to oppose the false pathos of Socialist Realism'.[14]

Wagner's reason for joining the Romanian Communist Party in 1972 was consistent with his view that all intellectual and artistic activity should have a political dimension: he hoped that, by opposing 'den real existierenden Schwachsinn' ('actually existing nonsense'), he could help to work towards a socialism which was more than 'nur das verzerrte Gesicht der Mächtigen' ('merely the distorted face of the high and mighty' – Csejka 1991: 2). Yet any high flying political hopes were soon brought down to earth by his sober artist's gaze, as he wryly commented in Keele: 'I still wanted to change society, but I was already writing my first poems',[15] and a subversive stance was always a characteristic of his writing, with implications for his everyday life. In his second volume of poetry *die invasion der uhren* (the invasion of the clocks, 1977) he quite literally says goodbye to his 'Frühlingshoffnungen' (spring hopes) in the poem with the same title as the collection, which begins: 'bye kosmische zeiten' (bye cosmic times). As Csejka comments, these poems mark a new note in Wagner's writing, 'ein erfrischend selbstironischer Ton' (a refreshingly self-ironising tone): influenced by the 'Neue Innerlichkeit' (new inwardness) trend in West German writing at that time, the poet records in sober, discursive language 'das Ausbleiben von reeller Erfahrung' (absence of real experience – Csejka 1991: 3). The predominant themes in this collection were to remain central in Wagner's work from now on: the increasing bankruptcy of utopian thinking and 'the manifold obstacles encountered in the attempt to experience reality in any way at all' (Csejka 1991: 3).[16] Wagner and others in the 'Aktionsgruppe' did, however, maintain their belief in the potential of literature for exerting a transforming influence on the conventional mechanisms of perception, a view to which he still holds, albeit now in terms of change on a purely individual rather than societal level.

From the mid-1970s onwards, Ceauçescu's move away from his policy of 'sozialistischen (Pseudo-)Pragmatismus' ('a pseudo-pragmatic form of socialism' – Huttenlocher 1998: 346) to despotic autocracy drove Romania to economic ruin and social chaos. Intellectuals such as those in the Banat Action Group, with its programme of open discussion of problems inherent in the socio-political system, were inevitably forced into the position of outsiders and dissidents. By 1975, the *Securitate* had already had enough of the man they called the 'Spaßguerrilla' (joke-guerrilla), arresting Wagner and three other members of the Action Group. However, as a result of the intervention of the Federal Republic, the three were released again and the authorities left them alone after imposing a temporary 'Publikationsversbot' on the Group, though one of them (William Totok) was held in custody for several months. Their arrests marked the end of the Banat Action Group. Its members who did remain in Romania engaged in a period of 'normale Dissidenz' (normal dissidence), as Wagner put it, but his own activities during his remaining time in Romania were under continual pressure from increasingly repressive measures. And by the end of the 1970s, Wagner, now disillusioned, realised that what was being practised in Romania under the guise of socialism was not reformable, 'daß mit dem System nichts mehr zu machen ist' (that nothing more could be done with the system').[17]

Richard Wagner was never actively involved in politics, but inevitably, 'politics was always a very important dimension' in his work (B, 20),[18] for, as he explained, 'in a dictatorship, politics is everywhere. I don't bring it into my poems, it gets there by itself' (F, 44 5).[19] Being able to publish was also vital, and this became more and more difficult in Romania after Wagner lost his position as Banat cultural correspondent for the German newspaper, the *Karpaten Rundschau*, in 1983 as a result of huge pressure from the editorial office. After several repeatedly unsuccessful applications for a post with the Bucharest-based German journal of the Romanian Writers' Union, *Neue Literatur* (New Literature), he was unemployed from now on. In 1983 he also left the Adam-Müller- Guttenbrunn Literary Circle when he saw how pointless everything appeared in the face of the disastrous effects of the now all-enveloping Ceauçescu dictatorship. '1983 is the year when everything collapsed' (B, 20),[20] recalls Wagner. He experienced a sense of increasing personal isolation, for Romanian-Germans had now started to emigrate in droves and many of his own friends left. But the main reason for the attitude of resignation so characteristic of his works written at this time, such as *Gegenlicht* (Contre-jour, 1983) and *das auge des feuil-*

letons (the eye of the feuilleton, 1984), was his recognition 'that people go along with everything and are prepared to help to carry the burden of all this madness and absurdity. And you are left there standing alone, looking ridiculous' (B, 20).[21] Another important reason for his decision to leave was the recognition that now he would only have been allowed to publish 'Nebensächliches' (trivial things), a factor which could have been used to legitimise the regime by making it appear to Western eyes to be more liberal than it actually was.

For Wagner, 'der logische Endpunkt' (the logical conclusion) was to apply for an exit permit. Yet the implications were severe for an author, namely the loss of his public – his most recent volumes of poetry, *Hotel California* I and II (of 1980 and 1981), in which he had returned to an aggressively defiant, rebellious tone, had been aimed specifically at his Romanian-German readership. His two major stories of the end of the 1980s were published in the West and are thus aimed at different readers. They have as their theme his departure from Romania (*Ausreiseantrag* – Application to Leave, 1988) and his arrival in the West (*Begrüßungsgeld* – Welcome-Money, 1989). Both are autobiographical, featuring the same central characters: a journalist called Stirner, clearly Wagner's *alter ego*, and his German-teacher-wife; and both are written in the form of a seemingly straightforward, anecdotal account of events which nevertheless subtly draws the reader into the narrative. Together the two stories form Wagner's concluding reactions to what had been a gradual process of profound disillusionment associated with the failure of a literary venture and a utopian sociopolitical model.

Ausreiseantrag portrays humdrum existence in a town in the Banat in the 1980s, recording the effects of the Ceauçescu dictatorship on everyday life which eventually drive the couple to leave the country. This fragmentary protocol, written 'in a sometimes laconically sober, sometimes bitterly ironic tone' (Huttenlocher 1998: 346),[22] shows how external social decline is relentlessly accompanied by the complete isolation and inner paralysis of the individual writer who, faced with the interminable monotony of each day, gradually loses his ability to think and to write. Stirner's capacity for recalcitrance (his name is a pun on the German idiom 'jemandem die Stirn bieten', to stand up to someone) is gradually eroded by the cumulative effect of a repressive totalitarian society. His ultimate state of bitter resignation comes when he recognises the submissive lethargy which this repression has produced in the Romanian people.

Begrüßungsgeld follows Stirner and his wife to West Germany, the title signifying the predominant factor of money in inter-human relationships in the Federal Republic, a theme which Wagner develops in his recent documentary novel *Lisas geheimes Buch* (1996). The story recapitulates the first six months which they spend after arriving at the transit camp in Nuremberg. Here, in his experiences in the capitalist, democratic society of the West, Stirner finds a grotesque counterpart to the deprivation of the right to self-determination which he experienced in the totalitarian state: interminable overstimulation, the dictates of fashion and the latent tyranny of 'the economy'.[23] The contrast between the transient arbitrariness of the West and the 'Eindeutigkeiten' (unambiguous nature) of the points of reference which he has left behind threatens him with loss of his intellectual identity. Symptomatic of this is the increasing discrepancy he experiences between the 'centre' and the 'periphery', between the German language spoken every day in the Federal Republic and the German he speaks and writes which marks him out as 'einer, der von außen kommt' (someone who comes from outside) and which is now becoming 'fremder' (more foreign), isolating him from those around him: 'Er war jetzt mit seiner Sprache allein' (he was now alone with his language – Wagner 1991: 159).[24] Stirner's inner turmoil and social disorientation are given striking expression in the form of the work: the sequence of events is more sharply broken up than in *Ausreiseantrag*, with fragments of experiences and memories intermingled with bits of dialogue, dream sequences and brief reflective passages as the past is interwoven into the present.

Berlin: Life at the 'Centre'

Since coming to the West, Wagner has published numerous literary texts in diverse forms: collections of essays such as *Mythendämmerung. Einwürfe eines Mitteleuropäers* (Twilight of Myths. Objections of a Central European, 1993); prose pieces and short stories such as *Giancarlos Koffer* (Giancarlo's Suitcase, 1993) and *Der Mann, der Erdrutsche sammelte* (The Man Who Collected Landslides, 1994); collections of poetry such as *Rostregen* (Rust-coloured Rain, 1986), *Schwarze Kreide* (Black Chalk, 1991) and Heiße Maroni (Hot Chestnuts, 1993); and three novels, *Die Muren von Wien* (Viennese Moraine, 1990), *In der Hand der Frauen* (In Women's Hands, 1995) and *Lisas geheimes Buch* (Lisa's Secret Book, 1996). He has also written two substantial political/historical works aimed at enlightening West German readers, *Sonderweg Rumänien* (Romania: The Special Way, 1991) and *Völker ohne Signale* (Peoples Without Signals, 1992), for, as he has put it so provocatively, 'the Federal Republic is a land without history' (Keele 1997),[25] since not only are West Germans for the most part unaware of their own history, they are ignorant of what has gone on in Eastern Europe.[26]

What is his position artistically and politically now that he has been in the West for some ten years? Of his departure from Romania, he writes in the essay collection *Mythendämmerung*: 'Ich ging und war ohne Hoffnung' (I left without any hope). Six years later, when interviewed in the Federal Republic in 1993, it appeared that his basic attitude on many issues had not changed, but, as he said: 'My life is different. Having a particular point of view is no longer so important. But I am for discussing problems' (B, 20).[27]

Like many writers in or from former Communist countries, Wagner has abandoned any utopian hopes: he now discusses all issues 'as dispassionately as possible' in the belief 'that passions have been exhausted by ideologies in this century' (B, 20).[28] Wagner now sees one of his tasks as 'writing about and attacking the political crimes in this century' (B, 20).[29] His first attempt to do this began with his story *Ausreiseantrag*.

Above and beyond purely aesthetic considerations, literature has for Richard Wagner a commemorative function: 'It describes life, real situations, and does this in a very concrete way, which is why it is more vividly graphic than academic texts are' (B, 20).[30] He wishes to give us some understanding of the things that went on under communism by transforming them in all their everyday dimensions into literature. But he is not only concerned with the past but also the way it lives on in the present, as he commented in Keele, 'Bei mir verzahnt sich alles' (With me everything is interlinked). Thus his roots as a Banat Swabian are always inherent in his writing, sometimes explicitly as a central theme, for instance, in his novel *Die Muren von Wien* (hereafter referred to as 'M'), in which he confronts the, for Banat-Germans, perennial question of their own identity: Benda, the main character, hopes to find his true home in Germany, but in the West, even though he speaks German, he is still an outsider and comes to realise that a Banat Swabian is neither a Romanian nor a German: 'His West had only been an illusion which he had thought up to counter the deadening banality of life in Romania' (M, 107).[31] And if elsewhere in Wagner's works the Banat Swabian issue is not an explicit theme, it is there, implicitly, in everything that he writes, as he explained in his Frankfurt lecture: 'The Romanian-German dimension is the thing which is absent but always present. It is simply there in what I write' (F, 41).[32] It is in this respect, too, that he expresses an affinity with Johannes Bobrowski:

> In this minority I had my home, but I was not at home, I do not mourn its way of life, but it haunts me. Now, in Berlin, I'm like Johannes Bobrowski with his oddball idea. 'It is inexpressible', writes Bobrowski, 'and it is the place where we live.' He writes. The Banat has Sarmatian repercussions, as it were.[33] (F, 46)

And even though, as we have noted, he adopted an oppositional stance towards them, his background was and remains the German minority: 'ohne sie ist diese Region für mich nicht existent' (without them this region has for me no existence – B, 20). Now, though, in Berlin and a long way from the Romanian reality of his childhood and youth, this part of his identity exists only 'in my head, as an integral part of me and my literature' (B, 20).[34]

His present stance *vis-à-vis* his departure from Romania is a positive one: 'My decision to leave was an option in favour of the West' (B, 20).[35] He is aware that his experiences in the West have changed his outlook, particularly since German unification: 'My view of things is a Western one ... One is at home wherever one recognises one's own thoughts' (B, 20).[36]

He sees his essays and his literary works written in the West as 'Selbstver-
ständigungsprozesse', part of a multiple process of self-communication and
self-understanding.

One theme with which he is preoccupied is the relationship of minorities to their language: 'I'm of the opinion that minorities have a different
relationship to their language because they see their language as being continually at risk' (B, 20).[37] Hence he is particularly interested in what he calls
'das Spannungsverhältnis zwischen Peripherie und Zentrum' (the tensions
in the relationship between the periphery and the centre), believing that
the German minority, from its position on the periphery in Romania, is the
only one since the Second World War to produce a German literature
which has in the meantime been completely integrated in the centre, i.e.,
the Federal Republic.

Though he now lives at the 'centre', in Berlin, Richard Wagner prefers
to see himself as a Central European, a concept which he investigates in his
essay *Völker ohne Signale* (Peoples without Signals) and one which had an
important significance for Eastern European dissidents. 'Central Europe is
the only concept that represents the great diversity which is there in Eastern Europe' (B, 20).[38]

Some of his views on literature are expressed in a short essay written for
the 'Kultur: Briefe' (culture: letters) section of *Literatur und Kritik* in April
1994, in which he explained the difference between writing under a dictatorship and writing in a more open, pluralistic society. What they do have
in common is: 'die Frage nach dem Sinn des Schreibens' (the question as
to the whole point of writing – Wagner 1994: 11), which remains the same
anywhere. It is the 'Schreibsituation', the situation in which the writer actually writes, which is different. Under Communist dictatorships there were
three categories of authors: those who were encouraged and supported,
those who were tolerated and those whose work was banned. Censorship
and repression thus created a false sense of importance for the writer – false
because literature gained a significance not through itself, through its inherent value as literature, but because it became the only arena where some
freedom was possible in terms of discussion of historical and political
issues, albeit 'between the lines' of published literary texts. This had the
effect of making writing too easy, with fame or notoriety becoming the
goal: 'Many authors no longer gave themselves up to literature, they
exploited it' (ibid: 11).[39] Their aim was not to be writers but to be historians, journalists, dissidents and resistance fighters, sometimes all rolled into
one. Yet the powers that be still controlled literary activities through a
combination of the carrot and the stick, through privilege and punishment.
And so writers knew they could afford to give the appearance of being subversive as long as they did not go too far. Thus they acquired a relatively
large readership, but literature itself suffered: 'Das hat die Literatur fade
gemacht' (it made literature bland, insipid – ibid: 11). Under socialism,
then, writers had no power as writers, but they did have the illusion that

they were literally making politics through their literature. With the *Wende*, though, the writing of history and journalism returned to their true domains, as Wagner wittily puts it: 'What was hitherto between the lines was now on television' (ibid: 11).[40] And literature thus lost its false significance, leaving many hitherto popular dissident authors suddenly at a loss as to how to proceed now.

Richard Wagner, though, is not and never was one of these authors. Indeed his poetological standpoint has consistently remained the same, as he explained in his Frankfurt Poetics Lecture in 1993. Whenever asked whether his writing had changed since emigrating, he would cautiously always try to give an answer:

> But the crux of the matter is that I write because I write. I started something that will never end. My writing was not a way of expressing myself under the dictatorship. I continued to write as soon as I arrived in Berlin. I was writing during the bewildering first year after my arrival and I am writing today too, now that I have settled in Berlin.[41] (F, 49)

Now that he is living in the West, though, he sees literature and the literature industry as being in a state of crisis in the chaos of the market-place. Yet he is prepared to accept the attendant difficulties, for literature is now measured not by what is written between the lines but by its own yardsticks: 'It no longer gets its aura from the fact that it is banned' (Wagner 1994: 11).[42]

Richard Wagner's own approach in his recent writing is encapsulated in the sentence which follows on from the one cited above: 'Beyond this, the past cries out and the present demands to be described in all its intricacy. Even though it looks as if no one wants to hear about the past and the present. Because now hardly anyone is able to extract any entertainment value from the whole disaster. Literature needs plenty of staying power.'[43] For Richard Wagner, then, writing involves giving literary shape to the interwoven complexity of the past and the present. It is my view that the diversity of the styles and forms of his works written in the West are testimony to the range of experiences which he has distilled into his literary works. By way of illustration, and given the constraints of space in this chapter, I shall conclude with brief comments on two of his most recent works not discussed in Graham Jackman's chapter.

Der Mann, der Erdrutsche sammelte (1994, hereafter referred to as 'E') is a collection of sixty-six 'Kalendergeschichten', short, often witty, usually humorous anecdotes in the tradition of Johan Peter Hebel, Bertolt Brecht and Günter Eich. The multifarious material for these pieces is drawn from Wagner's critical awareness of both the past and the present, from memories of the past, but also from humdrum events, everyday experiences in pubs, in the street and in shops, and newspaper, television and radio reports. The diversity of these little anecdotes and parables (most are less than one page in length) is indicated in the range of titles, from the everyday 'Der Mann, der in Westberlin lebte' (the man who lived in West

Berlin) to the seemingly fantastical 'Der Mann, der durch die Luft gehen konnte' (the man who could walk through the air). The collection is divided into four parts, each of which bears the title of one of the stories, indicating loose thematic connections between them as the author as literary *flâneur* meanders between past and present. The first section, 'Der Mann, der in Westberlin lebte', features life in Berlin east and west, reflecting Berlin as the city of Wagner's residential choice, Berlin as the 'centre' of the German cultural world, but also Berlin as unique, like no other city in Germany because of its cosmopolitan character, because of its links with socialism and the past and the 'periphery' of German culture, and because it is the only place in Germany where unification can be experienced directly. The second part of the prose collection, 'Der Mann, der Erdrutsche sammelte', shows the frequent topsy-turviness of everyday human activities and relationships. The third, 'Der Mann, der nach Pitcairn auswandern wollte', (the man who wanted to emigrate to Pitcairn), tells of wishes, dreams and aspirations, with its echo of the *Bounty* mutineers. And finally the section 'Der Mann, der durch die Luft gehen konnte' introduces more personal and private themes. Many of these short pieces have a grotesque twist in the tail where the ultimate absurdity of everyday routine is suddenly illuminated with a flash of black humour. Thus 'Der Mann, der in Westberlin lebte' goes once a week to an observation tower from which he can observe the other side beyond the wall. One day, after many years, the Wall is no longer there, so the man goes back into town to the station Bahnhof Zoo and buys a super-saver ticket – to Aachen! Other stories focus, too, on the absurdity of people's aspirations: the title story concerns a man who flies halfway around the globe to take pictures of landslides, building up a considerable collection of such photographs which he shows off at family gatherings; but when he dies, an event totally unrelated to landslides, his wife throws the entire collection away! Sometimes anecdotes become grotesque emblems of empty rituals and the pointlessness of much human behaviour: 'Der Mann, der Schlange stand' (the man who stood in a queue) tells of the man who stood in an official queue for years and who now sits at home because the queue was suddenly dispersed.

Recollections of life in the Banat intermingle with life in Germany after the demise of socialism, and Berlin forms the focal point, a city full of contradictions as in the story 'Der Mann, der mit einer Ananas über den Potsdamer Platz ging' (the man who crossed Potsdam Square with a pineapple). Here, it is as if the 'periphery' is now at the very centre: 'It was as empty on Potsdam Square as if Potsdam Square were the Central Europe of Berlin' (E, 18);[44] the man with the pineapple, though, is undaunted and carries on across the Square, proudly displaying his pineapple and looking as if he is 'walking through Central Europe', ready to be photographed by some news agency at any moment. Yet the humorous atmosphere suddenly changes to one of threat at the end as the past, too, seems to come alive for 'it seemed to him as if now and then he could hear shots' (E, 18).[45] Wagner's collection ends on a more serious personal note: the threat of loss of identity as writer in a world becoming empty of readers. In 'Der Mann, der Bücher las' (the man who read books), a first-person narrator recalls that once, long ago in a different, little known place, `he knew a man who read books. In the middle of the night, when he awakes from his dreams about this man, he can never get back to sleep again, and so he too reads books. One such sleepless night when he is reading, a puzzling sentence comes to him which he writes down here: 'I can say nothing about myself that I myself would find credible' (E, 90).[46]

The work was well received and critics praised, in particular, the laconic style and the precision and restraint of the language. Agnes Hüfner in the *Süddeutsche Zeitung*, for instance, comments: 'He relates it all in simple statements, in ordinary words of which there are astonishingly few' (4 October 1994).[47] Andreas Schäfer in the *Berliner Zeitung* (4 October 1994), on the other hand, praised the poetic quality of Wagner's prose: 'His sensitive gaze passes over everyday life as it flickers before his eyes; by observing the seemingly banal and the obvious with curiosity and amazement, he hammers poetic sparks out of it.'[48]

Richard Wagner's recent work *Lisas geheimes Buch* (1996; hereafter refrred to as 'L') is, by way of contrast, a documentary novel, based on an authentic protocol: over a period of six months, the author made tape recordings of his interviews with a prostitute, and, after some editing, worked much of this material verbatim into his literary text, weaving into it a fictional strand, thereby giving the novel a structure which creates effective tension between fact and fiction: Indeed, critics categorised the work as 'faction'. The purely fictional protagonist is the journalist Franck, the author's *alter ego*, who initially interviews Lisa for his newspaper and later feels drawn towards her. He looks her up again and she tells her story to him which he records on tape. Franck, though, distrusts his own investigative means of ascertaining the truth, and at one point thinks to himself: 'I mustn't show her that I am forming an impression of her which is not only being determined by her' (L, 62).[49]

Lisa, a former citizen of the GDR and thirty-year-old mother of three children is tired of her squalid flat and after the *Wende* sees only one way of achieving her wish to escape her drab situation. Without any illusions about what it implies, she turns to prostitution, coolly calculating what her chances are. And she gives a frank account of all the details of the double existence which she leads as prostitute and provider of luxuries for the family.

Wagner, partly through his narrative structure, avoids the twofold dangers of sentimental cliché and titilation in his portrayal of the prostitute. The level-headed, often likeable Lisa is not presented as the conventional victim of social circumstances but as someone driven by the irresistible lure of money. And she makes no bones about this: indeed, she adopts the principle of seeing men as walking thousand-mark notes: 'At that particular moment, you don't think of the man. Regard every man as a thousand-mark note, and you've got him. That became my principle!' (L, 48)[50]

Thus those critics who read the novel as an authentic 'Bericht über Prostitution' missed the point: for prostitution in *Lisas geheimes Buch* becomes an authentic metaphor for the principle which drives the new Germany, namely the misplaced belief that money enables people to be the architect of their own fate and happiness.

For Richard Wagner, the journey from the periphery to the centre, from the Banat to Berlin, has been one fraught with all manner of personal difficulties. Yet, as we have seen above, it has been a productive journey in terms of his achievements as a writer, which have already been widely recognised: since coming to the West, for instance, he has received numerous literary prizes, including the Darmstadt Leonce and Lena Prize for the best political poem in 1987 and the Andreas Gryphius Prize in 1988. He was a guest lecturer at the University of Ohio in 1992, and in 1993 he followed in the footsteps of other prominent contemporary German writers by giving the Frankfurt Poetics Lecture at the Goethe-University.

Richard Wagner is, then, a German writer with a unique voice that reflects the unique set of experiences which he briefly touches upon in his Frankfurt lecture: 'I sat there in my isolated Banat region and constructed for myself a periphery out of words. ... My origins in a minority in the East describe my relationship to language and to the world as periphery. My German origin makes it possible for my gaze from East to West to be a longing for the centre' (F, 36, 37).[51] He has recognised, too, the dangers of this 'longing for the centre': 'But whoever reaches the centre ceases to write: leaves the language of literature and finds the linguistic strait-jacket of society' (F, 36).[52] Thus for Richard Wagner, the journey from the Banat periphery to the German geographical and cultural centre has, paradoxically, been a journey back to the periphery in the recognition that, in modern societies, the writer remains necessarily on the fringe as critical outsider and *flâneur*: 'Literatur der Rand des Wirklichen' – literature, the periphery of reality (F, 49).

Notes

1. Mein Leben war sinnlos geworden und mein Schreiben auch.

2. Im Grunde sind alle Dinge, die ich in Rumänien so getrieben habe, gescheitert.

3. Some of these (and following) details about his life in Romania were described by Richard Wagner to me in several conversations and in three seminar discussions with colleagues and students at Keele in October 1997. Any quotations not otherwise identified stem from these conversations.

4. Wir versuchten, das zu leben, was wir leben wollten, Phantasie hineinzubringen und uns nicht der reglementierten Welt zu unterwerfen.

5. In den sechziger Jahren transportierte die Musik über Mauern und Zäune und Stacheldraht hinweg ein weltweit in der Jugend wirksames Lebensgefühl. ... Aus dieser Zeit und aus diesem Zusam-

menhang rührt wahrscheinlich meine Beziehung zur Populär-Kultur und ihren Formen. Das Ewige war mir egal. Ästhetik war Spaß und Provokation und Spaß.

6. In diesem Jahr war für mich poetisch meine Weltsicht angelegt.

7. Die Deutschen in Rumänien haben sich immer auf die Geschehnisse in der Bundesrepublik bezogen.

8. Als ich anfing zu schreiben, konnte man schreiben, was man wollte.

9. Ich bin ja in den Sozialismus geboren, ich kannte ja nichts anderes.

10. Wir haben diese Gesellschaft, wir nehmen sie an und versuchen, das Beste daraus zu machen.

11. Wenn sie betrunken waren, haben sie Landserlieder gesungen, die Generation meines Vaters war zu 90 Pozent in der Waffen-SS, die pseudo-intellektuelle Schicht, das waren die reaktionären Dorflehrer ... Gegen diese Leute, dieses Milieu habe ich geschrieben.

12. Wir schrieben eine ganz andere Sprache.

13. Wir saßen in Kneipen und erzählten uns Romane.

14. Ich suchte einen Ton gegen das Pathos der Heimatliteratur aber auch gegen das Pathos des Sozialistischen Realismus.

15. Noch wollte ich die Gesellschaft verändern, aber schon schrieb ich meine ersten Gedichte.

16. Die vielfachen Hindernisse beim Versuch, überhaupt Realität zu erfahren.

17. The example of *Solidarnocz* in Poland, however, did show him how the system could be opposed: 'Die Solidarnocz war die erste Bewegung in Osteuropa, die es geschafft hat, zentral gegen den Kommunismus vorzugehen, und sie mußte von den Kommunisten, wenn auch nur zeitweise, akzeptiert werden. Damit war der Kommunismus eigentlich gefallen' ('Solidarnocz was the first movement in Eastern Europe which managed to take assertive central action against Communism, and the Communists had to accept Solidarnocz, even if only temporarily. This actually signified the end of Communism' – B, 20).

18. Politik ist immer eine Dimension in meinem Schreiben, und das ist mir sehr wichtig.

19. In einer Diktatur ist überall Politik. Ich stelle sie nicht ins Gedicht, sie kommt von alleine hinein.

20. 1983 ist das Jahr, in dem alles weggekippt ist.

21. daß die Menschen alles mitmachen, daß sie bereit sind, diesen ganzen Wahnsinn, dieses Absurde mitzutragen. Und man ist allein und steht lächerlich da.

22. mal in lakonisch-nüchternem, mal in bitter-sarkastischem Ton.

23. See Huttenlocher 1998: 346–7.

24. For a more detailed discussion of this issue, see Graham Jackman's chapter 'Alone in a crowd', in this book.

25. 'Die Bundesrepublik ist ein Land ohne Geschichte.'

26. His essay *Völker ohne Signale* (Peoples Without Signals, 1992) offers an ironic answer to the words of the Communist Manifesto: 'Völker hört die Signale' (Peoples, listen to the signals); and in *Sonderweg Rumänien* (Romania: The Special Way, 1991), he explains the significance of events in Southeastern Europe over the last hundred years.

27. Ich lebe anders. Mir ist es nicht mehr so wichtig, eine Perspektive zu haben. Ich bin dafür, daß wir über Probleme reden.

28. , So leidenschaftslos wie möglich ... daß die Leidenschaften von den Ideologien in diesem Jahrhundert verbraucht worden sind.

29. über und gegen das politische Verbrechen in unserem Jahrhundert zu schreiben.

30. Sie beschreibt Lebensräume und tut dies sehr konkret, weshalb sie anschaulicher ist als wissenschaftliche Texte.

31. Sein Westen war eine Illusion gewesen, die er sich gegen die tötende Banalität des Lebens in Rumänien ausgedacht hatte.

32. Das Rumäniendeutsche ist das Abwesende, das immer präsent ist. Es schreibt mit.

33. 'Ich war in dieser Minderheit zuhause aber nicht heimisch, ich traure ihren Lebensformen nicht nach, aber sie geht mir nach. Jetzt, in Berlin, geht es mir wie Johannes Bobrowski mit seinem Käuzchen. "Das ist nicht ausdrückbar," schreibt Bobrowski, "und ist der Ort , wo wir leben". Schreibt er. Das Banat zieht sozusagen sarmatische Kreise.' Sarmatia, an actual area in the Southern Russian Steppes inhabited by a nomadic Slav people, was used by Bobrowski in his poetry as a central cipher for his main theme: the aggressive relationship, throughout history, of the Germans to their neighbours in the East (Poles, Lithuanians, Russians and Jews).

34. in meinem Kopf als Bestandteil von mir und meiner Literatur.

35. Meine Entscheidung, wegzugehen, ist eine Option für den Westen gewesen.

36. Meine Sicht auf die Dinge ist eine westliche ... Man ist zuhause, wo man sein Denken wiedererkennt.

37. Ich bin der Meinung, daß Minderheiten eine andere Beziehung zu ihrer Sprache haben, da sie ihre Sprache immer gefährdet sehen.

38. Mitteleuropa ist der einzige Begriff, der die Vielfalt in Osteuropa repräsentiert.

39. Viele Autoren setzten sich dem Schreiben nicht mehr aus, sie benutzten es.

40. Was bisher zwischen den Zeilen stand, war nun im Fernsehen.

41. Aber im Kern ist es doch so, daß ich schreibe, weil ich schreibe. Ich habe etwas angefangen, was nie wieder aufhört. Mein Schreiben war nicht eine Ausdrucksform in der Diktatur. Ich schrieb nach meiner Ankunft in Berlin sofort weiter. Ich schrieb in meinem verwirrenden ersten Jahr der Ankunft und ich schreibe auch heute, seitdem ich in Berlin heimisch geworden bin.

42. Ihre Aura entsteht nicht mehr unter dem Stern des Verbots.

43. Jenseits davon schreit die Vergangenheit und ruft die Gegenwart nach vertrackter Beschreibung. Auch wenn es so aussieht, als wollte keiner etwas über die Vergangenheit und von der Gegenwart was hören. Weil jetzt kaum einer dem ganzen Desaster einen Unterhaltungswert abgewinnen mag. Die Literatur braucht einen langen Atem.

44. Es war so leer auf dem Potsdamer Platz, als wäre der Potsdamer Platz das Mitteleuropa von Berlin.

45. Es war ihm, als höre er vereinzelt Schüsse.

46. Ich kann über mich nichts sagen, was mir selber glaubhaft erschiene.

47. Das alles erzählt er in einfachen Aussagen, in gewöhnlichen und erstaunlich wenigen Worten.

48. Sein sensibler Blick fährt über das alltägliche Gegenwartsgeflimmer; indem er das scheinbar Banale und Offensichtliche mit einer neugierigen Verwunderung betrachtet, schlägt er aus ihm poetische Funken.

49. Ich darf ihr nicht zeigen, daß ich mir ein Bild von ihr mache, das nicht nur von ihr selbst bestimmt wird.

50. Du denkst in dem Moment nicht an den Mann. Jeden Mann angucken wie einen Tausend-markschein, und dann hast du ihn. Das wurde mein Prinzip.

51. Ich saß in meiner isolierten Region Banat und baute mir einen Rand aus Wörtern. ... Die Herkunft aus einer Minderheit im Osten beschreibt mein Verhältnis zur Sprache und zur Welt als Rand. Die deutsche Herkunft ermöglicht mir den Blick von Ost nach West als Sehnsucht nach der Mitte.

52. Doch wer die Mitte erreicht, schreibt nicht mehr. Er verläßt die Sprache der Literatur und findet die Sprachregelung der Gesellschaft.

References

Primary Sources

Books published in Romania

Klartext. Ein Gedichtbuch, Bucharest, Albatros,1973.
die invasion der uhren. Gedichte, Bucharest, Kriterion, 1977.
Der Anfang einer Geschiche. Prosa, Cluj-Napoca, Dacia, 1980.
Hotel California I. Der Tag der mit einer Wunde begann. Gedichte, Bucharest, Kriterion, 1980.
Hotel California II. Als schliefe der Planet. Gedichte, Bucharest, Kriterion, 1981.
Gegenlicht, Temeswar, Facla-Verlag, 1983.
Anna und die Uhren. Geschichten für Kinder, Bucharest, Ion Creanga, 1981.
das auge des feuilletons, Temeswar, Facla-Verlag,1984.

Books published in the Federal Republic

Rostregen, Gedichte, Darmstadt, Luchterhand, 1986.
Anna und die Uhren. Ein Lesebuch für kleine Leute, Kinderbuch, Darmstadt, Luchterhand, 1987.
Ausreiseantrag. Eine Erzählung, Darmstadt, Luchterhand, 1988.
Begrüßungsgeld. Eine Erzählung, Darmstadt, Luchterhand, 1989.
Die Muren von Wien, Roman, Frankfurt, Luchterhand, 1990.
Schwarze Kreide, Gedichte, Frankfurt, Luchterhand, 1991.
Sonderweg Rumänien. Bericht aus einem Entwicklungsland, Essay, Berlin, Rotbuch, 1991.
Völker ohne Signale. Zum Epochenbruch in Osteuropa, Essay, Berlin, Rotbuch, 1992.
Der Himmel von New York im Museum von Amsterdam, Geschichten, Frankfurter Verlagsanstalt, 1992.
Mythendämmerung. Einwürfe eines Mitteleuropäers, Essays, Berlin, Rotbuch, 1993.
Heiße Maroni, Gedichte, Stuttgart, DVA, 1993.
Giancarlos Koffer, Prosa, Berlin, Rotbuch, 1993.
Der Mann, der Erdrutsche sammelte, Geschichten, Stuttgart, DVA, 1994 - all references to this are indi-cated by E followed by the page number.
In der Hand der Frauen, Roman, Stuttgart, DVA, 1995.
Lisas geheimes Buch, Roman, DVA Stuttgart 1996.

Essays in journals, newspapers and books

'Unter Brüdern. Ein osteuropäisches Haßregister', in: Christoph Ransmayr, ed. *Im blinden Winkel. Nachrichten aus Mitteleuropa*, Vienna, Verlag Christian Branstätter, 1985, pp.173-180.
'Berliner Überlegungen', in *Literaturmagazin* 22, 1988, pp.177–182.
'Der Tag hat angefangen', in Günter Kunert, ed., *Aus fremder Heimat. Zur Exilsituation heutiger Liter-atur*, Munich/Vienna, Hanser, 1988, pp. 83–86.

'Die Aktionsgruppe Banat. Versuch einer Selbstdarstellung', in: Wilhelm Solnus, ed., *Nachruf auf die rumäniendeutsche Literatur*, Marburg, Hitzeroth, 1990, pp.121–30.

'"Der Spiegel der Identität einer Minderheit ist ihre Sprache." Die Rumäniendeutschen zwischen Isolation, Stalinismus, Assimilation und Nationalismus', in: *Frankfurter Rundschau*, 22 July 1991.

'"Sie winkte nicht, ich winkte nicht." Wie ich von Rumänien nach Westberlin kam: Eine Mauerschau ohne Mauer', in *Die Presse*, 13 February 1993.

'Temeswar: Kulturbrief', in *Literatur und Kritik*, vol. 273/4, April 1993, pp.14-16.

'Die Bedeutung der Ränder oder vom Inneren zum Äußersten und wieder zurück', in *neue literatur: 'Ideen in Not'*, vol.1, 1994, pp. 33–49. (This was Wagner's 'Frankfurter Poetik-Vorlesung' [Frankfurt lecture on poetics])

'Kulturbrief aus Berlin', in *Literatur und Kritik*, April 1994, vol. 283/4, pp. 11–12.

Interviews

'"Wir sind fürs Lebendige." Interview mit Richard Wagner', in: Emmerich Reichrath, ed., *Reflexe II: Aufsätze, Rezensionen und Interviews zur deutschen Literatur in Rumänien*, Cluj-Napoca, Dacia, 1984, pp. 47–51.

'"Jetzt hoffen die Rumänen auf Gorbatschow". Die Schriftsteller Herta Müller und Richard Wagner über das deutsche Miderheit im Ceauçescu-Staat', Reiner Traub and Olaf Ihlau, in *Der Spiegel*, vol. 41, no.19, 4 May 1987, pp. 154–163.

'"Warum rebelliert Rumänien nicht, Herr Wagner?" Ein Interview mit Ferkas Piroshka', in *Frankfurter Allgemeine Magazin*, 14 April 1989, pp. 102–3.

'Gefangene im eigenen Haus. Gespräch mit Richard Wagner', Adelbert Reif, in *Die Welt*, 23 December 1989.

'"Blick über die Maisfelder hinaus." Gespräch mit Herta Müller und Richard Wagner', Ferenc Ührte and Bela Szendi, in *Neue Zeitung*, no. 12, 24 March 1990.

'Richard Wagner: Politik ist immer eine Dimension in meinem Schreiben', (Susanne Broos) in *Börsenblatt*, no. 87, 2 November 1993, p. 18.

Secondary Literature

von Bormann, Alexander, 'Einspruch. Widerspruch. Zuspruch. Zur Rhetorik des zeitgenössischen Gedichts. Am Beispiel der rumäniendeutschen Lyrik, insbesondere Richard Wagners', in *Wespennest*, no. 82, 1991, pp. 24–32.

Csejka, Gerhard, 'Richard Wagner', in *Kritisches Lexikon zur deutschsprachigen Gegenwartsliteratur*, ed. Heinz Ludwig Arnold, Munich, 1991, pp. 1–5.

Elsie, Robert (editor and translator), *The Pied Poets, Contemporary verse of the Transylvanian and Danube Germans of Romania*, London and Boston, Forest Books, 1990.

Gauss, Karl-Markus, 'Die alten Geschichten kommen wieder. Der rumäniendeutsche Schriftsteller Richard Wagner und die Aktionsgruppe Banat', in *Die Wochenzeitung*, 23 August 1991.

Hüfner, Agnes, 'Der Mann, der und die Frau die: Sechsundsechzig Kalendergeschichten von Richard Wagner', in *Süddeutsche Zeitung*, 4 October 1994.

Huttenlocher, Armin M., 'Richard Wagner' in Walter Jens, ed., *Kindlers Neues Literatur-Lexikon*, Munich, 1998, pp. 345–7.

Kraft, Thomas, 'Orte der Erfahrung', in *Neue deutsche Literatur*, vol. 2, no. 42, 1994, pp. 172–5.

Krauss, Hannes, 'Fremde Blicke. Zur Prosa von Herta Müller und Richard Wagner', in *Neue Generation – neues Erzählen. Deutsche Prosa-Literatur der achtziger Jahre*, ed. Walter Delabar, Werner Jung, Ingrid Pergande, Opladen, Westdeutscher Verlag, 1993, pp. 69-76.

Marin, Robert, *Kurze Geschichte der Banater Deutschen*, Temeswar, Facla Verlag, 1980.

Schäfer, Andreas, 'Sie schärfen den Blick. Kürzestgeschichten von Richard Wagner', in *Berliner Zeitung*, 4 October 1994.

Schuller-Weber, Annemarie, 'Nationale Identität im kulturellen Wandel. Bedürfnis nach kultureller Selbstbestätigung: die Rumäniendeutschen', in *Zeitschrift für Kulturaustausch – 'Migration und kultureller Wandel'*, vol. 45, 1995/1, pp. 55–9.

Wichner, Ernest, ed., *Ein Pronomen ist verhaftet worden. Texte der Aktionsgruppe Banat*, Frankfurt am Main, Suhrkamp, 1992.

Wichner, Ernest, ed., *Das Land am Nebentisch. Texte und Zeichen aus Siebenbürgen, dem Banat und den Orten versuchter Ankunft*, Leipzig, Reclam, 1993.

Wittib, Monika, 'Richard Wagner: *Die Muren von Wien*', review, in *INN*, Zeitschrift für Literatur, vol. 9, 28 April 1992, p. 104.

Chapter 8

' ... a form of literature which was intentionally political.'

Richard Wagner in conversation with David Rock and Stefan Wolff[1]

Q: Did you experience any problems of identity as a German in Romania?

A: I didn't have any problems of identity, on the contrary, I had a very clear sense of identity. With my compatriots too, amongst whom I grew up in a village which up to 1945 had been completely German and then approximately half German, there was a very strong sense of German identity. That prevented me, too, from having any doubts about the fact that I was a German. In addition to this, we were also regarded as Germans by the other sections of the population in the region, by the Hungarians and Serbs and by the Romanians who made up the majority in the state. German was not only my mother tongue but also the language of the cultural conception which I had of myself. I also went to a German school where I learnt German language, German literature and German literary history. So all the components of a German identity were already there, and for that reason, from the outset, I have regarded myself as a German writer and have written in this language.

Q: And now that you are living in Berlin – do you have the feeling of being at home there?

A: 'At home' is not the right term. I emigrated to Germany, but I have nothing to do with Germany in the territorial sense as I did not spend the first thirty-five years of my life in Germany. My Germany is a cultural concept – the cultural nation. And I didn't pick Berlin, you know, because it's so wonderfully German, but because that is precisely what it isn't, because it's a cosmopolitan city. Otherwise, I could of course have moved to a proper German city in West Germany at that time. And as far as Romania is concerned, Romania was for me always 'the state'. What I related to was the Banat, the region. In Eastern Central Europe, the regions are more important than the states, they are also older than them. For the minorities, it is quite natural to identify with the region first. That is why there is a regional identity, and why there is much less of a sense of identity in terms of nation-states. So that is why I have this territorial relationship to the Banat, the place where I grew up, and why I don't have it to Germany. But at the same time, I do have to say that I did not have an 'unbroken' relationship with my compatriots. This conservative, even reactionary section of the population, with its fundamentalism, I found repulsive, and in my early texts, I wrote in opposition to the culture which they practised, and did not identify with them. Nor did I feel the Banat to be the territory of this minority but a territory in which a variety of ethnic groups lived. The cultural background of the Banat that I mean is more the Habsburg base, whose influence is still felt today in the everyday culture of the region – culturally much more than politically.

Q: So do you feel at home in Berlin in a cultural sense?

A: I am at home in Berlin because I find a lot of my own ideas reflected there. But I'm not really at home in Berlin either.

Q: What do you associate with the term 'Heimat' [home, homeland]?

A: I wouldn't use the term at all, because it has bad associations for me, for two reasons. Firstly, 'Heimat' has connotations of that folkloric, conservative understanding of the German minority and thus it carries an unbroken sense of edification[2] to which I am very opposed. Secondly, the term 'Heimat' was a firmly established component of Communist propaganda and for that reason it is for me pretty well tainted.

Q: Which cultural traditions have you taken up?

A: For me, what was going on in Germany, in contemporary German literature, in modern writing, was always important. I was also always interested in things Western. Socialist Realism was, of course, binding in Romania right into the sixties, but later on, reception of modern literature from the West was possible. The ethnic Romanians were always oriented more towards France and Paris, whereas we writers from the German minority followed the arts and modern writing in Germany, Austria and Switzerland. I wanted to know what was going on, and I wanted to do something similar. In the sixties, of course, that also had a lot to do with music, and much of the reception of modern arts from the West came via music. I have always read a lot, very many different authors, and of course this changed from period to period in line with what I was doing myself, too. When I started writing, Brecht was an important author for me because of his terseness, his laconic style and the absence of any kitsch in his work. I also read the Viennese Group, and then what was written in the GDR in the wake of Brecht: Sarah Kirsch, Volker Braun, Günter Kunert. Amongst the lyric poets, it was Paul Celan who interested me most, partly on account of his biography. To sum up, then, there were three influences: modern Western writing in German, critical GDR literature and literature from the periphery, such as that from the Bukovina, which had similarities with my own situation.

Q: Did you see your own texts in terms of opposition to the Communist dictatorship?

A: That was, above all else, the stance of the Romanian-speaking writers who saw themselves as having a cultural role to play, in consequence of which opposition within the dictatorship for them meant survival of culture, too. For me that was an elitist idea which I never shared. Then in 1972, the German-speaking authors of my generation formed a group, 'the Banat Action Group'. It was our declared aim to write a form of literature which was intentionally political, not escapist. Thus, we wanted to write a kind of literature which was contemporary, topical and playful, which reacted to the political situation and took a social-critical approach. This was completely different from the approach of the Romanian writers. Our group functioned for three years, with publications, public appearances and influence, then we came to be despised.

Q: What role did your sense of identity play with regard to the socialist state, with its different ethnic majority, the state in which you lived and which you were critical of? And what role did your sense of identity play with regard to the German minority in Romania?

A: The two were linked. Even if I was critical of the Romanian-Germans, I was of course myself a product of this ethnic group. As a minority, we always kept our distance from Romanian culture, the Romanian nation and the Romanian state, and felt that we did not belong there. Because of this distance, it was easier for me than for an ethnic Romanian to have a critical perspective on many things – not only on communism, but also on Romanian nationalism, the role of culture, the value of criticism. At the same time, though, I saw myself as a citizen of the Romanian state, and took the view that one also had a job to do as a German-speaking writer. Otherwise my colleagues and I would indeed never have had the idea of social-criticism being part of the programme of the Action Group. Here again we differed from our German-speaking compatriots who were of the view that this was a matter for Romanians, were thus ethno-centric in their way of thinking and had their anti-Romanian prejudices. That was a convenient attitude for a minority to hold, but one which I did not share.

Q: What policy did the state pursue with regard to the German sense of identity, and, on the other side, how did the minority itself try to preserve its identity?

A: The Romanian population always regarded the minority as German, and there were no problems. The state adopted a tactical approach. During the first few years after the war, the minority had no rights and the theory of collective guilt prevailed. But in 1948 the Germans got official status as a minority, with all the cultural institutions, the media and the schools; these, however, did not belong to the minority, but to the state. This meant that the minority could not convey the way it saw itself via the media, but that the state used all these institutions for its propaganda. During Stalinism, the aim was to infiltrate the whole population as much as possible with Communism, and so with regard to the minority, it made sense of course to use their language. Then in the sixties it became more difficult for all the minorities in the period of 'openness' during which Ceauçescu installed his national-communism, based on communism and surreal Balkan nationalism, in order to win support amongst his own people. This had its effect on the minorities at the very moment when the nationalists in the Communist Party were trying to curtail the rights of the minorities. There was then a latent conflict situation which affected the Hungarian minority first and foremost, less so the German minority. There were even periods in which the German minority was used as an advertisement for national-communism when there was criticism from both East and West of Romanian policy towards minorities. In this way, the German minority ended up in a complex situation in which it was more object than subject.

Q: How was the German minority able, in spite of this, to preserve its identity?

A: The German minority changed in that it became more German and simultaneously modern through the reception of what was going on in Germany. Before 1918 the focal point was Vienna, and afterwards it gradually shifted to Berlin. Altogether, though, it was always a relatively uncritical adoption and simulation of the values from the metropolis of the time, including that of the Third Reich. Then after the Second World War it was the Federal Republic. Of advantage to this preservation of their identity were: the fact that the German minority had, for centuries, preserved traditions such as church consecration festivals; the fact that there were representatives of the minority in the Romanian state machine; and the fact that there were fairly close family ties with the Federal Republic through refugees with whom more intensive contacts were allowed again from the 1960s onwards.

Q: Were there attempts to assimilate minorities on the part of the Romanian state?

A: Yes, but only sporadically and not necessarily in a repressive way. That came about rather through the urbanisation from the mid-1960s and through mixed marriages. From the 1970s on, the state was not at all interested in assimilation any more but tried to make capital by 'selling' members of the German minority. And assimilation could not function for the simple reason that, for the German minority, ties to the Federal Republic were more valuable than those to Romania. Romania was a state in crisis, whereas the Federal Republic was seen as a state of the future.

Q: What are the prospects for the German minority in Romania today?

A: The German minority does not have a future. Most people had already emigrated by the end of the 1980s. And after the 1989 revolution, there were another 100,000 Romanian-Germans who did not believe that there was any future for them in this state. As far as I'm concerned, the future of a minority always depends on there being a cultural nucleus in which creativity comes into being. If that is no longer the case, as with the Romanian-Germans, then there is no future. For some time to come there will be a remainder of the German population with a disproportionately high percentage of old people who will gradually die out. For those Germans who do remain, Romania is no alternative because of the political and economic situation. There are, though, also people who live, work or study in both Romania and Germany, but they all have a German passport to be on the safe side. One consequence of emigration was also the fact that the formerly self-contained, 'closed' area where the Germans settled no longer exists and the remaining members of the minority are scattered all over the place and have lost their everyday German cultural environment.

Q: What sort of reception did Romanian-German emigrants get in the Federal Republic?

A: Romanian-Germans always had lots of information about the Federal Republic, a real live German-speaking culture and family connections with West Germany. Nevertheless, it's one thing knowing a lot about a country and another actually living in this country. On the other hand, Romanian-Germans experienced fewer difficulties integrating than German emigrants from Poland or the former Soviet Union, because they were taken in by relatives. That is why Romanian-Germans live mostly in the South and Southwest of the Federal Republic and to some extent have stayed together. All in all, though, the Romanian-Germans have integrated best of all the emigrant groups. You can see this, too, in the fact that Romanian-Germans are the only minority to have produced noteworthy writers in German contemporary literature – Oskar Pastior, Herta Müller or Werner Söllner. This was above all because of cultural developments in Romania. On the basis of this, too, something resembling a hierarchy of '*Aussiedler*' has now developed in which the Romanian-Germans see themselves as the most German of all the '*Aussiedler*'.

Q: Do the Romanian-Germans in the Federal Republic have a group identity?

A: They do, though not as Romanian-Germans but as Banat Swabians or as Transylvanian Saxons who have the longest history of all German minorities and were also partly recognised as a separate nation. The way these two groups saw themselves was also strongly tied to their dialect. Thus, in terms of their regional identity, they are no different from other sections of the German population. The problem is, however, that in the 'truncated' Germany of today (it lost one-third of its territory after 1945), there is no longer any awareness of the fact that there are also Germans outside Germany. Before 1945, people were conscious of the fact that there were Silesians, East Prussians etc. The thing that disturbs members of these minorities today and also causes them grief is the fact that in Germany, they are not recognised as Germans. This mainly has something to do with the lack of understanding of history in the Federal Republic.

Q: How far have you changed as a writer since you have been living in the Federal Republic?

A: It is of course for one thing also a difference of age. Like many other authors, I began writing lyric poetry in my youth. That also partly has something to do with the fact that, in a dictatorship, lyric poetry gets past the censor more easily. One has a public that is used to reading between the lines, and there is this complicity between author and reader which can be best conveyed via lyric poetry. I write more novels today and this has mostly to do with the fact I am older and living and writing in completely different conditions, not like in a dictatorship where the writer has no power, but great political and less literary significance. I don't see myself as an exile-writer either: I have always written in German and always dealt with contemporary themes which of course have also always been linked to the past in a certain way.

Q: You have a preference for the literary anecdote.

A: I have always been interested in the short and shortest forms of prose-writing. They go back to Hebel in the nineteenth century and find their counterpart in this century in Robert Walser and Franz Kafka where the anecdote develops in the direction of the parable. I find the 'Kalendergeschichte'[3] interesting too, likewise developed by Hebel, but then used above all by Brecht. In-between forms which I am also interested in are, for instance, grotesque tales. Unfortunately, all these forms are relatively little in evidence in contemporary German literature as they do not fit in with the law of the book trade which wants, above all, novels.

Notes

1. Interview conducted on 4 November 1997, transcribed by Stefan Wolff and translated by David Rock.
2. The original German ('und hat so einen ungebrochenen Erbauungssinn') is difficult to render here; 'Erbauungsbücher', for instance, are books which contribute to the moral improvement of the reader.
3. An edifying story or fable, published on a calendar. See Johann Peter Hebel's *Schatzkästelin des rheinischen Hausfreundes* (Rhenish Family-friend's Treasure-chest) (Karlsruhe, 1811) and Bertolt Brecht's *Kalendergeschichten* (Berlin, 1948).

Chapter 9

Millennium

Richard Wagner

And where do you come from, asked the young man suddenly. The question always does get to you. Although I expected it. Although I am prepared for it. Live with it. I have been living with this question for a decade. I have lived with it since leaving Romania.

We had been talking about football. But as expected, the conversation quickly went flat. The young man had soon noticed that I have no idea about football. That I was not on that wavelength. Football is not something you can simply talk about, just like that. Football is something you have to know all the ins and outs of.

You don't come from the former GDR, he said.

No, I said.

The young man nodded to himself and signalled to Manda, the barmaid. Same again. She nodded. Manda was smart. We all liked her. We? The men who sat in the Millennium Bar at midnight and competed for her attention.

You can sit here, sit here comfortably at the bar, ever intent on not losing your balance, not tipping off the stool. When speaking of the turn of the millennium, you have to appear to be sober, have a sobering effect. Just like a Roman M.

The bar is a good place for passing time. For passing the end of these times. You can talk about the fears that drive you from place to place and which preoccupy us all, incidentally, and already the century is creeping towards its close. Nothing is the way it once was any more. What can really be said about the nineties? Perhaps it is just the decade of things petering out. Simply there to make the numbers up. Two thousand is now everywhere. It all started quite some time ago. When somebody wanted to say something important, he started with: Two thousand.

We always did have a certain weakness for numbers. We, the Europeans. here at the bar. Nostradamus and so on. Always did make us predict everything. Tell fortunes. The entire history of European culture is just one fortune-telling after another. Told, warned. Forewarned. Cassi, I know, as someone once wrote. One of my fellow compatriots. In those days. A long time ago. With whole chunks of my life, a long time ago. Cassi, I know, he wrote. Whatever did become of him. I do not know, I cannot say. Cassi, like Cassandra of course.

If this compatriot of mine had lived in the GDR, he would certainly never have hit upon the abbreviation. Not with Cassandra. You see, they aren't amused by it. They aren't able take a joke. They always see something heading for them. Heading for them mercilessly. And this is beyond a joke. In view of the millennium, you've really got to go to Tibet.

Just around the corner, already a second esoteric book shop has opened. I have never been in. In either of them. When I walk past, though, over and over again I always catch a glimpse of a book-title. It is always something to do with numbers or meditation. Whenever I come to the Millennium Bar in the evening, my eye always falls on the shop windows as I go past. On these brightly lit shop windows. Numbers, meditation. Perhaps these are indeed the basic concepts of the decade. Numbers, and in between, meditation. What else is there to do? Politics you can forget. Women you can forget, too. After three glasses of wine, they start talking either about the absolute necessity of introducing an eco-tax or about Celine Dion.

What nationality are you then, asked my young interlocutor, now for the second time.

Oh, I see, I said. I come from the Banat.

Bannat, he said straight away. Bannat. He pronounces it with two Ns.

At first, I was still surprised that so many people in this city should have known the Banat. OK, they always pronounced it with two 'n's, Bannat, but they would say it without nodding their heads. Sometime later I discovered where the supposed knowledge came from. You see Bannat is the name of a well-known sports' shop in the city, a so-called globetrotter shop.

I looked at the young man.

I'm from the Banat, I said, but I have been living here for more than ten years.

When I came here, I said, people here were still talking about boycotting the national census.

What sort of national census, said the young man.

There, you see, I said, it was such a long time ago.

At the time, people were afraid of the see-through citizen,[1] I said.

The see-through what, he said.

Citizen, I said.

You're trying to take the piss, aren't you, he retorted. And already we were on familiar terms, using the 'du' form. In Germany, this often happens more quickly than you think.

At the time, people didn't want to be counted, I said, because they felt it was state-snooping.

Are you giving me history lessons, said the young man.

Go and ask your parents then, I said.

The young man cast a withering glance at me.

He had got drawn into something here alright. Well, I couldn't even tell one football club from another. I probably couldn't even name a single club. And even in other respects there were no mitigating circumstances as far as I was concerned. Not even a GDR past. Dynamo or whatever. All along the line I had to pass. Just to avoid any misunderstanding arising: I am not typical of my fellow-countrymen on this issue. I know innumerable people from the Banat who now, here, at the bar, could definitely have given the young man as good as they got on the football issue. What's more, I only have to think back to my early years in the Banat, the sixties, and how my fellow-countrymen there sat around on Sundays with their wine, mechanically reciting their way up and down the Bundesliga, with all the players' names and all the bullying done by the managers. As if their exit permits were dependent on their knowledge of the Bundesliga. Mechanically, they recited their way through the figures and forecasts for the games as if it actually involved their release from Romanian citizenship.

Romanian, asked my young friend who had once more signalled to the smart barmaid in unmistakable terms, did you say Romanian?

He looked at me with interest. But I looked at Manda's bottom.

We all know Manda, but we don't know anything about her. Word has it that Manda comes from Amanda, but she probably got the name as a baby in the eighties. I bet she's called Heike and only came across in the spring of eighty-nine with her parents. From Vogtland or somewhere. OK, you can't tell it from the way she speaks, but then that doesn't prove anything by a long chalk. And now, since the Wende, she's been living here in Schöneberg, on old West Berlin territory where we're all bustling about. Carefully, as if on some expensive plate. For West Berlin is endangered. To us, it seems as if it could break up at any moment. And then our home has gone for a burton.

The Ossis who got away right at the last minute, left with the very last train, they mostly come to a compromise with themselves. Go to West Berlin, to what once was, just about still counts as the West. Otherwise, well, it would be a going back. Voting with their feet and shortly afterwards in Köpenick again. How embarrassing. Got out too late to be able to be an old-owner. Heikeamandamanda knows where the borders are. She is pretty and smart, a woman with brains.

You did say Romania, my young neighbour whispered in my ear.

Yes, I said, the Banat is in Romania. Has been since 1918, I said. Before that, I said, but the young man interrupted me.

My name is Rüdiger, he said.

OK, Rüdiger, I said. It was time to use first names.

My name is Richard, I said, and thought to myself, I hope he doesn't ask me my surname.

Richard, he said, I have to tell you, I have been to Romania. It was a few years ago. I was in the Carpathians. At the time I had a girlfriend, he said. Her name was Heike. She came from there. From the Transylvanian Saxons. Are you one of them?

No, I said, I'm not one of them.

But you are also one of these Germans from Romania, one of these Romanian-Germans or German-Romanians or whatever you call it. Were you there for eight hundred years too?

I was speechless. Rüdiger's knowledge was considerable.

It was a really nice time we spent there, he said. Hay and meadows. Everything is still much more unspoilt, still not so dilapidated as it is here. And Heike's relatives, good people you know, some of them were super characters. Why is it that they are all coming here?

Do you know why, asked Rüdiger.

I said nothing. Was I supposed to give my lecture once again? I turned to that sight for sore eyes, Manda. Same again. But Rüdiger would not let it go.

So you don't know then either. No one knows, he said gloomily. Do they perhaps all want to come back to Germany because of the Millennium? Have they been waving their divining rods or something?

This subject, he said, was my only bone of contention with Heike. I said: Why do they all want to get away from here then. And she answered: What do you know about it anyway! Why do they want to get away and what do you know about it. This is how we split up. Because of this issue we split up. Can you understand that?

Yes, I said.

Rüdiger stared at me as if I was the hole in the ozone layer personified.

You understand that, he said slowly. Did I hear you correctly? You understand that.

Yes, I said.

Obvious, said Rüdiger, after all, you cleared off too. Yep, you are one of them. What's your Transylvania called again?

Banat, I said.

Oh yes, Bannat, he said. He pronounced it with two Ns. And why didn't you stay in your bloody Bannat? Where free-range hens and free-roaming cattle and sheep must still have been quite natural. OK, I don't know your Bannat, but I don't think I'm off course in assuming that, said Rüdiger. Why didn't you stay there?

Stop coming out with these xenophobic slogans, I said. I'm not going to go into it.

You must have been really driven into a corner then, said Rüdiger with a sly look. The fact that you now already feel like a foreigner. It's the first time I've heard that one of these Romanian-Germans feels like a foreigner. You're one hundred and fifty percent Germans aren't you? Not even the Waffen-SS were as German as you lot, were they? Ditch your excuses. Or else I'll get you to show me your German passport.

I shrugged my shoulders.

Well then, go on, out with it, said Rüdiger. I'll buy you one.

Do you know, he said, for two years I have been trying to understand why Heike left me. And I don't understand it. I don't understand anything at all. That's just what Heike always used to say. You don't understand anything at all, she used to say.

And now I go and meet you, he said, and think to myself, here's the man who can explain it to me. The man who can explain this Romanian-German woman to me. But you say nothing, he said reproachfully.

One can't explain everything, I said.

You're trying to talk your way out of it, said Rüdiger. We would have got on wonderfully well, Heike and I. If it hadn't have been for this Romanian-German thing, this Transylvania and this emigration and all that.

What's more, we could perhaps even have gone to Transylvania, said Rüdiger. I would have done that. For a few years, definitely. I liked it. But when I made the suggestion to her, something really snapped in her. You don't understand anything at all. You really don't understand anything, she said. And off she went.

Can you explain that to me, said Rüdiger.

No, I replied.

It was way past midnight. Slowly, the bar was getting empty. Manda had begun washing up and clearing away.

Rüdiger stood up, shaking his head, and marched off in the direction of the loo.

Will you drink a grappa with me, I said to Manda.

Notes

1. The German word 'gläsern' (literally 'glass') is here used figuratively to imply someone who has no secrets. Translation by David Rock.

Millennium

Und woher kommen Sie, fragte der junge Mann plötzlich. Die Frage trifft einen doch immer. Obwohl ich sie erwartet habe. Obwohl ich mit ihr rechne. Mit ihr lebe. Ich lebe nun schon seit einem Jahrzehnt mit dieser Frage. Seit meiner Ausreise lebe ich mit ihr.

Wir hatten über Fußball geredet. Aber die Luft war, wie zu erwarten, schnell raus. Der junge Mann hatte bald gemerkt, daß ich keine Ahnung von Fußball habe. Daß ich nicht dazu gehörte. Über Fußball kann man nicht einfach so reden. Über Fußball muß man Bescheid wissen.

Aus der ehemaligen DDR kommen sie nicht, sagte er.

Nein, sagte ich.

Der junge Mann nickte vor sich hin und gab Manda, der Barfrau, ein Zeichen. Noch mal das Gleiche. Sie nickte. Manda war fix. Wir mochten sie alle. Wir? Die Männer, die um Mitternacht in der Millenniums-Bar saßen und um ihre Aufmerksamkeit konkurrierten.

Man kann hier sitzen, bequem an der Theke sitzen, immer darauf bedacht, die Balance nicht zu verlieren, nicht vom Hocker zu kippen. Wenn man von der Jahrtausendwende spricht, muß man nüchtern wirken. Gerade, wie ein römisches M.

Die Bar ist ein guter Ort für den Zeitvertreib. Für den Endzeitvertreib. Du kannst von den Ängsten reden, die dich umtreiben und die uns im übrigen alle beschäftigen und schon schleicht das Jahrhundert auf sein Ende zu. Nichts ist mehr, wie es einmal war. Was läßt sich schon von den Neunzigern behaupten? Vielleicht ist es bloß ein Auslaufjahrzehnt. Nur da, damit die Zahl voll wird. Zweitausend steht jetzt überall. Das hat schon vor einer ganzen Weile begonnen. Wenn einer etwas Wichtiges sagen wollte, sagte er zuerst einmal: Zweitausend.

Wir hatten ja immer ein gewisses Faible für Zahlen. Wir, die Europäer, hier am Tresen. Nostradamus und so. Ließen uns doch immer alles voraussagen. Wahrsagen. Die ganze europäische Kulturgeschichte ist eine einzige Wahrsagerei. Gesagt, gewarnt. Vorgewarnt. Kassi, ich weiß, wie einer mal schrieb. Einer meiner Landsleute. Damals. Ist schon lange her. Mit ganzen Teilen meines Lebens ist es schon lange her. Kassi, ich weiß, schrieb er. Was bloß aus ihm geworden ist. weiß ich nicht, kann ich nicht sagen. Kassi, wie Kassandra natürlich.

Hätte dieser Landsmann von mir in der DDR gelebt, wäre er gewiß nie auf die Abkürzung gekommen. Mit Kassandra nicht. Da hörts nämlich bei denen auf. Da verstehen die keinen Spaß. Die sehen ja immer etwas auf sich zu kommen. Gnadenlos auf sich zukommen. Und da hört der Spaß auf. Angesichts des Jahrtausends mußt du schon nach Tibet gehen.

Gleich um die Ecke öffnete bereits die zweite Esoterik-Buchhandlung. Ich war nie drin. In beiden nicht. Im vorübergehen erhascht mein Blick aber immer mal wieder einen Buchtitel. Es ist jedes Mal etwas mit Zahlen oder Meditation. Immer wenn ich abends in die Millenniums-Bar komme, fällt mein Blick im Vorbeigehen auf die Schaufenster. Auf diese hell erleuchteten Schaufenster. Zahlen, Meditation. Vielleicht sind das ja die Grundbegriffe des Jahrzehnts. Zahlen, und dazwischen Meditation. Was soll man sonst machen. Die Politik kannst du vergessen. Die Frauen kannst du auch vergessen. Nach drei Glas Wein beginnen sie entweder von der absolut notwendigen Einführung einer Ökosteuer zu reden oder von Celine Dion.

Was für ein Landsmann sind Sie denn nun, fragte mein junger Gesprächspartner schon zum zweiten Mal.

Ach so, sagte ich. Ich stamme aus dem Banat.

Bannat, sagte er sofort. Bannat. Er spricht es mit zwei N aus.

Am Anfang wunderte ich mich noch, daß so viele Menschen in dieser Stadt das Banat kennen sollten. sie sprachen es zwar stets mit zwei N aus, Bannat also, aber sie sagten es mit kleinem Nicken. Irgendwann kam ich drauf, woher die vermeintliche Kenntnis kam. Bannat heißt nämlich ein stadtbekannter Sportladen, ein sogenannter Globetrotterladen.

Ich blickte den jungen Mann an.

Aus dem Banat bin ich, sagte ich, aber ich lebe schon seit mehr als zehn Jahren hier.

Als ich herkam, sagte ich, redete man hier noch vom Boykott der Volkszählung.

Was für eine Volkszählung, sagte der junge Mann.

Sehen Sie, sagte ich, schon so lange ist das her.

Man fürchtete damals den gläsernen Bürger, sagte ich.

Den gläsernen was, sagte er.

Bürger, sagte ich.

Du willst mich wohl verarschen, entgegnete er. Und schon waren wir beim Du. In Deutschland ist man oft schneller beim Du, als man denkt.

Damals wollten die Leute sich nicht zählen lassen, sagte ich, weil sie das als Staatsschnüffelei empfanden.

Gibst du mir Geschichtsunterricht, sagte der junge Mann.

Frag doch deine Eltern, sagte ich.

Der junge Mann warf mir einen vernichtenden Blick zu.

Da hatte er sich auf was eingelassen. Ich konnte ja nicht einmal die Fußballclubs auseinanderhalten. Wahrscheinlich konnte ich nicht einmal einen eigenen Club nennen. Und auch sonst hatte ich keine mildernden Umstände. Nicht einmal eine DDR-Vergangenheit. Dynamo oder wasweißich. Ich mußte auf ganzer Linie passen. Nur damit kein Mißverständnis aufkommt: Ich bin in dieser Frage nicht typisch für meine Landsleute. Ich kenne zahllose Menschen aus dem Banat, die jetzt, hier, an der Bar dem jungen Mann in der Fußballfrage durchaus Paroli hätten bieten können. Dazu muß ich mich bloß an meine frühen Jahre im Banat erinnern, an die Sechziger und wie meine Landsleute dort sonntags rumsaßen mit ihrem Wein und die Bundesliga runterbeteten, rauf und runter, mit allen Spielernamen und Trainerschikanen. Als hinge ihre Ausreisegenehmigung von der Kenntnis der Bundesliga ab. Sie beteten ihre Zahlen und Prognosen über die Spiele runter, als ginge es dabei um die Entlassung aus der rumänischen Staatsbürgerschaft.

Rumänisch, fragte mein junger Freund, der der fixen Barfrau wieder mal ein untrügliches Zeichen gegeben hatte, hast du rumänisch gesagt?

Er blickte mich interessiert an. Ich aber sah Manda auf den Hintern.

Wir kennen alle Manda, aber wir wissen nichts über sie. Manda soll von Amanda kommen, aber das hat sie sich wohl als Baby in den Achtzigern zugelegt. Sie heißt bestimmt Heike und ist noch Neunundachtzig im Frühjahr mit ihren Eltern rübergemacht. Aus dem Vogtland oder so. Hört man ihr zwar nicht an, aber das beweist ja noch lange nichts. Und jetzt, seit der Wende, lebt sie hier, in Schöneberg, auf dem alten Westberliner Territorium, auf dem wir uns alle tummeln. vorsichtig wie auf einem teuren Teller. Denn Westberlin ist gefährdet. Es ist uns, als könnte es jeden Augenblick auseinanderbrechen. Und dann ist unsere Heimat futsch.

Die Ossis, die noch in letzter Minute weg sind, mit dem letzten Zug abgefahren, die machen meistens einen Kompromiß mit sich. Gehen nach Westberlin, ins ehemalige, gilt grade noch als Westen. Sonst wäre es ja eine Rückkehr. Abstimmung mit den Füßen und kurz danach wieder in Köpenick. Wie peinlich. Zu spät weggemacht, um Alteigentümer sein zu können. Heikeamandamanda weiß, wo die Grenzen sind. Sie ist schön und fix, Frau mit Köpfchen.

Du hast Rumänien gesagt, flüsterte mein junger Nachbar mir ins Ohr.

Ja, sagte ich, das Banat liegt in Rumänien. Seit 1918, sagte ich. Davor, sagte ich, aber der junge Mann fiel mir ins Wort.

Ich heiße Rüdiger, sagte er.

Okay, Rüdiger, sagte ich. Es ist die Zeit gekommen, uns unsere Vornamen zu nennen.

Ich heiße Richard, sagte ich und dachte mir, hoffentlich fragt er mich nicht nach meinem Nachnamen.

Richard, sagte er, du mußt wissen, ich war mal in Rumänien. Das ist ein paar Jahre her. In den Karpaten. Ich hatte damals eine Freundin, sagte er. Heike hieß sie. Die stammte von da. Von den Siebenbürger Sachsen. Gehörst du zu denen?

Nein, sagte ich, zu denen gehöre ich nicht.

Aber du bist auch einer von diesen Deutschen aus Rumänien, von diesen Rumänisch-Deutschen oder Deutsch-Rumänen oder wie man das nennt. Warst du auch achthundert Jahre dort?

Ich war sprachlos. Rüdigers Kenntnisse waren beachtlich.

Es war eine schöne Zeit, die wir dort verbracht haben, sagte er. Heu und Wiesen. Es ist alles noch viel ursprünglicher, noch nicht so verkommen wie hier. Und die Verwandten von Heike, gute Leute sag ich dir, waren steile Typen darunter. Warum kommen die denn alle her?

Weißt du das, fragte Rüdiger.

Ich sagte nichts. Sollte ich jetzt wieder meinen Vortrag halten? Ich wandte mich der Augenweide Manda zu. Noch mal das Gleiche. Aber Rüdiger ließ nicht locker.

Du weißt es also auch nicht. Keiner weiß es, sagte er betrübt. Wollen die vielleicht wegen der Jahrtausendwende alle wieder nach Deutschland? Haben sie ihren Wünschelrutengang gemacht oder was?

Dieses Thema, sagte er, ist mein einziger Streit mit Heike gewesen. Ich sagte: Warum wollen die denn alle hier weg. Und sie antwortete: Was verstehst du schon davon! Warum wollen die weg und was verstehst du davon. So haben wir uns getrennt. Wegen dieser Sache haben wir uns getrennt. Verstehst du das?

Ja, sagte ich.

Rüdiger starrte mich an, als wäre ich das Ozonloch persönlich.

Du verstehst das, sagte er langsam. Habe ich richtig gehört? Du verstehst das.

Ja, sagte ich.

Klar, sagte Rüdiger, du bist ja auch abgehauen. Du gehörst ja dazu. Wie heißt dein Siebenbürgen noch mal?

Banat, sagte ich.

Achja, Bannat, sagte er. Mit zwei N sagte er es. Und warum bist du nicht in deinem verdammten Bannat geblieben? Wo die Bodenhaltung und das Neulandfleisch noch ganz selbstverständlich gewesen sein müssen. Ich kenne dein Bannat zwar nicht, aber ich glaube, ich liege nicht falsch, wenn ich das annehme, sagte Rüdiger. Warum bist du nicht dort geblieben?

Laß diese ausländerfeindlichen Parolen, sagte ich. Ich werde nicht darauf eingehen.

Du mußt ja ganz schön in die Enge getrieben sein, sagte Rüdiger mit schlauem Blick. Daß du dich jetzt schon als Ausländer fühlst. Das höre ich zum ersten Mal, daß so einer von diesen Rumänisch-Deutschen sich als Ausländer fühlt. Ihr seid doch Hundertfünfzigprozentige. So deutsch wie ihr war doch nicht einmal die Waffen-SS. Streich deine Ausreden. Oder ich laß mir deinen deutschen Paß zeigen.

Ich zuckte die Achseln.

Also, sags schon, sagte Rüdiger. Ich gebe einen aus. Weißt du, sagte er, ich versuche seit zwei Jahren zu verstehen, warum Heike mich verlassen hat. Und ich verstehe es nicht. Ich verstehe gar nichts. Das hat Heike nämlich immer gesagt. Du verstehst gar nichts, hat sie gesagt.

Und jetzt treff ich dich, sagte er und denke mir, hier ist der Mann, ders mir erklären kann. Der Mann, der mir diese rumänisch-deutsche Frau erklären kann. Du aber sagst nichts, sagte er vorwurfsvoll.

Man kann nicht alles erklären, sagte ich.

Du redest dich heraus, sagte Rüdiger. Wir hätten uns wunderbar verstanden, Heike und ich. Wäre nur dieses Rumänisch-Deutsche nicht gewesen, dieses Siebenbürgen und dieses Auswandern und all das.

Dabei hätten wir vielleicht sogar nach Siebenbürgen gehen können, sagte Rüdiger. Ich hätte das gemacht. Für ein paar Jahre bestimmt. Mir gefiels. Aber als ich ihr den Vorschlag machte, ist sie richtig ausgerastet. Du verstehst überhaupt nichts. Du verstehst wirklich nichts, hat sie gesagt. Und weg war sie.

Kannst du mir das erklären, sagte Rüdiger.

Nein, erwiderte ich.

Es war weit nach Mitternacht. Die Bar wurde langsam leer. Manda hatte mit dem Abwaschen und Abräumen begonnen.

Rüdiger stand kopfschüttelnd auf und marschierte Richtung Klo.

Trinkst du einen Grappa mit mir, sagte ich zu Manda.

Chapter 10

'Alone in a crowd': The Figure of the *'Aussiedler'* in the Work of Richard Wagner

Graham Jackman

Since his departure from Romania in 1987 with his then wife, Herta Müller, prose narrative has formed the larger part of Richard Wagner's literary output, and the experience of the *Aussiedler* one of its central concerns. I want here to look at three works from this point of view, *Ausreiseantrag* (Application to Leave) and *Begrüßungsgeld* (Welcome-Money), the two *Erzählungen* which he published in 1988, and the novel *In der Hand der Frauen* (In Women's Hands) of 1995, all of which have as their central figure a Romanian-German writer who leaves the Banat in southwest Romania for the Federal Republic and whose biographical details closely resemble those of Wagner himself.

As their titles indicate, *Ausreiseantrag* and *Begrüßungsgeld* (hereafter referred to as 'AB') portray respectively the events leading up to the submitting of an application by the writer Stirner and his wife Sabine for permission to leave Romania and their experiences following arrival in Germany, culminating in the obtaining of German citizenship. Together they provide a convincing and illuminating picture of the process of migration to Germany, above all in its psychological effects upon the *Aussiedler*.

In part the experience is pleasurable: in *Begrüßungsgeld* Wagner depicts Stirner's delight at specific phenomena of Western life, such as when he uses a left-luggage locker for the first time. However, he is also frequently disorientated and uncertain as to how to behave. Like anyone arriving in a new country, he and his wife discuss and criticise each other's behaviour: 'We've got to learn to cope, said Sabine. From all sides they heard the words "adapt yourselves", and they resisted. Every little thing made them nervous ... They recounted to each other their daily experiences, they compared notes. It was an adventure in which they were both the heroes and the spectators. They did their best to endure it' (AB, 156).[1]

Such, in themselves trivial, daily experiences form part of an overall sense of alienation probably common to all who exchange one country for another, for whatever reason. For an *Aussiedler* such as Stirner, however, more is at stake, his very identity. The structure of these two works – discontinuous sections from a few lines to several pages in length narrated through the optic of a single consciousness, the only substantial figure in the text – emphasises both the isolation of this figure and the fragmented, discontinuous nature of his experience of the world as he observes himself observing and comments on his behaviour, his 'performance' even, as he seeks to determine who or what he is in this Germany that he has hitherto known only at second hand.

Rosi Braidotti (1994: 21–5) has attempted to distinguish the mental attitudes of different categories of immigrant: the exile, the 'migrant' and the nomad, but none of these categories fits Stirner's case. The uniqueness of his position lies in his assumption that he is German: 'In Romania, he says, it was important to me to be regarded as a German. On official forms where it asked for your nationality I always wrote "German"' (AB, 205).[2] But in Germany, such claims, and the niceties of Braidotti's distinctions, are ignored: he is lumped in with the asylum-seekers and regarded simply as a 'foreigner'. When, despite the barriers between them, citizens from East and West Germany converse in a train, he is excluded: 'It was a conversation between natives. Stirner was a foreigner. Stirner did not exist' (AB, 263).[3] His paradoxical situation is brought out in another passage: 'But we are Germans. The Germans should go to Germany. Damned Germans, the Romanians said. At first he objected to being called an "emigrant". Emigration, how come?' (AB, 196).[4] But 'emigrant' is what he is:

> It was only when they left that it really became apparent how little he was at home in the German language. It offered him certainty only from a distance. He had clung to German while living as a foreigner in Romania. But now, in Germany? He was an emigrant after all. But one without a future. Emigrants hoped for things to improve in their own country, they hoped to return, some day. Stirner had no such hope (AB, 177–8).[5]

Even acceptance of the term 'emigration' is not the final step in this process of 'alienation': 'A year will pass and he will even accept the word "exile", it won't trouble him any more' (AB, 245).[6]

So, despite his abhorrence of the Ceauçescu regime and its security apparatus, whose impact on him as journalist and writer is a central theme of *Ausreiseantrag*, in Germany Stirner becomes more Romanian than ever before. Though he tries to distance himself from the typical behaviour of the exile, his desire to buy Romanian newspapers, his eavesdropping on conversations in Romanian and instinctive reactions such as when he sees a field of poppies and thinks 'Wie bei uns' (like at home) (AB, 239), are indicative of a sense of loss and displacement. Memories of his life in Romania and especially of his childhood become more insistent even as the process of adjustment to life in Germany takes place: 'He saw the city before him, and behind it another, his old city. The old city mustn't get too large, but it mustn't disappear either. Yes, it's a kind of grieving, he said to himself' (AB, 268).[7]

Paradoxically, it is language itself which Wagner depicts as being at the heart of the *Aussiedler*'s experience. In Romania the situation had been clear – to use Bakhtin's terminology, a struggle between a centralising 'monoglossia' (Romanian) and a centrifugal 'heteroglossia' represented by German and the other minority languages of the Banat, Serbian and Hungarian.[8] While Stirner was familiar with that situation, he had expected to feel linguistically at home in Germany. However, this assumption is challenged from the moment of arrival: 'Do you speak German, asked the official. Of course, said Stirner. Of course, he mumbled. Why of course. That was a long story' (AB, 141).[9]

Stirner's experiences in Germany reflect Bakhtin's insights in an unexpected and more disturbing way: German itself, on which Stirner has relied as the focus of his sense of self, which had defined him in Romania and which had made Germany the only possible destination for *Aussiedler* like himself, proves itself to be far from a unified language. Unlike the normal migrant or exile, he arrives in Germany as a native speaker of German, only to find that his Banat German accent makes him as much an outsider as he had been in Romania. His resultant insecurity affects not only his speech but through it his identity as German; Stirner finds that he uses different words and gets things wrong, and he has to make conscious efforts to learn the 'die Floskeln des Alltags' (the clichés of everyday speech). As a result, his German, which had been the source of his cultural and personal identity, begins to change: 'His German language was growing remote. He was moving towards a different German language' (AB, 195).[10]

As a writer too, he has lost his public, 'People that he could address, that his allusions and references were intended for, people of whom he knew that they understood what he meant.' But now that has gone: 'Now he was in no-man's-land. He spoke the same language as the people here, but he spoke it like one who comes from outside. He was now alone with his language' (AB, 159).[11]

Nor is it simply a question of varieties of German; it results from the wider, ideological dimension of the Bakhtinian model.[12] In Romania that model appeared to fit the case: Romanian represented not merely a language but an ideological discourse through which the state sought to impose its single version of reality. Wagner's depiction of Timisoara plastered with pictures of Ceauçescu, flags and slogans in preparation for the dictator's visit is a metaphor for a reality saturated with the signs of a discourse which seeks to preclude any alternative meanings: 'Whole facades were hidden beneath lettering. Hydraulic cranes lifted panels with slogans so high into the air that the view of the cathedral from the balcony was pretty well obscured' (AB, 17).[13]

Stirner's work as journalist and writer is in a double sense a challenge to this all-powerful discourse, both because of the German language and because of its dissident tendencies, feeble enough though these were, thanks to the operation of 'Selbstzensur' (self-censorship) (AB, 76). He had written *against* the power of the state: 'And there were enemies. It had been writing done under the shadow of state power' (AB, 159).[14] Sense and meaning were derived from this binary, oppositional structure. In the case of the official 'discourse', its meaning lay not in the words but in the assertion of power, in the denying of alternative meanings: 'The dictator's discourse is completely empty. It says nothing. The dictator's message is the dictator himself' (AB, 157).[15] Without the denied alternatives speaking becomes mere verbal activity, 'Wortlärm ... das Geräusch der Wörter' (verbal noise, the sound the words made) (AB, 43). Similarly, the alternative discourses, though numerous, all stand in a binary relationship to the dominant discourse: 'What one regarded as realistic oneself was labelled unrealistic, it was opposed to the state, anti-socialist. The words had two faces' (AB, 41).[16]

The prior assumption of such ideological dispute over meaning is that language was conceived as essentially meaningful, with clear monosemic significance – and in Romania, the regime's dominance means that for the most part its single meaning prevails: 'Under a regime that has occupied the language, one cannot express opinions. If one wanted to write realistically and said so, one immediately found oneself on the regime's terrain. For the regime too called for realistic writing. And the regime decided what was realistic' (AB, 41).[17] Stirner notes this later, in *Begrüßungsgeld*: 'He came from a country where everything still had its specific meaning. Torn trousers meant poor. Suit was Sunday, and women were for marrying' (AB, 249).[18]

In Berlin Stirner finds himself in a world whose linguistic contours are quite different, one to which Bakhtin's 'modernist' model no longer applies. Berlin too is saturated with language – but without the aspiration to monoglossia. 'There were too many words around him. Everywhere he was confronted with words' (AB, 212); 'The city was full of signs' (AB, 222).[19] Stirner has left the 'modernist' world of binary oppositions and has entered the 'postmodern' world of free-floating signifiers – the fleeting images and signs of advertising and the mass media – where there are no unitary, ideologically determined referential meanings. Words and ideas are no more than styles or designs for momentary effect and history only a wardrobe of them: 'We've just finished with the forties, soon we'll be taking the fifties down from the rail, and the sixties are rushing madly towards us' (AB, 222).[20]

It is this postmodern world which in large measure produces Stirner's sense of disorientation: 'He had to get used to the fact that everything was available, images, ideas. Everything was design, and design was transient, and transience was chic. So there was a sense of personal, arbitrary choice about everything. It was hard for Stirner to get used to it because until now he had lived among things that had only one meaning' (AB, 211).[21]

The world seems to Stirner to be like the peep-show which he frequents, where everything is ostensibly on offer but nothing is real: 'It was like being in a perpetual peep-show. You put a one-mark coin in and the curtain goes up. They show you what's on offer. They put on a show for you. The world takes the money out of your pocket. Then you're really living' (AB, 170).[22] Television reduces everything to 'a meaningless, unexciting continuum where everyone was putting on a show for everyone else, simply because there had to be something to watch' (AB, 188).[23]

Even politics is not exempt: not only are people unaware of the hardship and oppression in Romania, but there are no clear, principled positions. Left-leaning friends warn him of 'Beifall von der falschen Seite' (applause from the wrong side) (AB, 177), he is advised not to get involved in political activity and is described as 'an anti-Communist' (AB, 193). Symptomatic of the blurring of political lines is the use of hated Cyrillic characters as mere design: 'It was hard for him to get used to Russian letters on sweatshirts. CCCP as design. No, it could never be chic for him' (AB, 193).[24] Like everything else, politics is reduced to mere style, and all his understanding of the realities of Eastern Europe goes for nothing: 'I know something that I can find no use for, Stirner thought. And the reason why I can't find a use for it is that I cannot communicate it. Totalitarian thinking is only comprehensible for people who have lived in a totalitarian state' (AB, 259).[25]

So despite its 'postmodernity', its glittering surfaces and interreflecting signs and images, in this respect West Berlin suits Stirner; the clear polarities which existed there before 1989 through the existence of the Wall recreate for him the binary ordering of things with which he had always been familiar: 'In that respect Berlin corresponded to his way of thinking: the transit route, the border controls. That was something like the reality of travel as he had known it until now' (AB, 170).[26]

The final scene of *Begrüßungsgeld*, where Stirner and Sabine are formally recognised as German citizens, is shot through with irony: 'You have decided to become German', says the official, who asks them to help protect the delicate plant of democracy and 'not to give in to any totalitarian ideas.' 'You may perhaps have difficulty in getting used to things in Germany' (AB, 271),[27] he adds. But there is no such tidy ending to Stirner's crisis of identity, nor to the accompanying crisis in his writing, which stems from the cultural, rather than the purely linguistic disorientation which he experiences. There is at best a fragile *modus vivendi*. Some of his Romanian acquaintances have attempted to slough off their Romanian origins and create a new identity for themselves: 'they had spent years distancing themselves from themselves. They didn't want to be reminded of anything. They had painfully constructed a new identity for themselves, and they were afraid of losing this identity again' (AB, 213).[28] Others, by contrast, attempt to preserve their Romanian links: 'With his friends there was always the nostalgia. Yes, somehow they wanted to keep hold of their past, even if only through a few Romanian words' (AB, 225).[29] Stirner endeavours to avoid both extremes; he will neither cultivate nor suppress his Romanian origins but rather will endure the tensions that his dual identity engenders – such a duality is preferable to the dissolution which he begins to feel in West Berlin – even at the cost of the loneliness which ensues from belonging neither to the professional exiles nor to the entirely assimilated: 'It is simply my biography. I don't reject my biography' (AB, 226)[30] – and this enables him to write: 'I have memories of what I experience. I've had them for a little while now, he said, I can write again' (AB, 270).[31]

In der Hand der Frauen, which appeared in 1995 and is set in the Berlin of the 1990s, is not formally a sequel to *Begrüßungsgeld*: it has a first-person narrator who, despite a similar biography, is not identified with Stirner. For all that, the similarities are many; it is as if Wagner is providing an update on the process of integration – how is the Romanian writer and *Aussiedler* faring, seven or eight years later?

The narrowly linguistic concerns of *Begrüßungsgeld* have dropped away in *In der Hand der Frauen* (hereafter referred to as IHF). The narrator has no difficulties with German – on the contrary, he has a sharp ear for the latest big-city jargon and holds up its extravagancies and his own inventive formulations for the reader's amusement: 'I sit at the bar and look out. The ambience is dark-brown – it's the hazelnut, in techno-design. Rust-red. I hear a few snatches of conversation from brilliant-red mouths. Munch-red? Marxism meets bootlegging. I don't look at the woman behind the bar, she is probably an Interhotel blonde, softly obsequious' (IHF, 179–80).[32]

More even than in the earlier work, the focus of attention is the narrator's relationship to post-*Wende* Berlin. Though the book stands in some ways within the 'I am a camera' tradition of 'asphalt-literature' and of Berlin literature in particular, creating a sense of the city's panorama through reference to people and events currently in the news – mayor Diepgen, the bears in the zoo, the criminal Dagobert, division and reunification, the renovated houses in Prenzlauer Berg, the changing face of East Berlin – the city is seen mostly by night. We observe the narrator as he moves among its cafés, Kneipen (pubs) and cinemas and those who frequent them. Wagner again presents Western society, and more specifically Berlin, as a kaleidoscope of signifiers: advertising of various kinds, slogans and graffiti, the newspapers the narrator buys – a different one depending on which part of the city he is visiting – changing street and underground station names. Berlin is a 'postmodern' city, a Babel of interreflecting voices and jargons, styles and discourses, where truth and illusion are hard to distinguish from each other.

Richard Wagner has confirmed the influence of Walter Benjamin's portrait of nineteenth-century Paris in his *Passagen-Werk* (Paris Arcades project)[33] and his work on Baudelaire, and the narrator of *In der Hand der Frauen* shares Benjamin's 'Wollust im Benennen von Straßen' (pleasure in the naming of streets) (Benjamin 1982, 5: 644) as a way of creating local

colour, perpetuating the flatteringly romantic myth of Berlin which origi-
nated in the 1920s. But while the Marxist Benjamin emphasised *commercial*
names as the repository of the buried memories and dreams which lie
beneath the prosaic surface of the city,[34] in Wagner's Berlin these are
replaced by the names of cafés, Kneipen and cinemas – *Café Einstein,
Wiener Blut, Madonna, York, Rote Harfe, Milagio, Atlantik, Quasimodo,
Montevideo, Arsenal, Capri, Student von Prag, Brief an Felice, Estoril, Tati,
Pasternak, Romantic.* They constitute a repertoire of allusions and styles, to
be adopted and tossed aside in the effort to create a momentary personal
effect in the anonymity of the city.

Even more markedly than in *Begrüßungsgeld*, the permanent structures
of friend and foe which Stirner once knew are replaced by fleeting liaisons,
always threatened by the presence of alternative possibilities. On the third
page of the text this endless play of alternatives is illustrated: 'In the day-
time, preferably on Sundays, the animal protection people wait by their
stand at the entrance to the underground. They give out their leaflets
against animal-experiments and the Scientology people give out theirs:
The Path to Happiness. I have both leaflets at home. Against animal-experiments and for the path to happiness. I haven't read either of them' (IHF,
9).[35] The same instability penetrates personal relations too, as the opening
lines indicate: 'All relationships are three-way relationships, Ines says. But
there are only two people at every table' (IHF, 7).[36] Though people form
couples, the alternative third person is always implicitly present.

The narrator presents himself as being quite at ease within such a world,
an amused observer of Berlin life. He bears a decided resemblance to Benjamin's figure of the 'stroller' or *flâneur* (Benjamin 1982, 5: 524–69) and
cultivates, even in personal relations, the cool, ironic detachment which
Simmel, quoted by Benjamin, claims to be the effect of city life on the individual.[37] There is a fluidity and lack of fixity about the narrator, not only
in his movement through the city but also in his opinions, personal relationships and even his sense of identity, which might lead us to conclude
that he has overcome Stirner's sense of disorientation and has embraced
the 'postmodern condition', becoming what Braidotti calls a 'nomadic subject' who has 'relinquished all idea, desire or nostalgia for fixity' (Braidotti
1994: 22).

Several factors seem to suggest this. One is the abandonment of tradi-
tionally ordered narration. This episodic text as a whole has no direction
– its circularity is highlighted by the its final lines, which echo the opening.
The same absence of direction characterises the narrator's lifestyle. We first
meet him walking down the Kurfürstendamm 'as though I was going somewhere specific. But I'm not' (IHF, 7).[38] Later he asserts: 'It's as if I am letting myself drift. But I'm not drifting. I just like the feeling of drifting' (IHF,
105).[39] Yet this assertion stands at the end of a chapter, the action of which
is summed up as : 'I leave the house, it's midday, I usually go out at that

time under the pretext of going to have something to eat or wanting to buy a newspaper' (IHF, 93).[40]

Another marker is the tense structure which accordingly characterises the narrator's consciousness. The future tense of purpose and expectation is largely absent; the present tense predominates, marking the fleeting thoughts and moods of the narrator as he responds to his surroundings, yet without the consistency of true 'stream of consciousness'; it is, to use Braidotti's words 'an identity made of transitions, successive shifts and co-ordinated changes, without and against an essential unity' (Braidotti 1994: 22).

The most extreme indication of the narrator's unstable sense of identity is his reaction to television and film. These no longer have referential, informational value, as they did in Romania (AB, 106): in Berlin 'The cinema was no longer knowledge or experience. Before, it used to be a substitute for reality' (AB, 202).[41] Instead, he finds his behaviour and sense of self penetrated by the films he sees: 'I sit in the darkened cinema, and the story, the plot of the film, follows on my heels. I go out, unattached, into the dark, rainy city' (IHF, 15).[42] In Chapter 6, his confusion as to whether he has found his lost love Kathrin or whether Susanne is a different person is connected to a film: 'Alan Rudolph had told me. I had been to the cinema, to a film. I was in Alan Rudolph's film' (IHF, 121).[43] Not for nothing does the dustjacket bear the image of Rita Hayworth in *The Lady from Shanghai*.

Yet for all his air of ironic assurance, it gradually becomes apparent that the narrator is no more at ease amid the indeterminacy of the postmodern city than Stirner was. Braidotti's phrase 'nostalgia for fixity' aptly describes Wagner's narrator, for whom, and doubtless for many like him, emigration was a last resort rather than a deliberate strategy to develop a 'postmodern consciousness'. He remains an immigrant in Berlin, one who has carved out a niche for himself, who has become familiar with, and is a keen observer of, many of its facets but who still cannot take the city for granted. He comments ironically on his own relationship to the city: 'I travel across the town where I have been living for eight years. It's the city where I am at home, as I put it. Yes, I say that. I talk like one of those professional Berliners. Like those idiots who go around shouting: Berlin is the capital, Berlin is one of the world's great cities. As if they felt the need to persuade themselves that it really is' (IHF, 139).[44] Many of his own circle of friends, including most of the women, come from the East; as he remarks, 'in Berlin as a rule one meets only people who come from elsewhere' (IHF, 24).[45] His Berlin is essentially made up of such people: migrants, and 'foreigners', a floating population without long-term roots there.

For him and for them Berlin's cafés and *Kneipen* represent a surrogate home; they become the signposts within the labyrinth of the city by which the immigrant first charts his way, the havens from which he constructs a familiar world amid the initial strangeness of the metropolis.[46] The narrator appears to 'collect' cafés, taking possession of them rather as Walter Benjamin in his *Passagen-Werk* says of his 'Sammler' (collector) figure:[47] the collector detaches objects from their original function to embed them within a structure which he, the collector, has constructed. He assigns his meanings to these floating signifiers to construct an ordered cosmos of his own. In this, the *Aussiedler* may simply reflect in heightened form the experience of many in contemporary society. As Benjamin comments, 'To the flâneur – *even if he is born there*, (my italics – GMJ) like Baudelaire – his city is no longer his home. It represents rather a stage' (Benjamin 1982, 5: 437).[48]

In post-*Wende* Berlin there is no longer even the reassuring polarity of the East-West divide. When, in the final chapter, the narrator visits East Berlin, he finds that the old certainties no longer exist: 'Marxism meets bootlegging'. Postmodern flux has penetrated even East Berlin: in a café in the Oranienburger Straße he comments: 'Hier ist alles Kunst' (Everything is art here) (IHF, 185). Later he looks up and sees the television tower: 'I am in the street, and the television tower is everywhere. Centre. Centre centre centre' (IHF, 187).[49] The only centre to hold things together, it seems, is the symbol of the unreal and illusory.

Stable meanings and narratable events seem to be found only in the past, in the narrator's earlier life in Ceauçescu's Romania. These events are narrated in the past tense, indicating a caesura in the narrator's life and consciousness between the self now living, writing and thinking in Berlin and the life which he once lived in the Banat. Moreover, these past incidents are more sharply etched and, by contrast with the meaninglessness of the other incidents ('Everything is important and nothing means anything' – IHF, 130[50]), represent real events, marking changes and leaving permanent traces. The remarkably unironic passage in the final chapter about 'Täter' (perpetrators) and 'Handelnde' (those who perform the action) shows how deep those traces are, and so does the account, held back until Chapter 9, of the narrator's first marriage, his brush with the *Securitate* and his week in police custody, which led to the breach with his friend Bertram.

As against such harsh realities the narrator, like Stirner, is disconcerted to find that political life in the West has been reduced to the mere play of discourses. He recalls the two ex-GDR authors who '… spoke so sportingly about conditions in the only recently disappeared GDR that the listener might have thought that censorship was like the skilful presentation of a successful entertainment broadcast' (IHF, 102).[51] He himself speaks in an uncharacteristically uncompromising way, exempt from the general tone of irony or even cynicism, when he defends the West against presumably ex-GDR intellectuals (IHF, 166–7). When he withdraws a sexist remark made to Marie, he adds: 'I take everything back quite calmly, except the statements that I make about Communism' (IHF, 130).[52]

However, the most prominent symptom of, and metaphor for, the narrator's 'postmodern condition', and his unease with it, is his relationships with women. The Sabine figure from *Ausreiseantrag* and *Begrüßungsgeld* has disappeared, and the women who arrest or have arrested his attention are almost as numerous as the cafés. Some of these *affaires* and friendships are now over, such as those with Heike, Kathrin, Maja, Amalia, Gitta and Margrit. Corinna, Marion and Ursula call from time to time; there is Claudia in Amsterdam, Nina, once in Vienna, now in Strasbourg, to say nothing of the nameless ones: the girl on the plane, 'the girl from Wedding',[53] 'the eye-contact woman', two women in a bookshop, a journalist. At present there are, concurrently, Marie and Ines, who have at some time also been involved with the narrator's friend Hubert. The characteristic feature of all these relationships is their transience and instability – 'Der Reigen wird zur Hohen Schule' (the round-dance becomes an art-form) (Verdofsky 1995).

The narrator claims to cherish his freedom and to enjoy the single life: 'I can do what I want. I live alone. I like living alone' (IHF, 89).[54] However, the text tells a rather different tale. The title already suggests one who is in the power of women, who cannot live without them. His week in custody in Romania were 'the only days in my life without women. Without contact with women' (IHF, 158).[55] More importantly, in the round-dance of relationships, as in the endless play of signifiers, there is a hole at the centre. In a book where the narrator talks so freely and so unabashedly about his various female friends, one woman is excluded: his Romanian-German 'second wife, about whom I am saying nothing in this book' (IHF, 94),[56] as he repeatedly says. It reads like a joke with the reader – but hints here and there make clear that she has left him: 'my flat, in which hardly anything has changed since the departure of my second wife, about whom I will not say a word in this book' (IHF, 125).[57] He will not speak of her, yet does so by not doing so. By absence she is present, the void at the heart of the text, driving him perhaps, again and again, 'into women's hands' – and she is, of course, emblematic of his past life, in the 'homeland' which is left behind.

But though the male, 'logocentric' narrator is nostalgic for permanence – and by inference for stable binary, signifier–signified relationships for which male–female relationships may serve as a figure, it cannot be. After wandering rather forlornly through East Berlin in the final chapter the narrator decides, 'I'll go back to Schöneberg. I'll travel back. I'll go to my regular café again. Perhaps Marie will be there' (IHF, 187–8)[58] – and so she is. 'I enter the café and at once I am standing at the table where Marie and Tina are and I say hallo. May I join you, I say' (IHF, 190).[59] 'An allen Tischen sitzen zwei' (At every table there is a couple), the narrator concludes – but we suspect that the presence of a new woman, Tina, means that this too will soon be a 'three-way relationship'.

Beneath its flippant, amusing surface *In der Hand der Frauen* continues Wagner's exploration of what it is like to be from the East yet live in the West; to have adopted and to enjoy a mode of existence appropriate to one's circumstances yet to be keenly aware of what is lost in the process; to savour the delights of a city like Berlin and feel quite at home there, and yet remain 'allein unter vielen' (alone in a crowd)[60] a *flâneur*, strangely floating and susceptible to its deceptive surfaces; to be so profoundly marked by past experience, public and personal, that no present can be taken *quite* seriously afterwards.

For no matter how at home he may feel in Berlin, this narrator remains one identified by his Eastern origins. The sight of a man in a trenchcoat in the U-Bahn suddenly brings into his mind the word 'Securitate' (IHF, 144); before he drinks beer from a bottle he checks whether the bottle is still undamaged: 'It was a gesture from before, from the Banat' (IHF, 145).[61] A large proportion of his friends, male and female, turn out to have come from Romania or another East European country too. It is as if they seek each other out, as Gitta did the narrator, although long resident in Germany; they talk about 'coming from the East and remaining in the West. About the difference and the quarrels. About their difference from the aborigenes' (IHF, 170)[62] – an attempt to rediscover identity by re-mapping the world in terms of clear binary opposites. One is tempted to suggest that, just as his flirtations with the various women reflect the absence of 'my second wife', so too in a larger sense 'wir flirten mit dem Westen' (we are flirting with the West) (IHF, 57).

Notes

1. Wir müssen uns zurechtfinden, sagte Sabine. Sie hörten von allen Seiten das Wort 'Anpassen', und sie wehrten sich dagegen. Jede Kleinigkeit machte sie nervös ... Sie erzählten sich ihre täglichen Erlebnisse, sie verglichen. Es war ein Abenteuer, bei dem sie Haupthelden waren und zugleich Zuschauer. Sie suchten es auszuhalten.

2. In Rumänien, sagt er, war es mir wichtig gewesen, als Deutscher betrachtet zu werden. Ich schrieb in alle Behördenformulare, in die Rubrik Nationale Zugehörigkeit: Deutscher.

3. Es war ein Gespräch unter Inländern ... Stirner war Ausländer. Stirner war Luft.

4. Wir sind doch Deutsche. Die Deutschen sollen nach Deutschland gehn. Verdammte Deutsche, sagten die Rumänen ... Anfangs wehrte er sich gegen die Bezeichnung Emigrant. Emigration, wieso?

5. Erst durch den Weggang zeigte sich überdeutlich auch die Heimatlosigkeit im Deutschen. Das Deutsche war bloß aus der Entfernung eine Sicherheit gewesen. Sich am Deutschen festhaltend, lebte er in der rumänischen Fremde. Und jetzt, in Deutschland? Doch, er war ein Emigrant. Aber einer ohne Zukunft. Emigranten hoffen auf die Verbesserung der Zustände in ihrem Land, auf eine Rückkehr, irgendwann. Stirner hoffte nicht.

6. Es wird ein Jahr vergehn, und er wird auch das Wort Exil akzeptieren, es wird ihn nicht mehr beunruhigen.

7. Er sah die Stadt vor sich und hinter ihr eine ganz andere, die Stadt von früher. Die Stadt von früher, sie darf nicht zu groß werden, sie darf aber auch nicht verschwinden ... Ja, es ist Trauer, sagte er sich.

8. Bakhtin describes such a situation as 'The victory of one reigning language (dialect) over the others, the supplanting of languages, their enslavement, the process of illuminating them with the True Word, the incoporation of barbarians and lower social strata into a unitary language of culture and truth ... ' (Bakhtin 1981: 271).

9. Sprechen Sie deutsch, fragte der Beamte ... Ja natürlich, sagte Stirner. Natürlich, murmelte er. Wieso natürlich. Das war eine lange Geschichte.

10. Er entfernte sich von seiner deutschen Sprache, er näherte sich einer anderen deutschen Sprache.

11. Leute ... die er ansprechen konnte, an die Anspielungen, Andeutungen gerichtet waren, Leute, von denen er wußte, daß sie verstehen, was er meinte.. Jetzt war er im Niemandsland ... Er redete zwar die gleiche Sprache wie die Leute hier, aber er redete wie einer, der von außen kommt ... Er war jetzt mit seiner Sprache allein.

12. 'We are taking language not as a system of abstract grammatical categories, but rather language conceived as ideologically saturated, language as a world view, even as a concrete opinion, insuring a *maximum* of mutual understanding in all spheres of ideological life' (Bakhtin 1981: 271).

13. ... ganze Fensterfronten wurden von Buchstaben verdeckt ... Preßluftkräne [hievten] Losungswände so hoch in die Luft, daß der Blick vom Balkon auf die Kathedrale notdürftig verdeckt war.

14. Und es gab Feinde, es war ein Schreiben im Schatten der Macht gewesen.

15. Der Diskurs des Diktators ist völlig leer. Er sagt nichts. Die Botschaft des Diktators ist der Diktator selbst.

16. Was man selber als realistisch ansah, galt dann als unrealistisch, es war staatsfeindlich oder antisozialistisch. Die Wörter waren doppelgesichtig.

17. In einem Regime, das die Sprache okkupiert, kann man nicht Meinungen äußern. Wollte man eine realistische Literatur schreiben, und sagte man das, befand man sich bereits auf dem Terrain des Regimes. Denn auch das Regime forderte eine realistische Literatur. Und was realistisch war, bestimmte das Regime.

18. Er kam aus einem Land, wo alles noch (s)eine bestimmte Bedeutung hatte. Zerrissene Hose hieß arm. Anzug war Sonntag, und Frauen wurden geheiratet.

19. Es waren zu viele Wörter um ihn. Überall war er mit Wörtern konfrontiert. Die Stadt war voller Zeichen.

20. Die vierziger Jahre sind gerade vorbei, gleich nehmen wir die fünfziger von der Stange, die sechziger rasen mit einer irrsinnigen Geschwindigkeit auf uns zu.

21. Er mußte sich daran gewöhnen, daß alles zur Verfügung stand, Bilder, Ideen. Alles war Design, und Design war vergänglich, und Vergänglichkeit war chic. So hatten alle Auftritte eine Spur von Beliebigkeit ... Es fiel Stirner schwer, sich daran zu gewöhnen, da er bisher mit Eindeutigkeiten gelebt hatte.

22. Es war wie in einer immerwährenden Peepshow. Du wirfst die Mark ein, und der Vorhang geht auf. Man zeigt dir, was Sache ist. Man macht dir was vor. Die Welt zieht dir das Geld aus der Tasche. So hast du was vom Leben.

23. einem sinnlosen und lustlosen Kontinuum ... wo alle allen was vormachten, weil eben ein Programm abzulaufen hatte.

24. Es fiel ihm schwer, sich an die kyrillischen Buchstaben auf den Sweat-Shirts zu gewöhnen. CCCP, ein Design. Nein, für ihn wird das nie chic sein können.

25. Ich weiß etwas, dachte Stirner, mit dem ich nichts anfangen kann. Und ich kann damit nichts anfangen, weil ich es nicht weiter vermitteln kann ... Das totalitäre Denken ist nur für den faßbar, der in einem totalitären Staat gelebt hat.

26. Da kam Berlin seinen Vorstellungen entgegen: jedesmal die Transitstrecke, die Grenzkontrollen. Das hatte etwas von seiner bisherigen Reiserealität.

27. Sie haben sich entschieden, Deutsche zu werden; sich keinen totalitären Ideen hinzugeben. Vielleicht werden Sie Schwierigkeiten haben, sich in Deutschland zurechtzufinden.

28. sie hatten Jahre damit verbracht, sich von sich selber zu entfernen ... Sie wollten an nichts erinnert werden. Sie hatten sich mühevoll eine neue Identität gebastelt, und sie fürchteten, diese Identität wieder zu verlieren.

29. Bei seinen Bekannten war es das Immernoch, die Nostalgie. Ja. Irgendwie wollten sie sich ihrer Vergangenheit versichern, und sei es nur durch ein paar rumänische Wörter.

30. Es ist bloß meine Biographie. Ich stehe zu meiner Biographie.

31. Ich habe Erinnerungen an das, was ich erlebe. Seit kurzer Zeit habe ich sie, sagte er, ich kann wieder schreiben.

32. Ich sitze an der Bar und blicke hinaus. Ambiente, schwarzbraun, ist die Haselnuß, im Technozid-Design. Rostrot. Ich höre ein paar Gesprächsfetzen aus knallroten Mündern. Munchrot? Marxismus trifft auf Bootlegging. Ich blicke nicht auf die Barfrau, sie ist wahrscheinlich interhotelblond, softdevot.

33. The *Passagen-Werk* forms volume 5 of Benjamin's *Gesammelte Schriften* (Collected Writings).

34. 'Today the fantasies which one once imagined to be stored in the vocabulary of "poetic" diction are lodged within the names of businesses' (Heute nisten in den Firmennamen die Phantasien, welche man ehemals im Sprachschatz der 'poetischen' Vokabeln sich thesauriert dachte) (Benjamin 1982, 5: 235).

35. Tagsüber, mit Vorliebe sonntags, stehen die Tierschützer am U-Bahn-Eingang, an ihrem Stand. ... Die Tierschützer verteilen ihre Broschüre gegen Tierversuche, und die Scientology-Leute ihre Broschüre: Der Weg zum Glücklichsein. Ich habe beide Broschüren zu Hause. Gegen Tierversuche und für den Weg zum Glücklichsein. Ich habe sie beide nicht gelesen.

36. Alle Beziehungen sind Dreierbeziehungen, sagt Ines. Aber an allen Tischen sitzen nur zwei.

37. Das Aneinander-Gedrängtsein und das bunte Durcheinander des großstädtischen Verkehrs wären ohne ... psychologische Distanzierung ... unerträglich ... eine ... funktionelle Distanz zwischen [den] Menschen, die ein innerer Schutz ... gegen die allzugedrängte Nähe ... ist (The jostling crowds and the motley confusion of big-city streets would be unbearable without a psychological distancing, a functional distance between people which is an inner protection against the oppressive proximity) (Georg Simmel, *Philosophie des Geldes*, quoted in Benjamin 1982, 5: 561).

38. als hätte ich ein Ziel. Aber ich habe keines.

39. Es ist, als lasse ich mich treiben. Aber ich lasse mich nicht treiben. Ich liebe nur das Gefühl, sich treiben zu lassen.

40. Ich verlasse das Haus, es ist Mittag, da verlasse ich meist das Haus, unter dem Vorwand, etwas essen zu gehen oder eine Zeitung kaufen zu wollen.

41. Kino war nicht mehr Erkenntnis, Erfahrung. Früher hatte es Wirklichkeit ersetzt.

42. Ich sitze im dunklen Kinoraum, und die Geschichte, die Story des Films, folgt mir auf den Fersen. Ich gehe, ganz Single, aus dem Kino hinaus und in die nächtliche, nasse Stadt.

43. Alan Rudolph hatte es mir gesagt. Ich war im Saal gewesen und im Film. Ich war in Alan Rudolphs Film.

44. Ich fahre durch die Stadt, in der ich seit acht Jahren lebe. Es ist die Stadt, in der in zu Hause bin, wie ich sage. Ja, ich sage das. Ich rede wie ein Heimatist ... Wie diese Schwachköpfe, die herumlaufen und rufen: Berlin ist Hauptstadt, Berlin ist Weltstadt. Als müßten sie es sich einreden.

45. In der Regel begegnet man in Berlin ja nur Zugereisten.

46. Braidotti refers to the nomad or polyglot's 'need to take your bearings ... to draw maps' (Braidotti 1994: 16).

47. Benjamin describes the collector's activities as 'ein großartiger Versuch, das völlig Irrationale seines bloßen Vorhandenseins durch Einordnung in ein neues eigens geschaffenes ... System, die Sammlung, zu überwinden ... Er verliert sich, gewiß. Aber er hat die Kraft, an einem Strohhalm sich von neuem aufzurichten und aus dem Nebelmeer, das seinen Sinn umfängt, hebt sich das eben erworbene Stück wie eine Insel' (a great attempt to overcome the irrationality of his mere existence by incorporating it into a new, specially created system, the collection. He loses himself, certainly. But

he has the strength to pull himself up by a straw, and out of the sea of mists which envelops his sense the newly acquired piece rises like an island) (Benjamin 1982, 5: 271).

48. Dem Flaneur ist seine Stadt – und sei er in ihr geboren, wie Baudelaire – nicht mehr Heimat. Sie stellt für ihn einen Schauplatz dar.

49. Ich bin auf der Straße, und der Fernsehturm ist überall. Mitte. Mitte Mitte Mitte.

50. Alles ist wichtig und nichts von Bedeutung.

51. so sportiv über die Verhältnisse in der gerade erst untergegangenen DDR sprachen, daß man beim Zuhören die Zensur für die gekonnte Moderation einer erfolgreichen Unterhaltungssendung halten mußte.

52. Ich nehme alles leidenschaftslos zurück außer den Behauptungen, die ich über den Kommunismus mache.

53. Wedding is a mainly working-class district in the old West Berlin.

54. Ich kann tun und lassen, was ich will. Ich lebe allein ... Ich liebe es, allein zu leben.

55. die einzigen Tage in meinem Leben ohne Frauen. Ohne einen Bezug zu Frauen.

56. zweite Frau, über die ich in diesem Buch kein Wort sage.

57. [meine] Wohnung, in der sich kaum etwas verändert hat seit dem Auszug meiner zweiten Frau, über die ich in diesem Buch kein Wort sagen werde.

58. Ich will wieder nach Schöneberg ... Ich fahre zurück. Ich will noch ins Stammcafé. Vielleicht is Marie dort.

59. Ich betrete das Café und stehe schon am Tisch von Marie und Tina und ich sage hallo. Darf ich mich dazusetzen, sage ich.

60. The German phrase is the title of a review of *In der Hand der Frauen* by Jürgen Verdofsky in the *Frankfurter Rundschau*.

61. Es war eine Geste von früher, aus dem Banat.

62. das Herkommen aus dem Osten und das Bleiben im Westen. Über die Differenz und die Differenzen. Über den Unterschied zu den Aborigenes ...

References

Primary Sources

Wagner, Richard, Ausreiseantrag. *Begrüßungsgeld. Zwei Erzählungen*. Frankfurt am Main, Luchterhand Literaturverlag, 1988.
—— *In der Hand der Frauen*. Stuttgart, Deutsche Verlags-Anstalt, 1995.

Secondary Sources

Bakhtin, Mihail, 'Discourse in the Novel'. *The Dialogical Imagination*. trans. Caryl Emerson and Michael Holquist, ed. Michael Holquist. Austin, TX, University of Texas Press, 1981.
Benjamin, Walter, *Gesammelte Schriften*. 8 vols. Frankfurt am Main, Suhrkamp, 1982.
Braidotti, Rosi. *Nomadic Subjects. Embodiment and Sexual Difference in Contemporary Feminist Theory*. New York, Columbia University Press, 1994.
Verdofsky, Jürgen, 'Allein unter vielen', *Frankfurter Rundschau*, 15 September 1995.

Chapter 11

A Romanian German in Germany: The Challenge of Ethnic and Ideological Identity in Herta Müller's Literary Work

John J. White

Herta Müller, arguably the most important Romanian German writer since Paul Celan, succeeded in emigrating to the West in 1987 and has since then lived in the Federal Republic of Germany where she has continued to publish prolifically in her native language. Although her first four works of fiction, together with a substantial body of essays and poetry, had appeared in German before the watershed year of 1987, either in small Bucharest foreign-language publishing houses or as licensed editions in the West, it was with her 1989 novel *Reisende auf einem Bein* (Travellers on one Leg), focusing in some considerable depth on the ambivalent experience of coming to Germany, that Müller made her decisive breakthrough. This work, pre-published in serialised form in the West German *Frankfurter Allgemeine Zeitung*, was the first of many of Herta Müller's novels which were to be received extremely positively in the West. From this point onwards, her literary output has divided fairly evenly between vivid evocations of life in Romania under Ceauçescu and fictional accounts of the intolerable *Aussiedler* predicament in West Germany (invariably showing that there can be no absolute Year Zero, even for those who have left such a totalitarian regime long ago).

In addition to her many fictional attacks on West Germany's commercialism and her criticisms of the largely hostile treatment meted out to foreigners there, Müller has written two particularly disturbing accounts of the inexcusably unfeeling reception of Romanian Germans at the hands of the West German immigration authorities specifically responsible for processing ethnic German migrants from Eastern Europe. The more detailed, and by far the most ideologically revealing, is to be found in 'Und noch erschrickt unser Herz' (And still our hearts are startled), a paper, to some considerable extent based on first-hand experience, delivered at the 1993 symposium 'Berlin – tolerant und weltoffen' (Berlin – tolerant and open-minded), doubtlessly organised and provocatively so titled as a counter-measure to racist incidents in Germany at that time.[1] Herta Müller's second account comes in her 1989 novel *Reisende auf einem Bein.*

According to figures given in the official German government statistics on the subject (Info-Dienst Deutsche *Aussiedler,* No. 91, 1997), just under 14,000 *Aussiedler* came from Romania to settle in the Federal Republic of Germany during the year of Müller's arrival, a figure more or less consistent with those recorded for the preceding half dozen years[2] and one which would only be dramatically exceeded at the point where the collapse of the Ceauçescu regime cleared the way for a sudden influx of over 111,000 ethnic Germans. This tally was never to be matched again, primarily because by then the majority of ethnic Germans in Romania wishing to avail themselves of West Germany's immigration policy had by and large taken advantage of the opportunity to settle in the Federal Republic. By the mid-1990s the dramatic mass exodus of ethnic German Romanians was virtually over and numbers of *Aussiedler* were rapidly dwindling to the level they had maintained in the 1970s. What such an act of voting with their feet on the part of the ethnic German minority in Romania meant in practical terms can be easily gauged in the case of Herta Müller's home village of Nitzkydorf in the German-Swabian Banat region of Southwestern Romania. According to Glajar (1997: 539), at the time of Müller's departure,

> the local police officer had been the only ethnic Romanian. But prior to 1989 ethnic Germans had to sell their houses to the state if they wished to emigrate, and Romanians were encouraged to buy the houses of those who had left. In the summer of 1996, only 23 ethnic Germans were still living in Nitzkydorf. These ... all over 65 ... believed that a new beginning in the Federal Republic of Germany would be too difficult for them. Their children, however, all emigrated to Germany. Ethnic Ukrainians from Moldavia moved into the German houses of Nitzkydorf, and now they constitute the majority of the village population.

We never hear what eventually happened to Nitzkydorf's poor solitary ethnic Romanian policeman, but it is clear that the large Swabian German community of the Banat which Herta Müller wished to leave behind her in 1987 was soon no longer to exist in the form with which she was unhappily familiar. ('Unhappily' because for Müller such reactionary communities were as totalitarian in spirit as the socialist regime which was also doing its best to make it impossible for her to continue living in Romania.)

Around this time, a massive, pre-1989 emigration/immigration process (i.e. one preceding the collapse of the Berlin Wall) was already underway all across Europe, a phenomenon which Müller and her fellow German-Romanian dissident writers did much to document,[3] in her case both in respect of the leaving process (in *Der Mensch ist ein großer Fasan auf der*

Welt, published in English as *The Passport*) and – with the majority of her subsequent fiction and essays – with an eye to the specific difficulties encountered on arrival in the West and the problem of cultural integration faced by those still suffering under such a burden of traumatic experiences. Although now safely arrived in West Berlin, Irene, the protagonist of *Reisende auf einem Bein*, is haunted by the 'face of the dictator who had driven her out of the other country' (Müller 1989: 25)[4] and by other painful recollections of a past that would not allow itself to be laid to rest. When a German official declares 'One might get the idea that it is our country's job to make up for all the criminal mistakes your country committed' (Müller 1989: 51),[5] she dismisses the possibility that she might be able to turn over a new leaf. As virtually all of Müller's post-1987 fiction makes clear, the wounds of the past are not going to be quickly healed by any change of conditions in the present. 'Irene attributed the blame for all this to the other country' (Müller 1989: 142).[6]

'Und noch erschrickt unser Herz' is valuable, not just because of the information it supplies concerning the vagaries of the German *Aussiedler* reception process, but also for what it tells us about what it feels like to be on the receiving end of such hamfistedly unsympathetic treatment. It also has important implications for any consideration of Müller's own complex self-image as an ex-Romanian, ethnic German, literary dissident, would-be West German and hence someone necessarily having to remain enmeshed in a demeaning *Aussiedlungsverfahren* (immigration control procedure). Müller presents her initial brush with the German authorities as for the most part typical, although she invariably prefers the more neutral term 'Ausländer' (foreigner) to such official German categories as *Aussiedler* or *Übersiedler* (ethnic German immigrants):

> The first thing that a foreigner has to do, as far as the authorities are concerned, is to submit the relevant biographical details for scrutiny. Instead of letting the facts speak for themselves and narrating his CV, he has to submit the facts for scrutiny. This is the very opposite of telling. And in the light of the opportunity that is thus either granted or withheld from the foreign applicant, submitting for scrutiny is already putting into question (Müller 1995: 23).

However, matters were at the time also not helped by the indignity of being repeatedly shunted to and fro, while her own particularly recalcitrant status was being side-stepped by various bureaucrats responsible for her 'case' (*Sachbearbeiter*, as the German euphemism has it), and having to go back and forth between various inspection units ('Prüfstelle A and Prüfstelle B') equipped with a circulation permit (*Laufzettel*) and encounter *en route* such mocking notices as 'Ich nix verstehen deutsch' (Me no speak German) on interview-room doors. For anyone arriving at a reception centre already smarting from the specifically Romanian combination of bureaucratic chicanery and chauvinist contempt, such signals were anything but welcoming. However, Müller's presentation of her personal experiences has more fundamental implications than this. Rather than simply complaining about German xenophobia and officialdom's knack for administrative callousness, she brings out what she sees as the underlying significance of her initial treatment at the reception centre. At issue at the time, of course, was above all the question of whether she was applying for admission to the Federal Republic on the grounds of some claimed ethnic German status (i.e. as an *Aussiedler*) or whether she was really a political asylum seeker – in which case, the fact of her Germanness would have been virtually irrelevant:

> The fact that I in 1987, while laying my biographical details open for scrutiny, talked of the Romanian dictatorship was something that made the officials anxious. I left a dictatorship for political reasons, whereas the German officials wanted to hear about my German citizenship. When I answered the question whether I would have been persecuted for my views even if I had been a Romanian in the affirmative, the official in charge sent me to the police responsible for international affairs. He affirmed: either I was an ethnic German or a political refugee. There was no official form designed to take account of both statuses at the same time. The story I had to tell wreaked havoc in his filing-system. (Müller 1995: 25)[8]

Which is clearly not something to make a German immigration official disposed to be helpful beyond the call of duty.

So far, what we have been looking at is little more than a familiar snapshot of institutionalised xenophobia in action (contemporary German *Ausländerfeindlichkeit* with which the world has become all too familiar) coupled with Prussian bureaucracy, in a vivid account by someone who, in her speech upon being awarded the 1994 Kleist-Prize (Müller 1995: 7–15), was soon to betray a marked identification with the experiences of Kleist's horse-trader Michael Kohlhaas at the hands of the Electors of Brandenburg and Saxony.[9] Yet Müller detects more in these early experiences than the mere bureaucratic aspect of what Kleist called 'die gebrechliche Einrichtung der Welt' (the world's fragile constitution): in her eyes, such compartmentalised reactions possess an essentially moral dimension, and a by no means encouraging one at that. For Müller in fact, the ultimate question was not the bureaucratic issue of her legal status on entering Germany, but her consistently ethical stance, above all during her adult life in Nicolae Ceauçescu's Romania. That there might be a link between the two is not something with which the machinery of West Germany's *Aussiedlung* bureaucracy could be expected to cope. But Müller is not simply content to register the inadequacy of bureaucracy's taxonomic procedures: she homes in on the questionable position of the representative bureaucrat:

> Perhaps people in Germany never acquired the habit of asking about the personal moral dimension because it also intrudes into the life of the person asking the question. And because even here, in the freer country – where no-one's life is threatened – morality is often not compatible with one's own safety. While the officials who had been jolted out of their routine approach shunted my papers hither and thither, I felt obliged in my own mind to ask myself the question: how would they have reacted in my situation? (Müller 1995: 25)[10]

Tellingly, her paper then turns to the subject of the renascence of elements of fascist aggression in contemporary Germany. This is a significant step, for Müller's sceptical attitude towards both present-day Germany and contemporary Germans is more bound up with the past history of Germany, and the actions of former Nazi ethnic Germans in Romania, than any superficial lamentation at the resurgence of neo-nazism and bureaucracy without a human face might suggest.

Before pursuing the ideas in 'Und noch erschrickt unser Herz' further, I should like to juxtapose the material we have just been considering with the way in which a comparable encounter is handled in Müller's novel *Reisende auf einem Bein* (hereafter referred to as 'R'). Since this work had been published in 1989, that is to say four years before 'Und noch erschrickt unser Herz', one might be forgiven for assuming that Müller's Berlin paper was in part a gloss on the novel's rather laconic version of Irene's interview at the so-called *Übergangsheim* (transit hostel). Müller has often drawn attention to the elliptical nature of her literary works:[11] 'What keeps coming back and occupying my thoughts is what falls between the sentences ... . It is what is left out' (Müller 1991: 19) While ostensibly here talking of the sort of works she preferred to read, she was also indirectly making an admission about her own palimpsestic mode of writing. However, such a strategy was not without its problematic side when she was addressing a largely Western European readership: 'one needs to have had many experiences – daily experiences – to know what is being referred to ... . The trouble is that the reader here [in the West] lacks the necessary background to know what is meant.' (Vogl 1989: 7)[12] In fact, what remains to some considerable extent between the lines in *Reisende auf einem Bein* will become comparatively explicit in 'Und noch erschrickt das Herz'. As the reader soon comes to appreciate, the relationship between fiction and factual essays in Müller's *oeuvre* generally mirrors that between *Reisende auf einem Bein* and 'Und noch erschrickt das Herz'.

The first discordant mention of an interview with a West German official responsible for ethnic immigrant affairs (*Sachbearbeiter für Aussiedler*) comes in Chapter 4 of *Reisende auf einem Bein* (various further references to later 'difficult' encounters with the relevant authorities are scattered across the entire novel, as if to suggest that the initial *contretemps* was more typical than exceptional). Quite early after her arrival in the West, Irene, like Müller herself, is confronted with a question that has a direct bearing on her status in the eyes of the law: 'Did you, before coming to Germany, have any contact with the local secret police?' To which she responds unequivocally: 'I didn't with them, but they did with me. That is a different matter.' (R, 26)[13] Irene is understandably anxious to establish that she was a victim of the Romanian political system, not some *Securitate* informer, a point which does not go down well with her German interrogator: 'Please leave it to me to make distinctions of this kind for the time being. After all, that is what I get paid for' (R, 27).[14] Later, after various questions about acquaintances from her Romanian past, Irene is asked 'Wollten Sie die Regierung stürzen?' (Did you want to topple the regime? R, 28), a ludicrous suggestion to make to a single person (especially given what Manea [1992: 29f.] has so forcefully castigated as the relative paucity of organised resistance in his own country of Romania by comparison with Poland, Czechoslovakia and Hungary). This is clearly an inappropriate version of her dissident role *vis-à-vis* the Romanian regime, and Irene rejects it out of hand as a deliberate misrepresentation meant to trap her. 'None of his rubrics is able to account for me, Irene thought. This official is wandering lost across the fields. That was an idiom from the other country. It meant to insist on something without understanding it.' (R, 28)[15] It is not just that the assigned West German *Sachbearbeiter* lacks the requisite experience to comprehend Irene's circumstances; she for her part feels the need to resort to a phrase from the old country to sum up what is happening, as if she can only measure her German experiences with a Romanian yardstick. In fact, although this is presented in innocuous terms, her immigration interview inevitably conjures up painful memories of earlier *Securitate* interrogations: 'The official wore a dark suit, of the kind Irene knew from the other country.' (R, 26)[16] When she is eventually formally granted German citizenship, the immediate response of this particular 'Reisende auf einem Bein' (traveller on one leg) is far from ecstatic:

> On the letter-head: Bureau for Internal Affairs. Below: that she had been granted German citizenship. She was to report to Room 304 in a week's time to receive her state citizenship. Irene did not rejoice. She read on, as if this communication was not something that concerned her. Irene did not grasp the context in which the words 'Celebratory Meal' and 'Welcoming Address' occurred in the final paragraph. (R, 157)[17]

The whole atmosphere surrounding *Aussiedler* immigration to Germany is presented here as being unnecessarily inhospitable. According to Müller's novel, new arrivals are debriefed, i.e. interrogated by the 'Bundesnachrichtendienst'[18] about former contacts and activities (R, 26); they are on off-limits territory ('In front of the transit hostel there was a yellow sign with a picture of a camera crossed out in red' – R, 35);[19] a cold administrative order prevails ('in the waiting-room ... Irene received the queuing number 501 on a ticket, although no-one else was there, apart from her' – R, 95).[20] She is repeatedly belittled and patronised ('Down there, where you come from, was there an underground railway? No. Just as I thought, he said' – R, 35;[21] 'Just as I thought. You only speak German when you come to see me in my office' – R, 97).[22] It is thus hardly surprising that Irene's responses at times verge on the visceral. When an official proclaims the words 'Senat für Inneres' (Bureau for Internal Affairs), we are told: 'The way she pronounced the words "Internal Affairs" made them sound to Irene like stomach or intestines' – R, 122).[23] On receiving her 'Kleidergeld' (the money given to newly arrived immigrants as a one-off clothing allowance), Irene defensively engages in a grotesque fantasy: 'The official in charge of her case opened his mouth. He said nothing. His tongue stood in his mouth looking as if it hadn't any room. As if there was something else underneath his tongue. As if there was a finger under his tongue. A dry finger right in the middle of his mouth'. (R, 52)[24] There are many fingers, pointing fingers as well as accusing voices, in *Reisende auf einem Bein*.

Rejecting the suggestion that she might be suffering from any sense of homesickness ('Heimweh') for her native Romania (R, 51), Irene feels an 'Ausländerin im Ausland' (a foreigner in a foreign country – R, 61), as alienated from her new environment as previously from what she prefers to call 'das andere Land' (the other country). A discursive analysis of the reasons for such a sense of alienation is never given. Rather, the predicament is communicated impressionistically, at times even surreally, whereas in Müller's later autobiographical account a number of discrete plausible factors are identified giving a rational causality to the newcomer's sense of disenchantment. Thus, in *Reisende auf einem Bein* we are merely left with the impression that Irene is being grossly, perhaps wilfully, misunderstood by her interviewer and that she does not fit into his tidy set of 'Rubriken', whereas in 'Und noch erschrickt unser Herz' Müller makes it clear that, at the time, she had less rational reasons for her reluctance to be granted permission to stay in Germany on the grounds of being categorisable as an ethnic German *Aussiedler*, even though this was indubitably her right under German law (after all, her Swabian father had been an enthusiastic Nazi and had fought, like so many Romanian-Germans of conscriptable age, with the SS[25]).

One vital factor in this refusal to be both accomplice and victim of a bureaucratic fudge which would prefer to regard her dissidence in Romania as immaterial when compared with her ethnic German credentials (her 'Deutschtum'), is what might be thought of as an essentially ethical insistence on the truth. Indeed, one can appreciate her desire for absolute clarity: to accept automatic German citizenship as an *Aussiedler* would be tantamount to making things too easy for many of her ethnic German-Romanian compatriots who, as if in some grotesque latter-day re-enactment of the Nazi 'Heim ins Reich' programme,[26] were being offered German citizenship regardless of their political crimes and misdemeanours during Ceauçescu's dictatorship. Important though it clearly is, truth here is nonetheless less crucial as an ethical category *per se* than as an acknowledgement of the moral stance that Müller and some of her associates from the 'Aktionsgruppe Banat' (including Richard Wagner, Rolf Bossert and Roland Kirsch[27]) had taken. This was something that both her literary and essayistic writings would repeatedly put on record in the coming two decades. 'Deutschtum', in the uncritically patriotic sense in which it had been celebrated among the Romanian Germans of the Banat, Siebenbürgen (i.e., Transylvania) and the Bukovina, was hardly something Müller could associate herself with as a criterion of ethnic acceptability, without, that is, experiencing serious qualms. Rather than engaging in nostalgic, idealising evocations of her Banat home region, Müller concentrates – from *Niederungen* (Lower Reaches or Degradations)[28] and *Barfüßiger Februar* (Barefoot February) onwards – on the shameful past behaviour of her German compatriots in Marshall Ion Antonescu's wartime Romania and on what she held to be the continuing fascistoid and reactionary features of life in the ethnic German minority communities in Ceauçescu's time. To acknowledge one's 'Deutschtum' as a member of a Romanian ethnic minority entailed reminding oneself that of the c. 700,000 ethnic Germans living in the country in the early 1930s, more than 54,000 had served with the Waffen-SS, 15,000 in the *Wehrmacht* and the *Organisation Todt* and that the country had, like Hungary, been an ally of Nazi Germany. Her story 'Überall, wo man den Tod gesehen hat' (Everywhere where one saw Death, Müller 1987: 101–21) serves as a reminder that the numerous crimes perpetrated by Romanian-Germans during the Third Reich were by no means all carried out on Soviet territory and that a whole series of pogroms and mass executions had taken place in Romania itself. Even those who had not served with the forces of the Third Reich had on the whole, history records, been enthusiastic supporters of the Hitler regime.

To emigrate as an *Aussiedler* to a Germany which would itself always serve as a reminder of the role played by Germans in Romania's own dark twentieth-century history could well exacerbate Irene and Müller's pangs of historical conscience by forcing them to confront a whole series of painful reminders of Romania's own fascist dark past and its recent history of repression. There are in fact two junctures in *Reisende auf einem Bein* where Irene gives voice to such feelings of *déjà vu*. Walking along a Berlin street, she suddenly questions the façade that post-war West Germany reality presents her with: 'Irene was assailed by the feeling that everything in the town could suddenly become different. The old ladies with their white perms, polished walking sticks and healthy shoes could suddenly be young again and march off to join the Hitler Youth movement. Long, windowless vans would drive up to the shop doors. Men in uniforms would confiscate the goods from the shelves. And laws would be published in the newspapers as they were in the other country.' (R, 49)[29] As this shows: any resurgence of associations with the Nazi past automatically brings with it echoes of the Ceauçescu regime. But things can also be more irrational than this thinking-in-parallels suggests: when on a later occasion a West German child calls out 'Nutte' (tart) to Irene, her immediate reaction is to shout back 'Lieber eine Nutte als ein Faschist' (I'd rather be a tart than a fascist). But then, Irene 'took fright. The boy was at most five years old. He repeated the word: fascist'. (R, 153)[30] This is not the balanced critical response that we hear in the essays in *Hunger und Seide*, but the emotional hitting out of someone who remains deeply damaged by past experiences and for whom Nazi Germany (and even present-day Germany) and Ceauçescu's Romania have become impossible to keep separate. Clearly, there can be no Year Zero for an Irene or a Herta Müller coming to a new life in the West any more than there was for Germany in 1945. For a while Müller deceives herself: 'Since I had arrived in Germany, there was for me for the first time a sort of finality. It can't, I thought, just be the physical distance between the two countries.' (Müller 1995: 33)[31] But in due course she finds herself obliged to concede that no amount of geographical or temporal distance can make amends for the harm that her Romanian years have done to her: 'Driven into a corner by the *Securitate*, I finally myself sought the wide open spaces. Nothing was finished, only at an ending because it had been discontinued.' (Müller 1995: 34)[32]

This lack of any *tabula rasa* blessing to Müller's arrival in the West has had various repercussions in the intervening years. In her non-fictional work, she has consistently played the self-appointed role of expert on Romanian affairs, explainer of the Ceauçescu past and Eastern Europe-watcher for the media, above all for *Die Zeit*, the *Frankfurter Allgemeine Zeitung* and the *Hessischer Rundfunk* (see Eke 1997 on this). Her reactions to the civil war in the former Yugoslavia have inevitably been strongly influenced by her own ethnic minority background: 'For as long as they functioned', she once observed, 'the dictatorships [of Eastern Europe] were able to keep an effective stranglehold on the minority problems within the various states.' (Müller 1995: 160)[33] Müller has remained the committed chronicler of what has happened since: in Bosnia and Kosovo, in the former German Democratic Republic and, when it comes to the treatment of the Sinti, in her own post-1989 Romania and in Slovakia. Her campaign against all forms of totalitarianism has been very much predicated on her own minority background and her implacable refusal to submit to categorisation. Her own accounts of life in Romania under Ceauçescu may by and large do little more than reinforce the picture to be found in the writings of, say, Norman Manea and Katherine Verdery. But there is one notable exception: the disproportionate concern with the role of ethnic minorities in modern Romania, in particular the constant reminders of the activities of the ethnic German minorities during the wartime alliance between Antonescu's Romania and Hitler's Germany and the treatment of ethnic minorities in the Communist Romania of the 1970s and 1980s. The unfulfilled egalitarian promise of Romania's successful 1989 revolution and the manifestations of neo-Nazism and the persecution of foreigners, particularly in the reunified Germany, have inevitably attracted Müller's polemical attentions. When a gang of German skinheads apologised for 'mistakenly' beating up a German with the excuse 'Er sah aus wie ein Ausländer' (he looked like a foreigner), Müller sarcastically observed that, to avoid the recurrence of such a mistake, perhaps it would be best if in future foreigners were to identify themselves visually as such, preferably by wearing some sort of mark on their clothing: 'ein Zeichen an den Kleidern' (Müller, 1995: 45). Provocative remarks of this kind have helped make Herta Müller one of the gadflies on the surface of contemporary Germany. So have her complaints about the asymmetry of police response to left-wing and right-wing violence (Müller, 1995: 47), her analogies between 'die Täter und Schweiger Hitlers' – in other words, Hitler's willing executioners and those who keep silent about their crimes – and the accepted resurgence of 'Herrenmenschendenken' (the Master Race mind-set) in the Federal Republic (Müller, 1995: 42) and the way in which neo-Nazis have been tacitly permitted to assume the mantle of 'Vollstrecker einer öffentlichen Meinung' (i.e. those acting out the wishes of the public – Müller, 1995: 43), as well as her general tendency to equate all forms of utopianism, be they of the left or the right, with state repression and re-emerging totalitarianism.

The official *Sachbearbeiter*'s remark to Irene in *Reisende auf einem Bein* – to the effect that Germany would have to compensate immigrants for all the wrong done to them in their totalitarian homelands – was in Müller's own case soon to give way to another stock response from the host-community. Now that she was in the West, life in the new host-country was not simply expected to compensate her for the old one, she herself was expected to start showing signs of gratitude for this by writing positively about the new Germany. In fact, her usually polemical comments on German affairs were on the whole treated with a mixture of dismay and suspicion:

> people detected signs of inappropriate interference [in Germany's internal affairs]. ... I was directed back to my circumscribed realm: it was the place I came from that I had to write about. In my second, better homeland I had the right to gnaw at and swallow pieces of the German bread-crust. But with this once empty and now full mouth, a mouth which still remained alien, it was proper not to speak while eating. (Müller 1995: 30 f.)[34]

In what was virtually a mirror version of the Romanian regime's suspected covert policy whereby the early Müller was permitted to publish in the West, as long as her images of the Banat ethnic minority were negative enough for them to be advantageous to the state's process of minority persecution,[35] now in some quarters she was only going to find public acceptance if her picture of Germany was essentially an affirmative one. *Reisende auf einem Bein*, however, shows her taking a resolute stand against such knee-jerk expectations, albeit probably intuitively. 'In the other land, Irene said, I understood what it was that so completely destroyed people. The causes were there for all to see. It hurt me very much to see the reasons every day. ... And here, Irene said. I know there are reasons. But I can't see them. It hurts not to be able to see the reasons every day.' (R, 130)[36] At first, coming from an ostensibly socialist country, she is overwhelmed by the consumerist dimension of West German life. Chapter Ten's critical passages are predictable and not very profound as responses to newly experienced capitalism go, but no doubt at the time they represented a genuine reaction on the author's part.

> Irene wished she had many bodies in order to be able to wear all the clothes on display in the shop-windows. And enough money to be able to buy the clothes. ... But when Irene saw – on the same day in three different parts of the town – three different women with the same hair-clasp in the shape of an aeroplane, she was pleased that she had no money. And that her hair was too short for the clasps. And her head gradually grew heavy. And in the place between her nose and her lips her skin twitched like a huge insect. Then Irene knew: fashion shortens people's lives. (R, 75f.)[37]

When an advertisement for perfume appears in her letter-box some time later, such things now leave her unmoved. 'On the prospectus stood the words: the perfume that arouses feelings. Every drop a temptation.' (R, 77f.)[38] Such artificial promises are contrasted with the important letter from a friend still in Romania which Irene is about to open: 'The letter that arouses feelings, Irene thought. Every drop a seduction.' (R, 78)[39] By contrast to all the market hype, she recalls images of Germany's underclass hunting for shoe-bargains in the supermarket outdoor display-bins and remembers seeing poorly paid moonlighting workers (*Schwarzarbeiter*) decorating a flat. Pushing an empty trolley out of a supermarket, she congratulates herself on an admittedly small victory ('The person who buys nothing has stolen something, Irene thought, pleased, to herself' – R, 108).[40] But the novel's main concern is not so much what might be thought of as capitalism's soft targets as the general atmosphere of alienation and despair permeating the cold-hearted German society into which Irene is supposed to integrate. She recalls a notice she once stole from a Banat building-site with the warning 'Danger. Deep drop.' 'Even this sentence', we are now told, 'was something Irene had read in terms of her own life.' (R, 84)[41] Which is also true of graffiti she sees on the wall of a Marburg house: 'COLD LAND COLD HEARTS GIVE ME A RING JENS'. (R, 91)[42] She tries to picture what her *alter ego* Jens must be like, indeed she even tries to ring him up, but gets a wrong number. It is at this point that she thinks of the entire world as consisting of people vainly trying to arrive somewhere: 'Travellers ... Travellers on one leg and on the other one: lost people.' (R, 92)[43] When Irene eventually reproaches her husband with his failure to meet her at the airport, she gives expression to more than just the isolation of the moment: 'I had started off on my journey on my own and wanted to arrive as a pair. But everything was the other way around. I had started off as a pair. I arrived on my own.' (R, 126)[44] The symbolic truth of this remark is that while she had not yet reached Germany, Irene could live in the hope of finding companionship and integrating into a new way of life in the West. Once she arrives, all that faces her is isolation and an uncaring world.

The novels Herta Müller has written since *Reisende auf einem Bein* have on the whole done little to change that work's uncomfortable picture of Germany as experienced from the political asylum seeker's perspective.

The immigration and processing experience and the initial frustrated attempts at integration now figure less. Instead, Germany comes across as a rather desolate context in which Müller's various biographical surrogates gradually discover how impossible it is to escape the hold of Ceauçescu's Romania: either because they discover that 'friends' who come to visit them are actually informers acting on *Securitate* instructions (*Herztier*, The Land of Green Plums); or that they are continually being reminded of their 'Minderheitendeutsch' (*Barfüßiger Februar*, Barefoot February, passim), i.e., the German language even has a convenient compound noun for the inferior German that people from the German ethnic minorities in other countries speak; or because nightmares from the Romanian years break into the narratives just as for the first-person narrator of *Heute wär ich mir lieber nicht begegnet* (1997, Today I'd rather not meet myself) the shadow of imminent interrogation continually makes any semblance of normal life impossible ('Whenever I go to an interrogation, I have, from the outset, to leave my happiness behind me at home', [Müller 1997: 22][45] for an interrogation is a subtle process or 'Humiliation ... as if one felt barefoot over one's whole body'). (Müller 1997: 10)[46] Just as the characters of her fiction who do manage to reach Germany continually find themselves being transported by their feverish imagination or by their memories back to the world of Ceauçescu's Romania, a world in which they could not live any longer but which will not let them live independent of that past, so Herta Müller herself appears to remain an unfortunate prisoner of her Romanian years. This predicament of being an immigrant unable to settle and integrate, not simply because of the hostility of the receiving country but for psychological reasons, is something which is well summed up at one point in 'Und noch erschrickt unser Herz':

> Whenever I try to understand Germany, I inevitably come up against myself. In this I am no different to people who have always lived in Germany. Where I am different is in the way I am forced to come simultaneously up against myself here and myself in a country I left behind. Yet the two countries are so alien to one another that nothing in them and nothing in me (either then or now) is able to meet without this being damaging. That is probably the reason why I am unable to say anything definitive about the Germans. The reason why I can never belong now that I am in Germany and why I cannot leave Germany and go somewhere else. (Müller 1995: 30)[41]

Notes

1. This paper was originally serialised in the *Frankfurter Rundschau* of 15 and 22 May and 12 June 1993, then reprinted in *Hunger und Seide* (Hunger and Silk) (Müller 1995: 19–38).

2. This is hardly surprisingly, given the fact that the 1978 agreement between West Germany's Chancellor Schmidt and President Ceauçescu legislated for the release of at least 12,000 Germans per annum for the next five years. By then increasing the agreed ransom ('Kopfgeld') per German Romanian to DM 8,000, the West German government was able to extend this exchange agree-

ment for another five years, by which time Ceauçescu's regime was tottering on its last legs. Until then, 'the "free emigration" policy served the old nationalist dream of "purifying" the population and at the same time brought in hard currency as Israel and the Federal Republic of Germany paid for each freed citizen; meanwhile the policy gained Romania points with the U.S. Congress' (Manea 1992: 63).

3. This explains Müller's efforts to depersonalise the circumstances of her protagonist and generalise her material beyond any specifically Romanian background. 'Ich wollte mit der Person Irene von mir weggehen und verallgemeinern. Aus diesem Grund habe ich beispielsweise vermieden, Rumänien im Buch zu nennen. Ihre Situation trifft auf viele zu, die etwa aus Ländern aus dem Osten hierherkommen. Ich hätte am liebsten auch die politischen Gründe des Weggehens von Irene ausgespart, aber das konnte ich nicht, ich habe gesehen, daß ich ohne diese politische Dimension nicht auskomme' (With the figure of Irene I wanted to get away from my own situation and generalise. For the same reason I, for example, avoided mentioning Romania in the book. Her situation is that of many who have come here from countries in Eastern Europe. Ideally, I would also have liked to omit the political reasons for Irene's departure, but I couldn't do that, for I saw that I could not do without this political dimension; quoted in Eke 1981: 94).

4. Gesicht des Diktators, der sie vertrieben hatte aus dem anderen Land

5. Man könnte meinen, daß unser Land alles aufwiegen soll, was Ihr Land verbrochen hat

6. Die Schuld dafür schob Irene dem anderen Land zu

7. Bei den Behörden muß ein Ausländer als erstes seine Biographie offenlegen. Statt ihr noch einmal zu vertrauen und sie zu erzählen, muß er sie offenlegen. Dies ist das Gegenteil von Erzählen. Und angesichts der Chance, die ihm damit gegeben oder genommen wird, ist Offenlegen schon Infragestellen.

8. Daß ich 1987 bei der Offenlegung meiner Biographie von der rumänischen Diktatur redete, machte die Beamten nervös. Ich habe eine Diktatur aus politischen Gründen verlassen, und die deutschen Beamten wollten etwas über mein Deutschtum wissen. Als ich die Frage, ob ich mit meiner Haltung auch als Rumänin verfolgt gewesen wäre, mit Ja beantwortete, schickte der Beamte mich zur Ausländerpolizei. Er konstatierte: entweder Deutsche oder politisch Verfolgte. Für beides zusammen gab es kein vorgedrucktes Formular. Was ich erzählte, brachte sein Schubladen durcheinander.'

9. *Michael Kohlhaas* (1811): a story by Heinrich von Kleist chronicling a sixteenth-century German horse-dealer's struggle against state bureaucracy for what he conceives to be his God-given rights before the law. *Michael Kohlhaas*, which meticulously documents the stages by which a sense of natural rights rapidly gives way to taking the law into one's own hands and engaging in vengeful direct action, has had a strong appeal for subsequent writers. Both its images of the machinations of bureaucracy and the theme of rebellion have left their mark on fiction, from Kafka's early twentieth-century images of officialdom to E. L. Doctorow's *Ragtime* and Elisabeth Plessen's *Kohlhaas*.

10. Vielleicht hat man sich in Deutschland nie angewöhnt, die Frage nach der persönlichen Moral zu stellen, weil sie ins Leben des Fragenden hineinstößt. Und weil sich auch hier, in freierem Land – ohne Lebensbedrohung – Moral mit Lebenssicherheit oft nicht vereinbaren läßt. Während die Beamten, aus der Routine gerissen, meine Formulare hin und her schoben, mußte ich mir in Gedanken die Frage stellen, was aus ihnen geworden wäre in meiner Situation (25).

11. Das, was mich einkreist ist das, was zwischen den Sätzen fällt ... Es ist das Ausgelassene

12. Es sind sehr viele Erfahrungen – Alltagserfahrungen – nötig, um zu wissen, was ... gemeint ist. ... Nur: ein Leser hier [im Westen] hat nicht den nötigen Hintergrund, um das alles zu wissen.

13. Hatten Sie vor Ihrer Übersiedlung jemals mit dem dortigen Geheimdienst zu tun? Nicht ich mit ihm, er mit mir. Das ist ein Unterschied.

14. Lassen Sie das Differenzieren vorläufig meine Sorge sein. Dafür werde ich schließlich bezahlt.

15. Keine Rubrik hätte mich beschreiben können, dachte Irene. Der Herr vom Dienst irrt quer über Felder. Das war eine Redewendung aus dem anderen Land. Sie meinte, auf etwas beharren, ohne zu verstehen.

16. Der Beamte trug einen dunklen Anzug, wie Irene sie kannte aus dem anderen Land.

17. Senat für Inneres auf dem Briefkopf. Darunter: daß sie die deutsche Staatsbürgerschaft erhalten habe. Sie solle sich in einer Woche zur Überreichung der Staatsbürgerschaft auf Zimmer 304 melden. Irene freute sich nicht. Sie las weiter, als gehe es in dieser Mitteilung nicht um sie. Den Zusammenhang, in dem die Wörter 'Festessen' und 'Begrüßungsansprache' im letzten Absatz standen, verstand Irene nicht.

18. 'Bundesnachrichtendienst': Federal German agency charged with gathering intelligence about for-eign countries, particularly those behind the Iron Curtain. Founded in 1946 under the name 'Operation Gehlen' (after Reinhard Gehlen, who at the end of the Second World War transferred his *Wehrmacht* counter-intelligence group *en bloc* to the Americans), the 'Bundesnachrichtendienst' became part of the 'Bundesverfassungsschutz' in 1955. The unit's shady beginnings, and also the fact that it still had the same remit in the late 1980s, are probably seen by the author as too self-evident to require specific comment.

19. Vor dem Übergangsheim stand ein gelbes Schild mit einem rot durchgestrichenen Photoapparat.

20. im Warteraum ... hatte Irene die Wartenummer 501, obwohl außer ihr niemand da war.

21. Da, wo Sie herkommen, gabs da eine U-Bahn. Nein. Das habe ich mir gedacht, sagte er.

22. So hab ich mirs gedacht. Deutsch sprechen Sie nur, wenn Sie zu mir ins Büro kommen.

23. Wie sie das Wort Inneres aussprach, das klang für Irene wie Magen und Gedärme.

24. Der Sachbearbeiter öffnete den Mund. Er sagte nichts. Seine Zunge stand im Mund, als hätte sie keinen Platz gehabt. Als wäre unter seiner Zunge noch etwas gewesen. Etwas anderes als eine Zunge. Als wäre unter seiner Zunge ein Finger gewesen. Ein trockener Finger mitten im Mund.

25. Müller (1992a: 65f.) singles out one of her characters as 'einer der wenigen Rumäniendeutschen, die während des Zweiten Weltkriegs nicht in der SS waren' (one of the few Romanian-Germans who was not in the SS during the Second World War) and Richard Wagner once remarked: 'die Generation meines Vaters war zu 90 percent in der Waffen-SS' (90 percent of my father's gener-ation were in the Waffen-SS, Broos 1993: 20). See Glajar (1997), Komjathy and Stockwell (1980) and Nielsen (1993) on this dimension of Müller's work. According to Norman Manea's *The Black Envelope*, such Nazi sympathisers were referred to after the War as 'Heil Heil men' (Manea 1995: 14). 'Why is the subject [of genocide] covered up in this country' (Manea 1995: 139) is something that *The Black Envelope* seeks to uncover.

26. 'Heim ins Reich': the National Socialist campaign to orchestrate – and gain propaganda value from – the return of 'Volksdeutsche' (ethnic Germans) to the Reich. While the slogan is particu-larly associated with the return of Danzig and the Polish Corridor to Germany, the 'Heim ins Reich' policy embraces the Saar (transferred as the result of a plebiscite in 1935), the Sudetenland (returned to Germany under the September 1938 Munich Agreement), as well as the subsequent 'liberation' of ethnic Germans in Memel, Bohemia and Moravia and the Volga region.

27. Recording her pleasure at receiving the 1998 International IMPAC Award for Fiction for *The Land of Green Plums* (*Herztier*), Müller noted in an interview with Udo Scheer for *Die Welt* that it had been written 'für zwei Tote ... für die rumänien-deutschen Schriftsteller Rolf Bossert und Roland Kirsch. Roland haben sie kurz vor Ceauçescus Sturz in der eigenen Wohnung erhängt. [Bossert died shortly after arriving in the West.] Der Preis ist auch eine Hommage an die beiden. Es hat sich als richtig erwiesen, daß ich mir gesagt habe, ich muß ihnen etwas nachtragen' (for two dead

people ... for the Romanian-German writers Rolf Bossert and Roland Kirsch. Shortly before the fall of Ceauçescu they hanged Roland in his own home. The Prize is also an act of homage to the two of them. It turned out to be appropriate that I decided that I had to repay my debts to them). This Müller did with *Herztier*, a novel chronicling both the work of the 'Aktionsgruppe Banat' and the state's attempts to intimidate and neutralise its members. For further information about the membership and activities of the 'Aktionsgruppe Banat', see Richard Wagner, 'Die Aktionsgruppe Banat: Versuch einer Selbstdarstellung' in Wilhelm Solms (ed.): *Nachruf auf die rumäniendeutsche Literatur*, Marburg, Hitzeroth, 1990, 121–29: Nielsen (1993: 87–9) and David Rock's contribution to the present volume.

28. Müller observed of her treatment of the 'fascism' of the village described in *Niederungen* that it represented 'ein Schreiben gegen diese Identität, auch gegen dieses Banat-Schwäbisches Dorf, gegen diese sprachlose Kindheit, die alles unterdrückte' (an act of writing against this identity, also against this Banat-Swabian village, against this mute childhood which suppressed everything, quoted in Eke 1991: 11). Eke documents the vehemently 'völkisch' Banat-German response to *Niederungen* and *Barfüßiger Februar* (107–30). Her ethnic compatriots' reactionary conception of an idealising 'Heimatliteratur' led them to charge Müller with lacking the right 'volksbejahende Haltung' (positive 'folkish' attitude); and their 'gesundes Volksempfinden' (people's healthy instinct), as they called it, saw in her 'Greuelmärchen aus Nitzkydorf' (propaganda fairytales from Nitzkydorf) little more than washing one's dirty linen in public (Nestbeschmutzung). The 'Landsmannschaft der Banater Schwaben' even protested against her work being published at all.

29. Irene [fing] das Gefühl ein, es könnte plötzlich alles anders werden in der Stadt. Die alten Frauen mit den weißen Dauerwellen, polierten Gehstöcken und Gesundschuhen könnten plötzlich wieder jung sein und in den Bund Deutscher Mädchen marschieren. Es würden lange, fensterlose Wagen vor die Ladentüren fahren. Männer in Uniformen würden die Waren aus den Regalen beschlagnahmen. Und in den Zeitungen würden Gesetze erscheinen wie in dem anderen Land.

30. [Irene] erschrak. Der Junge war nicht älter als fünf. Er wiederholte das Wort: Faschist.

31. In Deutschland angekommen, gab es für mich zum ersten Mal eine Art Endgültigkeit. Die räumliche Entfernung zwischen den beiden Ländern, dachte ich, kann es nicht sein.

32. In die Enge getrieben von der Securitate, habe ich zuletzt selber das Weite gesucht. Nichts war beendet, nur zu Ende, weil abgebrochen.

33. Die Diktaturen haben, solange sie funktionierten, die Minderheitenprobleme im Inneren der Staaten durch den Würgegriff erstickt.

34. man wittert die illegitime Einmischung. ... Man verweist mich ins Abgezirkelte: wo ich herkomme, darüber habe ich zu schreiben. In meinem zweiten, besseren Leben hier an der deutschen Brotkante habe ich das Recht zu beißen und zu schlucken. Doch mit diesem damals leeren und jetzt vollen, aber fremdgebliebenen Mund gebührt es sich, beim Essen wenigstens zu schweigen.

35. As one detractor put it: 'H. Müller ist eine der wertvollsten Mitarbeiterinnen der Bukarester ZK-Propagandabteilung ... Sie schädigt das Image des Auslandsdeutschen im Mutterland, dessen Hilfe und Unterstützung im Banat und in Siebenbürgen so nötig ist. Deshalb durfte sie ihr Erstlingswerk im westlichen Ausland veröffentlichen, ein Vorrecht, das in der Regel nur sehr bekannten, besonders linientreuen Literaten zusteht' ('H. Müller is one of the most valuable collaborators working for the Bucharest Central Committee's propaganda department ... She damages the image of ethnic Germans in her own country [i.e., West Germany], a country whose help and support are so greatly needed in the Banat and Siebenbürgen regions. This is why she was allowed to publish her first work in a Western country, a privilege which as a rule is reserved only for very prominent, particularly party-line writers', H. Schneider: 'Eine Apotheose des Häßlichen und Abstoßenden. Anmerkungen zu Herta Müller's *Niederungen*', *Der Donauschwabe*, Christmas 1984, 10, quoted in Eke 1991: 127).

36. In dem anderen Land, sagte Irene, hab ich verstanden, was die Menschen so kaputt macht. Die Gründe lagen auf der Hand. Es hat sehr weh getan, täglich die Gründe zu sehn. ... Und hier, sagte Irene. Ich weiß, es gibt Gründe. Ich kann sie nicht sehn. Es tut weh, täglich die Gründe nicht zu sehn.

37. Irene wünschte sich mehrere Körper, um die Kleider aus den Schaufenstern zu tragen. Und Geld, um die Kleider zu kaufen. ... Doch wenn Irene an einem einzigen Tag, an drei verschiedenen Orten der Stadt, drei verschiedene Frauen mit der gleichen Haarspange, die ein Flugzeug war, sah, freute sie sich, daß sie kein Geld hatte. Und daß ihr Haar für die Spangen zu kurz war. Und ihr Kopf wurde langsam schwer. Und zwischen Nase und Mund zuckte die Haut wie ein großes Insekt. Dann wußte Irene: Die Mode verkürzt das Leben.

38. Auf dem Prospekt stand: das Parfum, das Gefühle provoziert. Jeder Tropfen eine Verführung.

39. Der Brief, der Gefühle provoziert, dachte Irene. Jeder Tropfen eine Verführung.

40. Wer nichts kauft, hat etwas gestohlen, freute sich Irene.

41. Gefahr ins Leere zu stürzen [literally: Danger of falling into the void]. Auch diesen Satz hatte Irene auf ihr Leben bezogen.

42. KALTES LAND KALTE HERZEN RUF DOCH MAL AN JENS.

43. Reisende ... Reisende auf einem Bein und auf dem anderen Verlorene.

44. Ich war allein abgereist und wollte zu zweit ankommen. Alles war umgekehrt. Ich war zu zweit abgereist. Angekommen bin ich allein.

45. Wenn ich zum Verhör gehe, muß ich von vornherein das Glück zu Hause lassen.

46. Demütigung ... , wie wenn man sich am ganzen Körper barfuß fühlt.

47. Wenn ich versuche, Deutschland zu begreifen, stoße ich notgedrungen auf mich selber. Darin unterscheide ich mich nicht von den Menschen, die immer schon in Deutschland gelebt haben. Wodurch ich mich unterscheide, das ist der Zwang, auf mich hier und auf mich in einem zurück-gelassenen Land gleichzeitig zu stoßen. Aber die beiden Länder sind einander so fremd, daß nichts in ihnen und nichts in mir (von damals und jetzt) sich ungestraft begegnen kann. Das ist wahrscheinlich der Grund, weshalb ich über die Deutschen nichts Verbindliches sagen kann. Weshalb ich in Deutschland nie dazugehören kann und weshalb ich aus Deutschland nicht wegge-hen kann.

References

Herta Müller: Principal Works

Niederungen. Bucharest, Kriterion, 1982; Berlin, Rotbuch, 1984; Reinbek, Rowohlt, 1993.
Der Mensch ist ein großer Fasan auf der Welt. Berlin, Rotbuch, 1986. English translation by Martin Chalmers: *The Passport.* London, Serpent's Tail, 1992.
Barfüßiger Februar. Berlin, Rotbuch, 1987.
Reisende auf einem Bein. Berlin, Rotbuch, 1989; Reinbek, Rowohlt, 1995.
Der Teufel sitzt im Spiegel: Wie Wahrnehmung sich erfindet. Berlin, Rotbuch, 1991.
Eine warme Kartoffel ist ein warmes Bett. Kolumnen 1990-92. Hamburg, Europäische Verlagsanstalt, 1992a.
Der Fuchs war damals schon der Jäger. Reinbek, Rowohlt, 1992b.

Herztier. Reinbek, Rowohlt, 1994. English translation by Michael Hofmann: *The Land of Green Plums.* New York, Metropolitan Books; London, Granta, 1996.

Hunger und Seide: Essays. Reinbek, Rowohlt, 1995.

Heute wär ich mir lieber nicht begegnet. Reinbek, Rowohlt, 1997

Secondary Literature on Herta Müller, the Romanian-German Minorities and the Ceauçescu Regime's Emigration Policy

Bauer, Karin, 'Tabus der Wahrnehmung: Reflexion und Geschichte in Herta Müller's Prosa', *German Studies Review*, 14, 1996, pp. 257–78.

Broos, Susanne, 'Richard Wagner: Politik ist immer eine Dimension in meinem Schreiben', *Börsenblatt für den deutschen Buchhandel*, 87, ii, 2 November 1993, p. 20.

Eke, Norbert Otto, ed., *Die erfundene Wahrnehmung: Annäherungen an Herta Müller.* Paderborn, Igel, 1991.

Eke, Norbert Otto, '"Sein Leben machen / ist nicht, / sein Glück machen / mein Herr." Zum Verhältnis von Ästhetik und Politik in Herta Müller's Nachrichten aus Rumänien', *Jahrbuch der Deutschen Schillergesellschaft*, 41, 1997, 481–509.

Glajar, Valentina, 'Banat-Swabian, Romanian and German: Conflicting Identities in Herta Müller's Herztier', *Monatshefte*, 89, 1997, 521–40.

Haines, Brigid, ed., *Herta Müller.* Contemporary German Writers Series. Cardiff, University of Wales Press, 1998.

Haupt-Cucuiu, Herta, *Eine Poesie der Sinne: Herta Müller's 'Diskurs des Alleinseins' und seine Wurzel.* Literatur- und Medienwissenschaft, Bd. 40. Paderborn, Igel, 1996.

Heinz, Franz, 'Kosmos und Banater Provinz: Herta Müller und der unliterarische Streit über ein literarisches Debüt', in Hans Schwob, ed.: *Beiträge zur deutschen Literatur in Rumänien seit 1918.* Munich, Verlag des südostdeutschen Kulturwerks, 1985, pp. 103–12.

Kegelmann, Ren, '*An den Grenzen des Nichts, dieser Sprache ... ': Zur Situation rumäniendeutscher Literatur der achtziger Jahre in der Bundesrepublik Deutschland.* Bielefeld, Aisthesis, 1995.

Köhnen, Ralph, ed., *Der Druck der Erfahrung treibt die Sprache in die Dichtung: Bildlichkeit in Texten Herta Müllers.* Frankfurt am Main, Lang, 1997.

Komjathy, Anthony and Stockwell, Rebecca: *German Minorities and the Third Reich.* New York, Holmes & Meier, 1980.

Manea, Norman, *On Clowns: The Dictator and the Artist.* New York, Grove Press, 1992

Manea, Norman: *The Black Envelope*, earlier version: *Plicul Negru*, Bucharest, Editura Cartea Românascâ, 1986, Trans. Patrick Camiller. New York, Farrar, Straus and Giroux, Inc., 1995.

Nielsen, Erika, 'Coming Home into Exile: The End of Romanian-German Culture' in *Cultural Transformations in the New Germany: American and German Perspectives*, eds. Friederike Eigler and Peter C. Peiffer, Columbia, SC, Camden House, 1993, pp. 81–90.

Ottmers, Clemens, 'Schreiben und Leben: Herta Müller, Der Teufel sitzt im Spiegel. Wie Wahrnehmung sich erfindet (1989)', in *Poetik der Autoren: Beiträge zur deutschsprachigen Gegenwartsliteratur*, ed. Paul Michael Lützeler. Frankfurt am Main, Fischer, 1994, pp. 279–94.

Tudorica, Cristina, *Rumäniendeutsche Literatur (1970–1990): Die letzte Epoche einer Minderheitenliteratur.* Tübingen-Basel, Francke, 1997.

Vogl, Bruno, 'Bewohner mit Handgepäck. Aus dem Banat nach Berlin ausgewandert – Herta Müller im Gespräch', *Die Presse*, Vienna, 7 January 1989, 5ff.

Zierden, Josef, 'Herta Müller' in *Kritisches Lexikon zur deutschsprachigen Gegenwartsliteratur*, ed. Heinz Ludwig Arnold, 50. Nachlieferung, Munich, Text + Kritik, 1995, 1–8 + Bibliography A–G.

Chapter 12

Günter Grass: 'The Man who Migrated across History'[1]

Julian Preece

> I have abandoned my original intention in my poems to depict the encounter between my people and the peoples of the East, an unhappy and guilt-ridden encounter ... All that is left are occasional utterances, which are nourished by memory, on my rooted-ness, which nothing can extirpate, in a landscape which we have quite rightly lost.[2]

> (Bobrowski 1987: 327)

The life and work of Günter Grass, born to mixed German–Slavic, Protestant–Catholic parentage in the independent city-state of Danzig in 1927, are riven by both history and geography. History because throughout his creative career he has wrestled with the moral enormity of the crimes committed by Germans in the name of National Socialism, a creed he and his family had supported during his youth; and geography because from the same age – seventeen – that he discovered the horrific reality which underlay National Socialist rhetoric, he was forced to start a new life hundreds of miles to the west of his native region as a so-called *Heimatvertriebener* or expellee. He lived first in Düsseldorf, then moved to West Berlin and finally Paris, where he wrote *Die Blechtrommel* (The Tin Drum, 1959), before settling once more in West Berlin. This divided city was for forty years a halfway house between the two German states, reflecting the unfinished postwar settlement more poignantly than any other part of the Federal Republic ever could. It fostered too a sense of eternal semi-permanence in its often transitory residents. Just as his East Prussian colleague and contemporary, Siegfried Lenz, settled in northern Hanseatic Hamburg, from the mid-1970s Grass owned a house near the western Baltic in Schleswig-Holstein, home from home for the exiled son of Danzig.

Salman Rushdie, a friend and fellow migrant, accounted for the feelings of loss and detachment which Grass must have experienced and suggested how these experiences – what Rushdie calls 'the triple disruption' suffered by migrants – shaped both his literary writing and his political views. The first disruption is the loss of 'roots', 'the sense of home as a "good" safe place'; the second is the loss of language, since, even though Grass continued to be surrounded by German speakers after 1945, the German language itself had to be reinvented, 'rebuilt, pebble by pebble, from the wreckage: because a language in which evil finds so expressive a voice is a dangerous tongue' (Rushdie 1991: 279). Finally, there is the loss of social and ideological orientation: 'Nazi Germany was, in some ways, another country. Grass had to unlearn that country, that way of thinking about society, and learn a new one' (Rushdie 1991: 280). For Grass, however, there could never be any doubt that because of the Second World War the geographical wrench and the heartache of loss stood in a morally just sequence. His view of his own past and his understanding of his own identity are fractured as a result: while he lovingly recreates his lost homeland on the printed page, he was one of the first public figures to argue for an acceptance of the post-1945 border, the so-called Oder–Neisse line, between Germany and Poland.

The proudly independent, historically wealthy and ethnically heterogeneous Hanseatic city of Danzig was predominantly German-speaking during Grass's childhood, but it had passed from German to Polish rule and back again repeatedly over the thousand years since Adalbert of Prague brought Christianity to the region at the end of the tenth century. As German Danzigers after the First World World War resented being cut off from the *Vaterland*, an above-average number voted for the NSDAP, which ran the city, ostensibly under the supervision of the increasingly ineffectual League of Nations, from as early as 1932, seven years before the whole of former West Prussia was seized by German forces in the autumn of 1939. The city's hinterland and the stretch of Pomerania which became known as the 'Polish Corridor' to its south still contained a rich and potentially explosive mixture of racial, religious and linguistic communities in the interwar years. According to a recent history:

> in Pomerania as a whole there were 919,102 Germans, 555,337 Poles, 106,598 Kaszubes and 20,456 Bilingual people. In Danzig itself, there were 315,281 Germans, 9,491 Poles, 2,124 Kaszubes, and 3,201 Bilingual ... The situation was further complicated by religion. Most Poles were Catholic, but not all Germans were Protestant and there were also German Jews and an increasing number of Polish Jews. (Tighe 1990: 90)

Grass's mother was of 'Kaszube' or Cassubian stock. While her three brothers were killed fighting for Germany in the First World War, a cousin took part in the defence of Danzig's Polish Post Office at the outbreak of the next war. Like Jan Bronski, Oskar Matzerath's uncle and putative father in *Die Blechtrommel*, 'uncle Franz' was executed by the Germans (Neuhaus 1997: 10–11). He was known either (in German) as Franz Krause or (in Polish) as Frantziek Krauze. His name may have been rarely mentioned in the Grass household after September 1939, but it is now commemorated on the monument to the Post Office workers. The Cassubians belong ethnically and linguistically more to the Slavs than the Germans and had historically stood between the two. The Nazis, however, generally counted them as *Volksdeutsche*, that is, aliens worthy of 'Germanisation' on the basis of German ancestry or kinship with the Germanic peoples. Anton Stomma from *Aus dem Tagebuch einer Schnecke* (From the Diary of a Snail, 1972), who shelters the runaway Hermann Ott in his cellar for the duration of the war, is Grass's most complete Cassubian. Born in 1888, he alternates all his life between the Polish and German language, while always speaking Cassubian at home, and between Germany and Poland, depending upon which is in the ascendancy. He treats Ott, whom he takes to be Jewish, as an insurance policy: in the event of a German defeat he can claim credit for having sided with the Germans' enemies and rescued a Jew; if, on the other hand, he needs to curry favour with the occupiers he can hand him over whenever he chooses.

In *Hundejahre* (Dog Years, 1963) it is clear that all the ethnic and religious groups, which the Nazis set on one another, have been mixed from the beginnings of settlement in the region. Under a regime obsessed with the purity of genealogy, not even the pedigree German Shepherd is 'pure' because three generations back Hitler's favourite dog is descended from an indisputably Slavic she-wolf. The origins of the human figures and the names of their towns and villages are even less uniform, as Harry Liebenau, the morally compromised narrator of the middle section, demonstrates with respect to his cousin Tulla and her family village:

> You were baptised under the name of Ursula but were called Tulla from the beginning. This nickname probably derives from the Koschnäwjer water spirit Thula which lived in the Osterwick Lake and whose name had various spellings: Duller, Tolle, Tullatsch, Thula, or Dul, Tul, Thul. When the Pokriefkes still lived in Osterwick they were settled as tenants on the Mosbrauchsbäsch next to the lakę, on the road to Konitz. From the fourteenth century to the year Tulla was born, in the year twenty-seven, Osterwick was spelt in the following ways: Ostirwig, Ostirwich, Osterwigh, Osterwig, Osterwyk, Ostrowit, Ostrowite, Osterwieck, Ostrowitte, Ostrów. The Koschnäwjer said: Oustewitsch. The Polish root of the village name Osterwick, the word ostrów, means river island or island in a lake, for the village of Osterwick had originally, that is in the fourteenth century, been situated on the island in Osterwick Lake. (Grass 1997: V:153)[4]

Attempts to deny or conceal ethnic mixture and the resultant ambiguity in identity never fail to earn the disapprobation of Grass's narrators. Pilenz in *Katz und Maus* (Cat and Mouse, 1961) takes a dim view of the 'Germanisation' of Polish-sounding names and emphasises that Mahlke's family resisted the opportunity to take up this offer which could have been advantageous to them.

When it comes to deciding whether the entire region belongs rightfully to the Germans or the Poles, the Baltic Sea, according to Grass in an autobiographical poem, 'Kleckerburg', speaks more sense than human beings from either side:

> What noise does the Baltic make? – Blubb, piff, pschsch ...
>
> In German, in Polish: Blubb, piff, pschsch ...
>
> But when at the Refugees' Congress, everyone
>
> weary of celebrating their tradition
>
> after journeys on special buses
>
> and federal railways, I asked the officials,
>
> they had forgotten
>
> the noise of the Baltic Sea and invoked
>
> the Atlantic.
>
> I stood my ground: blubb, piff, pschsch ...
>
> They all shouted: strike him dead!
>
> He has given up on human rights and pensions,
>
> on compensation and his native city.
>
> Listen to his accent:
>
> that's not the Baltic, that's treason. (Grass 1997: I:197)[5]

Grass has never been popular with the majority of ex-Danzigers: the Refugees' Association journal, *Unser Danzig* (Our Danzig), greeted *Die Blechtrommel* less than warmly (Loschütz 1968: 25–6); and Sudeten German extremists then set his Berlin frontdoor on fire in the dying days of the 1965 election campaign to let him know what they thought of his arguments in favour of *Ostpolitik* and reconciliation. He, on the other hand, can accept the loss of his native city because of its historical heterogeneity and the redundancy of all national claims to it.

None of the major characters in Grass's earlier fiction quite understands where he or she belongs, while the Nazis attempted to force everyone to declare a fixed allegiance by adopting a racial identity where ambiguity has no place. The mixture of Catholic and Protestant, German and Slav in Grass's own family reflected the historic hybridity of the people in the region and helps explain why so many of his fictional characters straddle ethnic and linguistic boundaries. Eberhard Starusch in *örtlich betäubt* (Local Anaesthetic, 1969) is half-German, half-Cassubian, like his creator; Oskar Matzerath never finds out whether his father was the Polish Jan or the German Alfred: he sides, however, with the Germans since that was the choice made by the majority in his immediate milieu and this choice is one of the greatest sources of his guilt. Joachim Mahlke in *Katz und Maus* has Polish sympathies, even though he dedicates his life to winning the highest German military honour and goes into battle with Germany's Slavic enemies in order to win it. Eddi Amsel in *Hundejahre*, on the other hand, is half-Jewish, half-Gentile, and models his identity, as his assimilated Jewish father had done, on stereotypical notions of how Jews and Gentiles are supposed to behave. The real Eddi Amsel alias Haseloff alias Brauxel (or Brauchsel or Brauksel) is impossible to pin down. His different names and the different ways he spells them signal this ever-shifting identity, his passport to survival during the Third Reich. While Hermann Ott is persecuted as a Jew for practising solidarity with the Jews, he has unimpeachable Aryan credentials and is descended from sixteenth-century Dutch Mennonite immigrants. The lesson Grass puts across is that ethnic or religious identity, whether for an individual or a whole nation, is a wholly artificial construct. This is how he, an expellee who mourns his lost homeland, rationalises his loss.

Making Danzig into the centre of his fiction for more than thirty years of his career was Grass's one way of coping with his personal loss. His fiction would run the risk of nostalgia were it not for the knowledge, which permeates its every narrative pore, that he is evoking a landscape where evil flourished. The places and place-names, the streets of suburban Danzig and the villages along the Baltic coast and down the course of the Vistula river were robbed of all the innocence which childhood would otherwise have lent them in the five years which began on 1 September 1939. Until then Stutthof, for instance, was the name of a small village on a coastal spit to the east of Danzig, separated from the city by the mouth of the Vistula, on either side of which perch the villages of Schiewenhorst and Nickelswalde, where the blood brothers Matern and Amsel grow up in *Hundejahre*. On the second day of the war, work started in the woods on the outskirts of Stutthof to build a concentration camp, the plans for which had evidently been carefully laid well in advance of the German invasion. It was an ideal location, concealed by woodland yet connected to Danzig by road and rail and surrounded on all sides by water, making escape especially difficult (Grabowska 1995). The camp was fully integrated into the local region: prisoners were sent out to the fields and to local factories to work; local Germans or Poles who fell foul of the authorities, by trading in ration coupons, for instance, were sent there for 're-education' from October 1941. This is what happens to the schoolmaster Oswald Brunies in *Hundejahre*, whose story is a fictional reconstruction of an incident Grass recalls from his own childhood. In *Hundejahre* the bones at Stutthof pile up into the sky, visible to all who wanted to see them.

As he never tires of reminding his readers, Danzig/Gdansk was built by a colourful array of nationalities. He takes the 'melting pot' of the city and its frequent changes in government down the ages to challenge national territorial claims on it after 1945. In a polemic against ungenerous German attitudes to Poland and the Poles in the aftermath of reunification he attempts to show the absurd irrelevance of chauvinistic attitudes given the relative newness of the concept of the nation-state: 'Flemish architects, settlers from the Netherlands and Scotland, Mennonites and Huguenots, English merchants and Jews, either from the city or from outside, have influenced the culture of this city' (Grass, 1997: XVI:314).[5] The chronicle of German and Polish competition for Danzig was itself highly contentious and used to underpin claims on it. The different ways of spelling the city's name are loaded with importance: to name something is to possess it, as Oskar had already hinted: 'From Gyddanyzc they made Danczik, from Danczik came Dantzig, which was later spelt Danzig, and today Danzig is called Gdansk' (Grass 1997: III:520).[6] Any unitary interpretation, such as that favoured by the radicals in *Der Butt* (The Flounder, 1977), is woefully insufficient. Not only Danzig was ethnically mixed, however. The rest of Germany was not much different. What attracted Grass possibly most powerfully to Theodor Fontane in his recent novel *Ein weites Feld* (Too Far Afield, 1995) was the Prussian novelist's French Huguenot ancestry, which made him a Prussian and yet by origin not a Prussian, accounting in part for his ever-evolving attitude to the whole project of nineteenth-century German nationalism. Grass loves the idea that the electoral principality of Brandenburg, the core of the kingdom of Prussia created in 1701, benefited to such a great degree from an influx of French-speaking expellees: Prussia is in some part a French creation.

Der Butt (1977), published exactly mid-way between his other two great novels, *Die Blechtrommel* (1959) and *Ein weites Feld* (1995), is a 'counter-narrative' to conventional historical accounts both of Danzig/Gdansk and the whole of Europe. The fact that history belongs to the victors is one of the few history lessons contained in the novel, but in the case of Germans writing about Danzig, history has belonged to the defeated in so far as their narrative continued to wield influence. One clear purpose of this novel is thus to correct popular German historiography of the region which was guided exclusively by the desire to demonstrate the 'Germanness' of the city from the days of the medieval Teutonic Knights to 1945, thereby proving the Germans' rightful claim to it (Rühnau 1971). The Communist Polish authorities too had reason not to like Grass's fictional accounts, not merely his portrayal of the violence in the Lenin Shipyards in 1970. None of his books was officially available to Polish readers until the 1980s since his use of German names for places and streets now in Polish hands was incompatible with the Polish authorities' claim that the newly acquired western territories had been an intrinsic part of Poland from time immemorial (Tighe 1990: 268–88). While Grass believes that the Polish acquisition of German land in the west, to compensate for the pre-war territories lost in the east to Lithuania and the Ukraine, to have been justified, he refuses to accept the wilder Polish claims of legitimacy. It would be necessary to start as far back as the *Völkerwanderungen* (tribal migrations) in the Roman epoch, which would clearly be ridiculous, to settle these rival claims (Grass and Giroud 1989: 78). Yet however ridiculous that might sound to rational observers, the *Völkerwanderungen* are precisely where the nationalists on both sides *do* start.

Like Grass's own family, characters in his first six prose works make the journey from Danzig to the western zones of occupied Germany in 1945. They have neighbours or relatives who are not so fortunate. Tens if not hundreds of thousands of civilians lost their lives on the hazardous trek or maritime evacuation to the west: Starusch's mother, clockmaker Laubschad and Herr and Frau Scheffler in *Die Blechtrommel*, and Walter Matern's family from *Hundejahre* are all drowned by Soviet U-boats (Bond and Preece 1991–92: 147–63). Like Frau Greff in *Die Blechtrommel* and Sibylle Miehlau from the 'Vatertag' chapter of *Der Butt*, the women left behind in Danzig were raped by victorious Soviet soldiers, a fate which befell Grass's own mother. Grass's major postwar characters, Oskar and Pilenz, the *Dog Years* triumvirate, Starusch and Sibylle Miehlau all remain unsettled in their private lives. Aged between their late twenties and early forties, none is married. All are still obsessed with their past.

The physical suffering, attacks by marauding Poles, who hold up the train carrying Oskar and his surviving family members, and the loss of life made the whole subject of expulsion especially fraught after the end of the war. The great majority of *Vertriebene* were wholly innocent of wrongdoing, like civilians in every other country. While they had certainly supported the war in overwhelming numbers as long as it promised them victory, they were victims of its outcome nonetheless. The fact that they had brought their fate on themselves hardly lessened their pain; it merely made it more complicated. Yet since acknowledgement of their suffering could be seen to imply a legitimisation of the claims for the 'return' of the vast areas, stretching eastwards along the Baltic Coast to the borders of Russia and Lithuania, the question of the expellees' suffering could not easily be addressed, neither the physical suffering on the trek west nor the mental anguish in the years after 1945. It remained, like so many other matters which pertained to the legacy of National Socialism, an area riddled with taboos; addressing the question at all meant treading on a minefield of grievances. The thinking that underscores Grass's treatment of expulsion from *Die Blechtrommel* to his post-reunification novelette *Unkenrufe* (The Call of the Toad, 1992) is that the Holocaust overshadows everything that happened in its aftermath. While the Poles are guilty of chauvinistic distortion themselves, they are historically in the right because of the scale of the atrocities committed by the Germans between 1939 and 1945, both in Poland itself and elsewhere in Eastern Europe. At the same time German pain is real and must be respected. During the election campaign of 1969, when Grass played a pivotal role in getting the architect of *Ostpolitik*, Willy Brandt, elected to the Chancellorship, he accused the CDU of manipulating the expellees' anguish by promising them that the former German territories would somehow be won back peacefully. As a result the older generation in particular refused to settle in the new Federal Republic:

'Ready to leave at any moment, they sat among their packed suitcases, placing their trust in a policy called a "Policy of Strength", whose sandpit victories have since been disproved by reality' (Grass 1997: XIV:503).[7] The generation of his parents and grandparents carried the greater historical burden because they were more weighed down by memories and least able to adapt to new surroundings. He exhorted them in the 1965 election to found new cities in underpopulated areas of the Federal Republic and to emulate emigrants to the New World by calling them Neu-Breslau, Neu-Königsberg and Neu-Danzig. This would underline their commitment to their new home and keep alive their memory of their old one.

Grass found CDU intransigence on the Oder–Neisse line doubly counterproductive since it might have been possible to negotiate the return to Germany of the border city of Stettin and part of the Lausitz, both of which were, as German maps of the time expressed it, 'under Polish administration' but would have acceded, of course, to the GDR. The lip-service paid by CDU politicians to unification clearly angered him. During Adenauer's long Chancellorship (1949–63) and even beyond they refused to recognise the GDR in any shape or form, thus ruling out any dialogue, while misleading voters by claiming that the lost provinces could somehow be got back and 'the borders of 1937' somehow reconstituted. Grass's desire for a peace treaty which would recognise the Oder–Neisse line became a reality after Brandt's election in 1969. It was entirely appropriate that Grass, along with Siegfried Lenz, accompanied Brandt on his historic visit to Poland in 1970 when he knelt at the monument in the Warsaw ghetto to Holocaust victims, a gesture intended to illustrate German acceptance of guilt.

Grass's biographical experience has clearly powered his fiction and shaped the nature of his comments in his second chosen role, that of public campaigner: his comments on German nationalism and the German nation in the 1960s, the period of his first great preoccupation with the national question, as well as in 1989–90, and latterly his support for 'asylum seekers' and gypsies. Grass has argued repeatedly for a multicultural Germany, which, despite official pronouncements to the contrary, is a centuries-old reality. The unification of the two German states was his single greatest theme in the federal elections of 1966, when he launched himself on what amounted to a one-man campaign on behalf of the ex-émigré Willy Brandt. Grass's sense of what constituted the nation and what was meant by national unity (he has consistently favoured a loose confederation) was undoubtedly sharpened by the fact that his Danzig no longer belonged to either part of it. As far as unification in 1965 was concerned, he saw part of the problem to be the unwillingness of the Christian Democrats to accept the new postwar borders of Germany, which meant in particular the new border between the GDR and Poland which marked *de facto* the eastern boundary of German territory. The clear losers here were the citizens of the GDR. From fear of displeasing the *Vertriebene* lobby, the CDU would not publicly accept the postwar settlement which had deprived the combined GDR and FRG of one-quarter of the prewar German territory. Grass stressed that he knew all too well how difficult it was to accept these realities:

> Silesia, eastern Pomerania, East Prussia – as someone who comes from down there, I can only gnash my teeth and beat my breast as I utter the truth: we have gambled them away, lost our chance, by taking on the world, we lost them (Grass 1997: XIV:113).[8]

This reveals one of the great creative tensions in his work: his emotional attachment to his home and his grief over its loss jostles with an understanding of German guilt and a rational appreciation of the justice of what happened. Reason wins out over emotion; guilt leaves no room for resentment.

After the successes of the SPD's *Ostpolitik*, first under Brandt (1969–74) and then Helmut Schmidt (1974–82), which was continued by Helmut Kohl and the CDU after 1982, the whole issue of reunification and the German–Polish border lay dormant until 1989–90. When it re-emerged in the wake of the fall of the Berlin Wall, Grass became the most vociferous critic of Kohl's march to a new unified Germany. In *Unkenrufe*, which challenges both German and Polish chauvinism, he returned to the subject of expulsion and the new strains in German–Polish relations after the upheaval of 1989. He also explored a view latent in all his fiction that the very notion of ethnic identity is both chimerical and profoundly poisonous. What his hero, a German professor of art history, born in German Danzig which is now Polish Gdansk, and heroine, a Polish restorer born in Polish Vilnius which is now Lithuanian Wilna, want to do is to bury the whole issue once and for all by allowing the *Vertriebene*, whether German or Polish, to return to their respective native city for burial. Yet they inevitably stir up irredentist longings in the Germans (the Polish–Lithuanian part of the project never properly gets off the ground) and their whole enterprise goes horribly wrong when it is taken over by Germans with an eye to more than just business expansion. The 'Polish–German–Lithuanian Cemetery Society' keeps memories of the past alive, however genuine the spirit of reconciliation which inspired it. Through the figure of the Bengali rickshaw entrepreneur Mister Chatterjee (based unmistakably on Salman Rushdie), Grass presents an alternative view of the future. In Chatterjee's vision all religious, linguistic and ethnic groups should merge through interbreeding and form a new, dynamic entity. Europe and Germany in particular can only profit through contact with a foreign influx of Bengali-speaking Hindus, who by the end of the millennium have transformed the whole region. Yet this utopian alternative has its darker side and does not by any means stand as a blueprint. On the last page of *Unkenrufe*, Reschke and Pitkowska are killed on their honeymoon in a car crash in Italy. They are buried in a double, nameless grave overlooking the coast. The narrator speaks in more than just their name when he ends his reconstruction of their ill-fated good intentions with the words: 'Let them lie there' (Grass 1997: XII:246).[9]

Grass's more pessimistic predictions have not been born out in the decade since German reunification. The expellees really are a spent force now that anyone with even a childhood memory of their lost homeland has reached retirement age. Time has healed wounds and German–Polish relations have normalised. Grass recognised this in his second and far more substantial work of fiction to address the question: *Ein weites Feld* makes no mention of Danzig/Gdansk. This is surely a sign that he has finally moved on from this once all-consuming theme.

Notes

1. Quotation from Rushdie 1991: 279.

2. Eine ursprüngliche Absicht, mit meinen Gedichten zu einer Darstellung der Begegnung meines Volkes mit den Völkern des Ostens zu kommen, einer unglücklichen und schuldhaften Begegnung, ist aufgegeben ... Es bleibt bei gelegentlichen Hervorbringungen, die von der Erinnerung genährt sind, von der unlösbaren Verwurzelung in einer Landschaft, die mit allem Recht verloren ist.

3. Du wurdest auf den Namen Ursula getauft, aber von Anfang an Tulla gerufen. Wahrscheinlich leitet sich dieser Rufname von dem Koschnäwjer Wassergeist Thula her, der im Osterwicker See wohnte und verschieden geschrieben wurde: Duller, Tolle, Tullatsch, Thula oder Dul, Tul, Thul. Als die Pokriefkes noch in Osterwick wohnten, saßen sie als Pächter auf dem Mosbrauchsbäsch nahe dem See, an der Landstraße nach Konitz. Osterwick wurde von der Mitte des vierzehnten Jahrhunderts bis zu Tullas Geburtstag, im Jahre siebenundzwanzig, so geschrieben: Ostirwig, Ostirwich, Osterwigh, Osterwig, Osterwyk, Ostrowit, Ostrowite, Osterwieck, Ostrowitte, Ostrów. Die Koschnäwjer sagten: Oustewitsch. Die polnische Wurzel des Dorfnamens Osterwick, das Wort ostrów, bedeutet Flußinsel oder Insel in einem See; denn das Dorf Osterwick hatte sich ursprünglich, also im vierzehnten Jahrhundert, auf der Insel im Osterwicker See befunden.

4. Was macht die Ostsee? – Blubb, piff, pschsch ...

   Auf deutsch, auf polnisch: Blubb, piff, pschsch ...

   Doch als ich auf dem volksfestmüden,

   Von Sonderbussen, Bundesbahn

   gespeisten Flüchtlingstreffen in Hannover

   die Funktionäre fragte, hatten sie

   vergessen, wie die Ostsee macht,

   und ließen den Atlantik röhren;

   ich blieb beharrlich: Blubb, piff, pschsch ...

   Da schrien alle: Schlagt ihn tot!

   Er hat auf Menschenrecht und Renten,

   Auf Lastenausgleich, Vaterstadt

   Verzichtet, hört den Zungenschlag:

   Das ist die Ostsee nicht, das ist Verrat.

5. Flämische Baumeister, Siedler aus Holland und Schottland, Mennoniten und Hugenotten, englische Kaufleute und ansässige wie eingewanderte Juden [haben] diese Stadt kulturell geprägt.

6. Aus Gyddanyzc machte man Danczik, aus Danczik wurde Dantzig, das sich später Danzig schrieb, und heute heißt Danzig Gdansk.

7. Aufbruchbereit saßen sie zwischen gepackten Koffern, vertrauend einer Politik, die sich 'Politik der Staerke' nannte, und deren Sandkastensiege inzwischen von der Realität widerlegt worden sind.

8. Was jene Provinzen angeht ... Schlesien, Hinterpommern, Ostpreußen, – kann ich, also jemand, der von da unten kommt, nur zähneknirschend und gegen die eigene Brust schlagend die Wahrheit aussprechen: Wir haben diese Provinzen vertan, verspielt, eine Welt herausfordernd verloren.

9. Laßt sie da liegen.

References

Bobrowski, Johannes, *Gesammelte Werke in sechs Bänden*, ed. Eberhard Haufe. Berlin, Union Verlag, 1987, vol. 4.

Bond, D. G. and Preece, Julian, '"Cap Arcona" 3 May 1945: History and Allegory in Novels by Uwe Johnson and Günter Grass', *Oxford German Studies* 20/21, 1991–2, pp. 147–63.

Grabowska, Janina, *Stutthof. Ein Konzentrationslager vor den Toren Danzigs*. Bremen, Edition Temmen, 1995.

Grass, Günter, *Werkausgabe*, ed. Volker Neuhaus and Daniela Hermes. Göttingen, Steidl, 1997.

Grass, Günter and Giroud, Françoise, *Wenn wir von Europa sprechen. Ein Dialog*. Frankfurt am Main, Luchterhand, 1989.

Lenz, Siegfried, *Heimatmuseum*. Munich, dtv, 1981.

Loschütz, Gert, ed., *Von Buch zu Buch. Günter Grass in der Kritik*. Neuwied and Berlin, Luchterhand, 1968.

Neuhaus, Volker, *Schreiben gegen die verstreichende Zeit. Zu Leben und Werk von Günter Grass*. Munich, dtv, 1997.

Rühnau, Rüdiger, *Danzig. Geschichte einer deutschen Stadt*. Würzburg, Holzner, 1971.

Rushdie, Salman, *Imaginary Homelands. Essays and Criticism 1981–1991*. London, Granta, 1991, pp. 273–282.

Tighe, Carl, *Danzig/Gdansk. National Identity in the Polish-German Borderlands*. London, Pluto Press, 1990.

Chapter 13

From 'Sudetendeutsche' to 'Adlergebirgler': Gudrun Pausewang's *Rosinkawiese* Trilogy[1]

Kati Tonkin

It is customary to refer to the Germans who were expelled from Central and Eastern Europe after the Second World War in terms of their place of origin – they are East Prussians, Pomeranians, Silesians, Sudeten Germans and so on. This is reflected in the names of the major expellee organisations which formed after 1949, such as the *Sudetendeutsche Landsmannschaft*, and certainly the evidence points to the expellees' own strong identification in these terms during the early postwar period. As time passed, however, the expellees increasingly became part of the national culture of Germany and their expellee identity gradually diminished. But this did not indicate that all feeling of belonging in terms of their place of origin was relinquished. It is the aim of this article to demonstrate, using the example of the Sudeten Germans, that there was a corresponding consolidation rather than weakening of the sense of local identification, which came to supersede identification as Sudeten German. The argument falls into three parts: firstly an explanation of the genesis of Sudeten German identity and an examination of its nature; secondly a description of how this identity became localised in the postwar period; and thirdly the analysis of a concrete example of localised identification in three texts by an expellee from the Sudetenland, Gudrun Pausewang: *Rosinkawiese: Alternatives Leben in den zwanziger Jahren* (Rosinkawiese: Living the Alternative Life in the 1920s, 1980), *Fern von der Rosinkawiese: Die Geschichte einer Flucht* (Far from Rosinkawiese: Story of a Flight, 1989), and *Geliebte Rosinkawiese: Die Geschichte einer Freundschaft über die Grenzen* (Beloved Rosinkawiese: Story of a Friendship over Borders, 1990). Here the author revisits the 'Rosinkawiese', a two-hectare plot of land where she spent her childhood. Together the books reveal a narrowly delineated sense of belonging and can be used to illustrate the split between a localised identity and the more politically charged Sudeten German identity.

Sudeten German: Genesis of an Ethnopolitical Identity

The term *Sudetendeutsch* is relatively recent, having first been used as a collective name for the ethnic Germans in Bohemia and Moravia–Silesia in 1898. It was coined by Franz Jesser in an attempt to sidestep the problem of having to use the cumbersome phrase 'die Deutschen aus Böhmen, Mähren und Schlesien' every time he wanted to refer to his German-speaking countrymen. Following the example of the term 'Alpendeutsche' for the Germans in the Alpine country, Jesser suggested the names 'Sudetenländer' and 'Sudetendeutsche', after the mountain range Sudetengebirge (Habel 1984: 94). In 1901 the phrase 'die Deutschen in den Sudetenländern' was used in the German-Bohemian weekly *Der Deutsche Volksbote*,[2] and in 1903, in an article that has been attributed to Jesser,[3] the 'Alpendeutschen' were contrasted with the 'Sudetendeutschen'.[4] However, it was not until the creation of the state of Czechoslovakia in 1918 that the term began to be understood generally to refer to all of the ethnic Germans in Bohemia and Moravia–Silesia.

The so-called Sudeten Germans in fact formed eight distinct groups with their own dialects and distinctive cultural traits.[5] This situation developed as a result of the migrations of centuries earlier, the first German settlers in these areas originating from different German tribes – the Central and North Bavarian, East Franconian, Upper Saxon and Silesian tribes. Over the centuries, the descendants of the settlers experienced different lines of development from the groups from which they had originally come, partly through the intermingling of two or more tribes, partly through cross-cultural contact with Czechs and other Slavic peoples. This resulted in the emergence of dialects which differed somewhat from the original dialects,[6] and the development of a great cultural diversity (Hemmerle 1957: 144–5).

Nevertheless we can speak of these people as an ethnic group[7] prior to 1918. Along with Czechs and Slovaks, as well as Poles, Ruthenians, Hungarians and others, they comprised the multiethnic Austro-Hungarian Empire. However, the lack of a common name prior to the creation of the Czechoslovak state does suggest that this category of collective identity was neither very significant in people's everyday lives nor particularly problematic. The potential for ethnic conflict had certainly been present since at least 1848,[8] and sparks had flown from time to time, but it took a sudden and dramatic change in political circumstances to precipitate the crystallisation of German identity and the assumption of the name *Sudetendeutsche*. Until that point in time their 'German' identity existed at some

level, but other – named – categories of identity held more immediacy
(Jaworski 1995: 33).[9] The self–perception of the Sudeten Germans as members of an ethnic group distinct from other ethnic groups in the
Austro-Hungarian Empire, then, undoubtedly predates the emergence of
their name, but before this identity became problematic they were what
has been termed an ethnic *category*, having 'only a dim consciousness that
they form[ed] a separate collectivity', rather than an ethnic *community*,
where 'community' connotes a subjective sense of identity as a collective
(Smith 1991: 20–1).

The briefest glance at a map showing the population distribution of the
'Sudeten Germans' reveals that there were considerable obstacles to the
development of a common sense of identity among these people,[10] spread
out as they were in a relatively long and in parts very narrow crescent with
a high percentage of Germans but also significant numbers of Czechs, and
several German linguistic enclaves (*Sprachinseln*) in the predominantly
Czech-speaking parts.

With the dissolution of the Austro-Hungarian Empire and the founding
of the Czechoslovak Republic in 1918 the Germans in Bohemia and
Moravia–Silesia experienced a sudden and profound change in status.
Within the Austro-Hungarian Empire all ethnic groups had been recognised as ethnic national groups with equal rights, but in practice the
Germans had been in a position of dominance.[11] Within the newly created
state of Czechoslovakia, however, they officially constituted a minority,
and although the Czech Constitution enshrined generous laws protecting
minority rights, and the Czechs made further significant concessions to the
Germans,[12] the Germans felt themselves to be dispossessed and under-
privileged. It is in this political context that a sense of solidarity emerged
uniting the various German groups in Bohemia and Moravia–Silesia, and
it is due to this sense of solidarity that the term *Sudetendeutsch* came into
popular usage to describe the group. The ethnic Germans in Bohemia and
Moravia–Silesia, who prior to this had identified more strongly on other
levels, now perceived a need to unite in order to further their political interests.[13] It was the political situation of 1918, then, which sparked the
transformation from ethnic category to ethnic community. Between 1918
and the annexation of the Sudetenland to the Reich in 1938, Sudeten German identity strengthened and became more highly politicised as relations
between Czechs and Germans deteriorated.

Expulsion and Identity Transformation

In the aftermath of the War the majority of the Sudeten Germans were
expelled from Czechoslovakia, most of them settling in what in 1949
became the Federal Republic of Germany. While the highest concentration of expellees from the Sudetenland was in Bavaria, they were spread

throughout the four occupied zones. Despite this fragmentation, however, cohesion within the Sudeten German expellee community was strong in the early postwar period. Just as the initial catalyst for the crystallisation of Sudeten German identity had been a political event, here too, the impetus for an increase in the strength and vitality of this identity was political.

The leaders of the various Sudeten German groupings[14] soon realised that in order to gain political power they needed to unite all Sudeten Germans in one organisation (Luza 1964: 308). This was the function of the *Sudetendeutsche Landsmannschaft* (Luza 1964: 309), the political and cultural basis of which was *Heimatpolitik* – the struggle for recognition of a 'Recht auf die *Heimat*', or a right to return to the Sudetenland.[15] The East Prussian, Silesian and other expellee *Landsmannschaften* shared this goal. However, the *Sudetendeutsche Landsmannschaft* became more highly politicised than other groups because it felt marginalised by the policy of the umbrella organisation, the *Bund der Vertriebenen* (BdV), to promote the goal of a return to the borders of 1937, which excluded the Sudetenland. Gatz contrasts the isolationist stance of the Sudeten Germans with the East Prussians, who tended to work in organisations encompassing many other expellee groups (Gatz 1989: 344). The East Prussians had been included within the greater German Reich and thus felt no need to develop a strong, distinctive subgroup identity prior to the expulsion. The Sudeten Germans, by contrast, had been repeatedly excluded and were less secure in their German identity (Gatz 1989: 486). Through the experience of exclusion from the Reich and then incorporation as a minority within the Czechoslovak Republic, they had developed a strong group consciousness and a tradition of political activism (Gatz 1989: 254, 486).[16] Thus the Sudeten German expellees maintained some distance from other expellee groups in West Germany, so strengthening their inner cohesion.

A further factor in the solidarity of Sudeten German expellees was a sense of alienation. Upon their arrival in occupied Germany, expellees from the Sudetenland, as well as those from the Oder–Neisse territories and Eastern Europe, experienced a profound culture shock. To be sure they spoke German (with the colouring of dialect) and were issued with German papers, but they had lost their familiar environment and accepted forms of communication:

> The differences in regional culture between the host society and the refugees in everyday life and material culture, in intellectual and religious thought and behaviour patterns, in living arrangements, in clothing, in work and eating patterns and so on were at first largely experienced as 'foreign'. (Tolksdorf 1990: 110)[17]

This sense of alienation in postwar Germany strengthened the internal cohesion of the various expellee groups, despite their geographical dispersion. In his examination of the processes of sociocultural integration, Kurz cites the example of the village of Gersdorf in Hesse, which in 1949 had a population of 176. Postwar expulsion brought 128 people to the village, of whom 109 were Sudeten German. The original inhabitants of Gersdorf were used to an austere existence and avoided close contact even with their neighbours. Seventy-seven of the newly arrived Sudeten German expellees came from southern Moravia, where work and living conditions had been easier and social relations were more congenial and demonstrative. Such differences in modes of behaviour led to clashes between the established residents and the expellees and an initial intensification of Sudeten German identity (Kurz 1950: 35–6).

However, tensions not only arose between the indigenous population and the Sudeten German expellees. Within the Sudeten German community itself differences soon began to make themselves felt. In Gersdorf, for example, the other thirty-two Sudeten German expellees hailed from northern Moravia, where life had been harder than in the south. They were industrial workers and tended to be serious and reserved, in stark contrast to their southern Moravian countrymen, with whom they were supposed to share a strong identification. The differences also made themselves felt in everyday communication, since the southern Moravians spoke a Bavarian–Austrian dialect and the northern Moravians a Silesian dialect. The original inhabitants of Gersdorf tended to use a combination of High German and their own local dialect (Kurz 1950: 35–6). Thus there was a high level of incompatibility in traditions, norms and dialects not only between the locals and the expellees, but also within the Sudeten German community.

Such experiences are evidence of the persistence and re-emergence of localised identities alongside Sudeten German identity. As the expellees gradually integrated into West German society and the desire of the majority to return to the Sudetenland abated, these localised identities began to predominate. The political influence of the *Sudetendeutsche Landsmannschaft*, with its aim of return or restitution, also diminished in the context of the 'Ostpolitik' of postwar German governments, as the attendance at annual reunions illustrates. From the beginning, the reunions had combined nostalgia with nationalistic fervour (Gatz 1989: 440). They were social events which provided an opportunity to meet up with former neighbours and friends and to celebrate the cultural heritage of the various provinces through the wearing of *Trachten* (regional costumes), the singing of traditional songs, and taking part in traditional dances and eating the culinary specialties of the region. But from their inception, they had been dominated by the political rhetoric of the Sudeten leaders, who maintained that the meetings were demonstrations of the desire of all Sudeten Germans to return to their *Heimat*. As the expellees successfully integrated into West German society, the political backdrop to the occasions lost importance for the majority of those attending, and socio-cultural aspects assumed greater significance. There were signs of this development as early as 1960: the Sudeten German *Bundestreffen* of that year was attended by 350,000 Sudeten German expellees, but the main political event of the

Treffen, the rally, attracted a mere 80,000, and their response to the speeches was less than enthusiastic.[18] The increasing integration of the expellees into West German society, then, was accompanied by the beginning of a shift from a predominantly political identification as Sudeten German to one which emphasised sociocultural aspects of belonging, aspects which had a much narrower and more differentiated focus than 'the Sudetenland'.

Attendance at the annual reunions decreased sharply in the 1970s. The signing of the Prague Treaty recognising the border between the Federal Republic and Czechoslovakia[19] in 1973 made it virtually impossible for the expellee leaders to maintain the illusion of a real possibility of return. What continued and strengthened in place of this political interest and engagement was a desire simply to remember, to reminisce with neighbours and friends from the old village or town (Strothmann 1995: 267). A further development was the wave of return visits: '"Homesickness Tourism", facilitated by the treaties, took the place of *Heimat* polemic' (Strothmann 1995: 268).[20] The *Heimat* polemic of the *Sudetendeutsche Landsmannschaft* had been predicated on an ethnic identity which would legitimize political and territorial claims. 'Homesickness tourism', on the other hand, evinced more conciliatory aims and had a narrower focus. 'The old village, the former town, the countryside of an earlier time' (Strothmann 1995: 269)[21] were visited for the sake of memory, personal and private associations, and cultural maintenance. Importantly, the people revisiting the place of their childhood generally expressed no desire to return permanently – a significant change from the initial years after the expulsion.[22] Thus with the decline of the political imperative of a cohesive Sudeten German group to promote the goal of return, localised identities began to supersede Sudeten German identity. What we are seeing here, then, is a reversion to older, more local units of pre-ethnic identity after the failure of consolidation of the relatively recent 'Sudeten German' identity and in the light of formative events: the dissolution of the Habsburg Empire and foundation of the Czechoslovak Republic, the inclusive ethnic movement of 'Heim ins Reich' and its disastrous failure, and the integration into West Germany as an economically and socially successful Western European capitalist state.

'Wir Adlergebirgler': Gudrun Pausewang's Expression of Belonging

The shift of focus from Sudeten German to localised pre-Sudeten German identities is evidenced in the publication from the end of the 1970s and increasingly in the 1980s of hundreds of village histories and autobiographical accounts of childhood in the provinces or return journeys. In addition, since the late 1980s an increasing number of reunions of villages and towns have taken place every year (Tolksdorf 1990: 123). Most of this cultural activity has occurred independently of the *Sudetendeutsche Lands-mannschaft*, which continues to call for a right of return and for compensation from the Czech government (Tolksdorf 1990: 123–4).[23]

Gudrun Pausewang's *Rosinkawiese* trilogy is an example of the autobiographical expellee literature published since the late 1970s, and can be used to illustrate my thesis. Pausewang was born in 1928 in Wichstadtl in the Adlergebirge in eastern Bohemia and fled with her family in 1945. The first of her *Rosinkawiese* books, published in 1980, takes the form of letters from Pausewang's mother to the fictitious grandchild of an old friend, who wants to live an alternative and self-sufficient lifestyle and is interested in learning about the Pausewangs' attempt to do that on their Rosinkawiese in the 1920s. Pausewang was fifty when she began this book and had never before felt the desire to write about her childhood, although she had already published more than a dozen novels (Pausewang 1990: 28). *Rosinkawiese: Alternatives Leben in den zwanziger Jahren* is an expression of identity rooted firmly in the Adlergebirge in eastern Bohemia, a mainly agricultural and very poor area of the Sudetenland. The particularities of life in 'Wichstadtl im Adlergebirge' form the core of the narrative. The house the Pausewangs build on the Rosinkawiese is 'a timber house with a natural stone foundation, typical of the Adlergebirge' (Pausewang 1980: 29).[24] They have patchwork rugs woven by one of the many weavers in the area, 'as [the rugs] could be found in farm houses everywhere in the Adlergebirge' (Pausewang 1980: 87).[25] The reader learns about the food eaten in these parts: 'Potatoes with linseed oil [was] typical poor man's food in the Adlergebirge' (Pausewang 1980: 35)[26] and '[t]he Adlergebirgler enjoyed mushrooms and ate them often (Pausewang 1980: 80).[27] Traditions and customs are also described and, significantly, these are mostly quite specific to the Adlergebirge, or at least are remembered as such:

> The old village customs, which still survived in the Adlergebirge, meant a great deal to us. On the first of May, we went into the village with our children after the lads had erected the maypole at dawn. Then there was *Schmeckostern, Kaiserkermest mit dem Hahnschlagen*, the solstice bonfire in the mountains and the Saint Nicholas and *Krampus* processions in December (Pausewang 1980: 97).[28]

The selective nature of this expression of cultural identity is striking. The reader senses that beyond the Adlergebirge life is quite different. Pausewang writes not of the 'Sudetendeutschen' but of the 'Adlergebirgler' and the 'Wichstadtler', and the only time she mentions 'Deutsche' is in a political context: the author's father needs to find work but knows it will be difficult: 'As a German I have no chance of finding work here with unemployment so high. Most of the unemployed are German. Why should I be any luckier than anyone else? (Pausewang 1980: 104).[29] This is not primarily a statement of ethnic identity but a political categorisation – as a German-speaker he has little chance of finding work while there are so many unemployed Czechs in Czechoslovakia. There is a clear division of

identification into sociocultural identity, which is located in the Adlergebirge and Wichstadtl, and political categorisation, which is German.

The juxtaposition of (Sudeten) German identity, where the emphasis is
on the political community, and identity as Adlergebirgler, which operates
outside the political sphere, is most evident in the second book of Pausewang's trilogy, which focuses on her family's flight from Wichstadtl to
Winsen near Hamburg in 1945. The first chapter is entitled: 'How the war
came upon us – or: How we ourselves moved towards war';[30] Pausewang
is clearly at pains to demonstrate her acceptance of the connection
between the unleashing of the war by Nazi Germany and the expulsion of
the Germans from Central and Eastern Europe. She writes that in order to
understand the causes of their flight, it is necessary to look back to 1938
when 'the fervent hope of the Sudeten German' (Pausewang 1989: 15)[31] of
being annexed to Germany had just been fulfilled. The political character
of this Sudeten German identity is immediately apparent: the desire of
Sudeten Germans to have 'their' territory incorporated in the German
Reich was primarily a *political* wish which stemmed from their sudden
change in status from dominance within the Austro-Hungarian Empire to
a minority in the Czechoslovak state. Throughout the text, Pausewang consistently uses the terms 'deutsch', 'Deutsche' 'sudetendeutsch' and
'Sudetendeutsche' to denote political community, while questions of sub-
jectively experienced identity centre on East Bohemia, the Adlergebirge,
Wichstadtl and the Rosinkawiese.

The people of the Adlergebirge identify as a 'compatriot' (*Landsmann*)
only somebody who speaks their dialect (Pausewang 1989: 20). Although
the border is only a few kilometres away and on the other side of it they
would be 'Germans ... among Germans, and thus safe from partisan bul-
lets' (Pausewang 1989: 34),[32] the Wichstadtler cannot imagine leaving 'their
houses, their village' (Pausewang 1989: 36)[33] and so they at first stay despite
the approach of the Russians. Pausewang, too, defines herself not as Sudeten German, but as coming from the Adlergebirge, as she tells her son in
the letter to him which opens the book: 'A few years ago I showed you my
Heimat: Wichstadtl im Adlergebirge, situated in the north of Czechoslovakia... ; it belonged to Austria-Hungary before 1918, then to Czechoslovakia,
from 1938 to the "Greater German Reich", and since 1945 it has been part
of Czechoslovakia again' (Pausewang 1989: 5).[34] It is not that the author
seeks to deny the German nature of this *Heimat* and of her identity: she
writes that Wichstadtl was 'German-speaking, whichever state it belonged
to' (Pausewang 1989: 5).[35] But it is not simply a German identity. It is not
even Sudeten German identity – when she speaks of her *Heimat*,[36] the
word 'Sudetendeutsch' is conspicuously absent. Her personal sense of
identity and belonging is specific to the Adlergebirge.

When Pausewang does identify herself as part of the German or Sudeten German collective, it is in political contexts, and generally in cases
where somebody outside the collective instigates the categorisation. For

instance, when Czechoslovakia is liberated from the Nazis, notices are put up by the local Czech authorities telling the inhabitants what they may and may not do. Pausewang writes that these notices 'were addressed to us, the German inhabitants of the town' (Pausewang 1989: 54),[37] and later she comments: 'So much was forbidden to us Germans at that time' (Pausewang 1989: 96).[38] For her, it is the Czechs who categorise the Adlergebirgler as German. The collective name is accepted by the writer as an objective description of who they are, but when she is writing about her own subjective experience and feelings, they revolve around the Rosinkawiese, Wichstadtl and the Adlergebirge. The distinctions Pausewang makes are clearly problematic; however, the issue here is her self–identification.

The difference between categorisation by others and Pausewang's own subjective sense of belonging is evident again when she writes of the rumours circulating among the refugees, who are mainly from Pomerania and Silesia. Upon hearing that there is 'a flood of Sudeten German refugees'[39] making its way along the roads about a week's journey behind them, the Pausewang family try to imagine them, and it is not Sudeten Germans in general they think of, but 'the Wichstadtler' (Pausewang 1989: 105). The only instance of a self-identification as Sudeten German occurs when Pausewang's mother writes a letter to the locals in Lübz, a town in the Soviet Zone of Occupation where the family stays from July to October 1945. She asks them to donate clothing, linen, anything they can spare, and identifies herself and her children: 'I am a war widow and had to flee the Sudetenland with my six children' (Pausewang 1989: 168).[40] The Sudetenland is the smallest identifiable unit for outsiders. This is thus not so much a declaration of ethnic identity as a means of allowing the locals to understand where the family has come from.

The third of Pausewang's books, *Geliebte Rosinkawiese*, is an example of the many accounts of visits to the former *Heimat* written by expellees after the lifting of travel restrictions in the 1960s, which sparked the so-called 'homesickness tourism'. The area with which Pausewang identifies is apparent from her description of one of the journeys she makes to the Rosinkawiese between 1964 and 1989. As they draw nearer she describes 'the Adlergebirge's coniferous forests, the mountain pastures and narrow valleys with their white water rapids, which for me were no longer part of the journey, but signalled having arrived' (Pausewang 1990: 41).[41] When Pausewang and her brother visit their former home for the first time in 1964, she describes the purpose of their visit: 'We wanted to take in everything, wanted to see the old sights, smell the old smells, hear the old sounds, wanted to touch whatever tempted us to touch it' (Pausewang 1990: 20).[42] But when asked by the present owners of their former home whether they would like to live there again their answer is unequivocal: 'No. We would never live here again permanently, as lovely as it once was. We feel at home somewhere else now' (Pausewang 1990: 22–3).[43] This statement is indicative of a successful integration into West Germany, which can be said to have been accomplished when the expellees give up the idea of a permanent return.

Thus Pausewang's accounts of her childhood in the Adlergebirge, the flight of her family and her return visits reflect the shift that has occurred for the majority of Sudeten German expellees since the 1970s, from a highly political and suspect Sudeten German identity to a much more narrowly defined sense of belonging, where the focus is on sociocultural rather than political elements of the place. The place is no longer the object of concrete aspirations, but has become the locus of personal memories.

Sudetendeutsch – A Transitory Identity?

The *Sudetendeutsche Landsmannschaft* of today recognises the diversity of the people it claims to represent and acknowledges the political factors which led to the unification of the group as the Sudeten Germans after 1918:

> The Sudeten Germans are a thoroughly heterogeneous group. They differ in terms of dialect, descent and regional culture ... . Their fate since 1918, however, has caused them to form a political unit.[44]

But whether they still constitute a political unit is questionable. More than fifty years after their expulsion from Czechoslovakia, the Sudeten Germans are part of the fabric of German society, and very few of them express a desire to return to the 'Sudetenland', a large majority agreeing: 'It is now time to declare this chapter closed.'[45] Sudeten German identity is perhaps best thought of as transitory: surfacing under particular political conditions, it flourished in the political climate of the 1920s until the 1960s, at least partly obscuring older categories of identification. In the 1970s this situation was reversed: the political aspect of identity having diminished in importance, the more localised identities underwent a revival. During the last three decades, Sudeten German identity has lost significance for most expellees and, more importantly perhaps, for their offspring. More localised identities such as Pausewang's 'Adlergebirgler', based on the individual's sense of language (dialect), place and custom, have re-emerged as more potent, and certainly more enduring.

Notes

1. I am indebted to my colleague, Associate Professor Peter Morgan, who read and commented on this chapter.

2. *Der Deutsche Volksbote*, 27 October 1901; cited in Habel 1984: 94.

3. By Edgar Pscheidt 1983, '80 Jahre 'Sudetendeutsch'?', in *Mitteilungen des Sudetendeutschen Archivs* 73, 1–3; cited in Habel 1984: 95.

4. 'Zweiteilung?' 1903; cited in Habel 1984: 94.

5. These eight groups can be further divided into subgroups – one source distinguishes twelve different types of Bohemian Germans alone: Göttinger Arbeitskreis 1954: 19.

6. For instance, the linguistic island of Schönhengst was settled mainly by East Franconians, but in the north there were strong Silesian influences and in the south North Bairisch and in the east Middle Bairisch influences. Thus several very distinct subordinate dialects developed. Phonetic changes also occurred as a result of close contact with the Czech linguistic group. Thus the name Senftenberg became Zamberk (Senftenberg would have been pronounced Schenftenberg up to 1300): Meynen 1954: 9.

7. I am drawing here on A.D. Smith's definition of an ethnic group as a cultural collectivity, sharing a collective name, a myth of common ancestry, historical memories, an association with a specific 'homeland' and elements of a common culture which differentiates it from other groups: Smith 1991: 21.

8. Luza writes that from 1848 most of the German speakers in Bohemia and Moravia-Silesia thought of themselves as belonging to the German nation (in a cultural rather than political sense): Luza 1964: 23.

9. More keenly felt identities prior to 1918 were, for example, class-based identities, which often conflicted with ethnic identities. Indeed very often economic contrasts between the upper and lower classes 'prompted the German and Czech workers to make common front against their employers, who likewise belonged to both ethnic groups': Stier 1957: 112–13. See also Cohen 1981: 25–6; Habel 1984: xx.

10. This despite the impression which is conveyed by the enormous amount of literature on the long history and culture of the 'Sudeten Germans' that has been generated since the expulsion. In fact, it may be that this vast body of literature exists precisely *because* there was no cohesive sense of identity – it is being 'created' in retrospect. See Cohen 1981: 17.

11. See, for example, Jaworski 1995: 33.

12. For example, wherever there were more than forty German children, a German primary school was established. This meant that 96.2 percent of German school children attended schools controlled by German school councils. A minority language could be used as an official language in districts in which more than two-thirds of the inhabitants spoke that language, and where the proportion was between 20–66 percent, the language was permitted to be used in public instruction and official communications. Only 130,000 of more than 3 million Germans lived in districts in which they were under 20 percent of the population: Luza 1964: 33–8.

13. It should be pointed out that previous experiences of exclusion, from the German confederation in 1866 and from Bismarck's Reich in 1871, paved the way for this politicisation of the Sudeten Germans in 1918. A sense of cultural belonging with Germany rather than with the newly created Czechoslovak Republic also played a role. However, this had clearly not been enough in itself to precipitate the crystallisation of Sudeten German identity prior to the change in political circumstances.

14. For example: the 'Ackermann-Gemeinde', a Catholic group closely associated with the CDU/CSU (Gatz 1989: 362); the 'Adalbert-Stifter-Verein', which aimed at preserving and fostering Sudeten German culture (Gatz 1989: 371); the 'Seliger Gemeinde' which was formed by Sudeten German SPD members (Gatz 1989: 378); and the 'Witiko Bund', a right-wing group which adopted Nazi doctrines and had as its main goal the regaining of the Sudetenland (Gatz 1989: 378).

15. See the various declarations by Sudeten German organisations in Habel 1984, especially pp. 307–33.

16. This contrast between the the two groups of expellees continues to the present day: in the changed political climate since the end of the Cold War, the unification of the FRG and the GDR, and the final recognition of Germany's eastern borders by the first government of the unified state, other *Landsmannschaften* have relinquished their claims to the east, but the *Sudetendeutsche Landsmannschaft* continues to maintain that the last word is yet to be spoken on the question of their *Heimat*: Erich Wiedemann, 'Der Tschech is an Freund', *Der Spiegel*, 2 September 1996: 175. See the official homepage of the *Sudetendeutsche Landsmannschaft*: http://www.sudetendeutsche.de/

17. Die kulturellen regionalen Diskrepanzen zwischen Aufnahmegesellschaft und Flüchtlingsgruppen in Alltagsleben und materieller Kultur, in mentalen und religiösen Denk- und Verhaltensmustern, in Wohnkultur und Arbeitsrythmus, in Kleidung und Ernährung usw. [wurden] zunächst in hohem Maße als 'fremd' empfunden. (All translations from German into English by me.)

18. Karl Feuerer, '"Selbstbestimmungsrecht" mit Trommeln und Fanfaren: Bemerkungen zum Sudetendeutschen Tag 1960', *Die andere Zeitung*, 16 June 1960; cited in Gatz 1989: 455–6.

19. 'Vertrag über die gegenseitigen Beziehungen zwischen der Bundersrepublik Deutschland und der Tschechoslowakischen Sozialistischen Republik', reproduced in part in Habel 1984: 381–2.

20. 'Heimweh-Tourismus', durch die Verträge wesentlich erleichtert, nahm den Platz der Heimatpolemik ein.

21. Das alte Dorf, die frühere Stadt, die Landschaft von damals.

22. In 1996, an EMNID survey revealed that 85 percent of Sudeten Germans would not go back to live there given the choice: "Tu Oma den Gefallen", *Der Spiegel*, 20 May 1996: 33.

23. See also the homepage of the Sudetendeutsche Landsmannschaft: http://www.sudetendeutsche.de/

24. ein Holzhaus mit einem Natursteinsockel, wie es im Adlergebirge üblich war.

25. denn diese Fleckelteppiche waren im Adlergebirge überall in den Bauernhäusern zu finden.

26. Leinöl auf Kartoffeln [war] ein typisches Armeleute-Essen im Adlergebirge.

27. Die Aldlergebirgler aßen oft und gern Pilze.

28. Die alten Dorfgebräuche, die hier im Adlergebirge noch lebten, schätzten wir sehr. Wir gingen mit unseren Kindern ins Dorf, nachdem die Burschen in aller Frühe des Ersten Mai den Maibaum aufgestellt hatten. Da gab es auch das Schmeckostern, die Kaiserkermest mit dem Hahnschlagen, das Sommersonnwendfeuer auf den Bergen und im Dezember die Umzüge von Nikolaus und Krampus.

29. Als Deutscher habe ich keine Chancen, hier in der Tschechei bei dieser Arbeitslosigkeit eine Stellung zu finden. Die meisten Arbeitslosen sind Deutsche. Warum sollte gerade ich Glück haben?

30. Wie der Krieg auf uns zukam – oder: Wie wir uns dem Krieg näherten.

31. der sehnliche Traum der Sudetendeutschen.

32. Deutsche ... unter Deutschen, also vor Partisanenkugeln sicher.

33. ihre Häuser, ihr Dorf.

34. ich habe Dir vor ein paar Jahren meine Heimat gezeigt: *Wichstadtl* im Adlergebirge, im Norden der Tschechoslowakei gelegen ... vor 1918 zum alten Österreich-Ungarn, danach zur Tschechoslowakei, ab 1938 zum 'Großdeutschen Reich', ab 1945 wieder zur Tschechoslowakei gehörend.

35. deutschsprachig, welchem Staat auch immer es zugehörte.

36. The word *Heimat* is loaded with political connotations as a result of its appropriation in Nazi propaganda (see: Tonkin 1997: ch. 1). Pausewang is clearly not using the term in this way, and indeed avoids it altogether in her next book. She addresses the question of the misuse of the term, then says that she prefers to describe her relationship to the place thus: 'As a child I felt safe there. During the first years of my life it was for me the centre of the world': Pausewang 1990: 5.

37. waren an uns, die deutsche Bevölkerung des Ortes, gerichtet.

38. Es war uns Deutschen damals so vieles verboten.

39. Eine Flut von sudetendeutschen Flüchtlingen.

40. ich bin Kriegswitwe und mußte mit meinen sechs Kindern ... aus dem Sudetenland flüchten.

41. die Nadelwälder, die Bergwiesen und schmalen Wildbachtäler des Adlergebirges, das ich schon nicht mehr mit zur Fahrt, sondern zum Angekommensein zählte.

42. Wir wollten uns alles ganz genau sehen, wollten die alten Gerüche riechen, die alten Geräusche hören, wollten berühren, was uns zu berühren reizte.

43. Nein. Nie wieder für dauernd hier leben, so schön es auch einmal gewesen war. Wir fühlten uns jetzt woanders daheim.

44. 'Die Sudetendeutschen sind in sich durchaus heterogen. Sie unterscheiden sich nach Mundart, Herkunft und regionaler Kultur ... . Ihr Schicksal seit 1918 hat sie jedoch zu einer politischen Einheit werden lassen.' From 'Die Sudetendeutschen: Eine Volksgruppe in der Vertreibung', http://home.t-online.de/home/sudeten/frame1a.htm; consulted 3 October 1998.

45. 'es sei Zeit, nunmehr einen Schlußstrich zu ziehen'. Eighty-three percent of Sudeten Germans questioned responded positively to this statement in an EMNID survey conducted for *Der Spiegel* in 1996: '"Noch weit entfernt": Die deutsch-tschechische Aussöhnung kommt nicht vom Fleck', *Der Spiegel*, 2 September 1996: 173.

References

Ackermann, V. , 'Integration: Begriff, Leitbilder, Probleme', in Bade 1990, pp. 14–36.

Bade, K.J., ed., *Neue Heimat im Westen: Vertriebene, Flüchtlinge, Aussiedler*. Münster, 1990.

Benz, W., ed., *Die Vertreibung der Deutschen aus dem Osten: Ursachen, Ereignisse, Folgen*. Frankfurt am Main, 1995.

Cohen, G.B., *The Politics of Ethnic Survival: Germans in Prague, 1861-1914*. Princeton, NJ, 1981.

Gatz, K.L., *East Prussian and Sudeten German Expellees in West Germany, 1945-1960: A Comparison of their Social and Cultural Integration* (PhD. dissertation, Indiana University, 1989.)

Göttinger Arbeitskreis, ed., *Sudetenland: Ein Hand- und Nachschlagebuch über die Siedlungsgebiete der Sudetendeutschen*. Kitzingen, 1954.

Habel, F.P., *Dokumente zur Sudetenfrage, Veröffentlichungen des Sudetendeutschen Archivs. München*, Munich, 1984.

Hemmerle, R., 'The Christmas Story in Sudeten Folk Art', *Sudeten Bulletin*, December 1957, pp. 144–5.

Jaworski, R., 'Die Sudetendeutschen als Minderheit in der Tschechoslowakei 1918–1938', in Benz 1995, pp. 33–44.

Kurz, K., 'Der Wandel des Dorfes Gersdorf, Kreis Hersfeld, durch das Einströmen der Heimatvertriebenen', in Lemberg and Krecker 1950, pp. 32–44.

Lemberg, E. and Krecker, L., eds., *Die Entstehung eines neuen Volkes aus Binnendeutschen und Ostver-triebenen: Untersuchungen zum Strukturwandel von Land und Leuten unter dem Einfluß der Vertriebenenzustroms*, Schriften des Instituts für Kultur- und Sozialforschung 1, Marburg, 1950.

Luza, R., *The Transfer of the Sudeten Germans. A Study of Czech-German Relations, 1933-1962*. New York, 1964.

Meynen, E., ed., *Sudetendeutscher Atlas*. Munich, 1954.

Pausewang, G., *Rosinkawiese: Alternatives Leben in den zwanziger Jahren*. Munich, 1980.

——, *Fern von der Rosinkawiese: Die Geschichte einer Flucht*. Munich, 1989.

——, *Geliebte Rosinkawiese: Die Geschichte einer Freundschaft über die Grenzen*. Munich, 1990.

Schillinger, R., 'Der Lastenausgleich', in Benz 1995, pp. 231–43.

Smith, A.D., *National Identity*. Harmondsworth, 1991.

Stier, A., 'Bruex in Sudetenland', *Sudeten Bulletin* October 1957, pp. 112–13.

Strothmann, D., '"Schlesien bleibt unser": Vertriebenenpolitiker und das Rad der Geschichte', in Benz 1995, pp. 265–276.

Tolksdorf, U., 'Phasen der kulturellen Integration bei Flüchtlingen und *Aussiedlern*', in Bade 1990, pp. 106–27.

Tonkin, K., *Identity on the Border: The Concept of Heimat in Horst Bienek's 'Gleiwitzer Tetralogie'* (MA dissertation, University of Western Australia, 1997.)

Chapter 14

'... for an artist, home will be wherever he can freely practise his art.'

Walter Grill in conversation with David Rock

Walter Grill was eight years old at the end of the Second World War when, together with his family, he was driven from his home in Carlsbad in the Sudetenland. He has spent most of his career as a sculptor in Bavaria and only returned to his former home in 1990, when he was one of the first Sudeten German artists to exhibit his works in the Czech Republic.

Q: Walter Grill, in this interview, I would like to ask you about your ethnic and territorial sense of identity and the extent to which this has influenced your work before and after 1990. First, do you actually have any clear sense of a Sudeten German identity; and if so, has this had any implications in terms of your work as a sculptor?

A: As I see it, I am unable easily to describe my Sudeten German identity in the way that older colleagues do in relation to their work, the ones who completed their studies in the country of their birth. I have never been confronted with the question of having to change my whole approach to my art. True, as a child I was forced to leave my homeland. But for me, it has never been like it was for those who had already made their names in the Sudetenland, older, well-established colleagues such as Fleissner, Losert, Lohwasser, Teuber and others. For them, the chaotic circumstances of the early post-war era had all sorts of consequences for their work: in a foreign country, they had to change their approach, reorientate, some even abandoned it altogether.

In my view there is no modern art being produced today which is typical of a specific country, and certainly not of a specific region. Art will stand for itself, and for an artist, home will be wherever he can freely practise his art.

Although borders (of every kind) have repeatedly been subjects and themes of artistic works (in mine, too), borders of countries have never played a significant role for me as a sculptor, someone involved in the plastic arts. However, the sense of wellbeing in a particular place (or its opposite) can have a positive (or negative) effect on one's artistic work.

Q: Can you tell us something about how you started your career as a sculptor in the Federal Republic? Did you experience any specific difficulties as a Sudeten German in Bavaria?

A: I started my studies at the Academy of Plastic Arts in Munich in the middle of the student troubles of the late sixties, and it was an institution in a state of flux. Most of the students of '68 were convinced that conventional modes of creation no longer applied; and I had (and still have) my own view: that the prerequisite for sculpture is a detailed study of nature. After completing my studies, I experienced all the difficulties of actually establishing myself as a sculptor. Success as a sculptor involves, amongst many other things, huge financial outlay in terms of materials and space. Asking the state for help, as many often do today, was out of the question for me, for obvious reasons. Personal initiative was called for. It was when I started to build my atelier that I really experienced the feeling of not being one of the locals: I restored part of the monastery in Rottenbuch, a protected monument. I noticed how others who had been resident in the area for generations found it much easier to get support for similar ventures.

Q: Can I now ask you about the more distant past: what do you remember of your family background and your childhood years in Carlsbad?

A: One thing I do remember are my parents' and grandparents' vivid accounts of an incident which took place when I was still a baby; it was Autumn 1938, the station in Reichenberg, my father was standing there with me, my mother and my sister on the platform, waiting for the train to take us north to Sweden. The Gestapo were checking everybody's papers as they waited for the train, and we were detained while the details of our identity papers were checked. Afterwards we were sent back to our place of residence in Altrohlau in Carlsbad. My father was terribly worried, suspecting that our failed attempt to get out (we had delayed it for too long) would have repercussions for us as a family. The decision to leave the country had been made because the family were long-standing supporters of social democracy. Our grandparents wanted to stay on, but the younger members of the family tried (as it turned out, unsuccessfully) to emigrate to Sweden.

From amongst my other more distant relatives, several families emigrated to Sweden and England. My father's cousin Martin Grill, born in 1908, made a new home for himself in Sweden, working as a journalist and a writer. In one of his books, *So waren unsere Tage* (That's what our days were like), he demonstrates how difficult it was to have any sense of identity in the early post-war years. The following conversation takes place in an employment agency in Sweden:

'You come from Austria?' 'Yes!' 'But you aren't an Austrian, are you?' 'I was Austrian up to 1918.' 'And then you lived in Bohemia?' 'I've always lived in Bohemia, I was born there, too.' 'So you're Czech then?' 'No I'm not, I'm German, Sudeten German.' ... 'So you are German then after all? Why didn't you go to Germany then?' 'I've never been a German, a German from within the Reich, I mean, from Germany itself. I'm a Czechoslovakian citizen, a former Austrian. My forefathers even came from Sweden, once upon a time ...'

Q: When did you and your parents leave Carlsbad?

A: In October 1946, my family, along with many others, was driven out by the Czechs and taken to Bavaria.

Q: Did your family ever express the wish to return to Carlsbad?

A: My father's attitude to his homeland was so negative that he never considered taking us back again for what would have been for him 'a journey into the past'. He said that he never wanted to set foot on this land again. Of course, I could understand his point of view: he had suffered for his socialist views under Hitler, and now he could not forgive the brutal destruction of his hopes for democratic, socialist coexistence, which he had held to through all the years of suffering, by others who thought differently in that country at the time.

Q: Did you ever want to go back to see your childhood home again?

A: I was proud of the way my father behaved during the Nazi period; but my memories of this time did not exactly inspire me to preoccupy myself with the past and my childhood. Today I suspect that I was subconsciously repressing a lot of things. I did not have to involve myself directly again with my past in the land of my birth until 1990, when an exhibition of my work and that of other colleagues was planned in Pilsen. Now my memories of things long past caught up with me again. I tried to imagine specific places and paths, to link paths with specific points of reference. It was all so near and yet so blurred and hazy. I was uncertain as to whether what I was imagining also corresponded to reality.

Would I still be able to find my way back to those surroundings once so familiar after such a long time, after a journey of forty-five years? Already, 20 kilometres away from my parents' house as the crow flies, the surroundings were surprisingly familiar. Street after street – it felt as if it was just yesterday that I had gone past these rows of houses. At a crossroads I went the wrong way, drove straight on, but noticed my error right away: I had made it because a house on the corner was missing – it had been badly damaged by bombs and later demolished. On I went, straight ahead again, then fourth street on the left, and there I was, standing in front of my parents' house. It had hardly changed, it just looked rather in need of repair. My wife, who had accompanied me, found it hard to believe that I had been able to find my way back after such a long time, remembering every detail so accurately.

I was apprehensive as I walked down the path to my grandfather's grave: it was oppressive, evoking nasty memories from those war days. The graves were overgrown with weeds, most of the gravestones had been overturned. I could no longer find the family grave. The beautiful countryside had changed as a result of collective farming; tortuous streams had been blocked up, small meadows and fields had disappeared, the fields full of wild flowers which I remember from childhood. Nearly all the things of which I had positive memories had disappeared.

Q: Did your visit bring back any other memories?

A: Yes: the schoolhouse; starting school; raising my arm hesitantly for the Nazi salute; being reprimanded by the teacher; punishment; the teacher asking me if I knew the 'dong-dong, dong-dong' sound (the signal for the enemy transmissions from England); memories of the wailing of the sirens, meaning 'no school'; bomb attacks; staying a long time in the cellar; trees covered in tinfoil, just like Christmas, to create interference; U.S. tanks; black soldiers giving us oranges; later on, Russian, Mongolian soldiers, ponies, Mahorkas,[1] schnaps; hunger.

I remember it being a shock to be back at school again, after a short interruption, but not understanding a word of the lesson in Czech. Now we were 'German swine'. My grandmother and aunt had to leave their house and home first (we knew that they would probably come to Bavaria), and a Czech house-block manager and his family, installed by the new military government, moved into the rooms vacated by them. My grandparents on my mother's side, together with one of my aunts, had already been driven out of their home, with just one hour's notice and hand luggage (probably into the Russian zone, so they were told).

In October 1946, my family too (my parents, two sisters and me) were 'evacuated' in a cattle-truck and 'resettled' (as the Czech authorities put it). From the time of our arrival in Germany until eight days before Christmas, we stayed in the O.T.[2] barracks near Mettenheim in Bavaria – we were cooped up in the huts like sardines in a tin. Then we were loaded back into the cattle-truck, sixty of us; it was bitterly cold; my father warmed up the milk for my little eleven-months-old sister on a spirit stove which he held between his legs. And then we finally arrived at the last stop of our odyssey, Riederau on Lake Ammersee.

The first glimpse, which I had when the doors of the truck were pushed open, was, for my child's eyes, quite beautiful; the lake lay in pre-Christmas splendour, set in the rolling foothills of the Alps which were covered in deep snow. Next day, we were sent to a small farm in Holzhausen. Christmas 1946 in our new home: we were taken in, no more and no less. It was cold, we were hungry; our Christmas present from our hosts was a bowl of flour, three eggs, a small portion of butter and for the children, a few Christmas biscuits. Nevertheless, for us children it was all new and wonderful – coming from a small town to the land of times gone by, and then into a farmhouse. Back to school again, with German as the language, and straight into the second half of the third year, although one hadn't understood anything in the second year; it was so nice to be able to understand the teacher again. The fact that there were no schoolbooks didn't matter either.

These were the memories that gradually came back during my first trip back to Czechoslovakia.

Q: Did these memories affect your first encounter with your old homeland and the people there?

A: Only in so far as my mood was one of tense expectancy as to how they would behave towards me: I said to myself: 'Let's just wait and see how they react'. But at the same time, I felt that now it was essential to face the present. I was in this country to mount an exhibition of artistic works by colleagues and by myself, and to make contact with Czech colleagues. The opening of the exhibition was marked by mutual fear of contact, with people on both sides putting out cautious feelers. There was an exchange of ideas between artist-colleagues about the past: how was it for a Czech artist to live and work in the former Sudetenland, and what was it like for a Sudeten-German artist to live and work in Germany? We came to the conclusion that the brutal past was suppressed on both Czech and German sides, and that, superficially at least, life for an artist could run a similar course in a socialist or a capitalist system. Artists in Czechoslovakia, though, enjoyed much higher social standing than their counterparts in Germany; but at the same time, this also implied total conformity to the regime: any deviation could be life-threatening for the person in question.

Nevertheless, this meeting encouraged me to accept the offer to exhibit my work in the city where I was born, Carlsbad, and in the capital, Prague. The official guidelines specified that the exhibition was to be organised in such a way as to promote social interaction and mutual understanding between the two sections of the population. The actual mounting of the exhibition in Carlsbad, though, involved overcoming considerable prejudice and many obstacles. It was only after the exhibition in Prague that I hit upon the explanation for this. In Prague, without exception, people reacted without prejudice, doors were opened as soon as I presented them with my request to mount the exhibition. I came to the inevitable conclusion that the capital Prague, along with its surrounding area, had always been predominantly Czech–Bohemian in character. The people I met there were, in contrast to those in Karlsbad (which is an area from which all the Germans have been evacuated and replaced by Slovakian Czechs), self-confident, open-minded, enthusiastically open to any sort of exchange of views, and free from prejudice.

Q: How did the Czech press react to your exhibition?

A: I was continually asked by the press why I, as a Sudeten German, was putting on an exhibition of my work here in Prague and Carlsbad of all places, and what my feelings were today standing in front of my parents' house. I could always sense the astonishment of my interlocutors when they heard my answer: that it was high time to come together again, and that I knew that the present owners of my parents' house had legally acquired it from the Czech state and paid for it, and so I could not object in any way.

To make my point clearer, I would just like to recount a meeting that I had with a Czech artist. I had been invited to his home and it was all going very cordially. But as I stepped into his very fine house, which dated back to the turn of the century, I noticed straight away the numerous antiques of German origin, all of which had been maintained with loving care. My admiration for this immediately triggered off feelings of unease, uncertainty or guilt in my host. When I noticed this and emphasised how much I appreciated the fact that these German cultural possessions had been preserved and cared for by him, and how happy I was that not everything had been senselessly destroyed during the war and the postwar period, the tension eased. I was deeply affected by the fact that an artist of all people, and one who had been humiliated first during the Third Reich and then by his own government after the Prague Spring and had suffered a great deal, should experience feelings of guilt on account of his appreciation of objects of German culture.

Q: Was there much interest in your exhibition amongst the Czech population?

A: With both exhibitions, the interest of the Czech population in my artistic work was considerable. At the opening of the exhibition in Carlsbad, for instance, the top class of the local grammar school were very keen to get involved.

Q: Did these exhibitions and your experiences in Czechoslovakia influence your subsequent work in any way?

A: Looking back today, I can say: Yes, they certainly did. In the wake of these experiences, I created a number of works, such as 'Spaltung' (split).[3] It is easy to explain how such an inspiration, and the form it took, came about. All this time, I had just been suppressing my childhood years up to the time of our expulsion. All at once, the past suddenly ran before my eyes again like a film. Today, I have to admit that the place in which I was born and grew up during the first few years of my life, also represents part of myself and my sense of home. Up to the point of my return, I had always been of the opinion that my only home was here in Bavaria where I went to school, where my family lives and where I work. But then suddenly I experienced a sense of being inwardly torn apart. Where is my home? Where my roots are or in the place where my family and I found ourselves linguistically back home again, in Bavaria, in West Germany?

Recently, I decided to participate in the competition for the new memorial, 'Flucht und Vertreibung' (flight and expulsion), to be built in the centre of Nuremberg in time for the millennium. Reflecting on the theme of this competition, I immediately saw myself as a nine-year-old again, sitting cooped up day and night in a goods wagon, looking at the seemingly endless tracks, travelling through a land that I did not know. I can still hear the rolling noise of the railway wagon on the tracks. Imprinted on my memory, too, is the suffering, the pain, the hunger, the despair and the anxiety of those around me. Then come the positive memories of my first impressions of Bavaria, the Ammersee, the landscape. I tried to give expression to these memories and impressions in the sculpture that I have recently planned for this competition. My piece is a three dimensional representation: chaotic ways – tracks – embankment – suffering – destruction – transition to order – clear paths – integration.

I regard myself as very fortunate in being able to live and work as a sculptor in a free country. I was spared the difficulty of having to express myself in a foreign tongue. I feel close to the land of my birth, but it has become so foreign that I can no longer imagine living my life there. But my wishes for the people who live there today are: that they really do feel that it is their homeland, and are able to lead their lives in harmony and peace in a united and free Europe.

Notes

1. Cigarettes which Russian soldiers rolled themselves using tobacco of that name.

2. *Organisation Todt.*

3. See frontispiece/cover.

Conclusion

Coming Home to Germany? Ethnic German Migrants in the Federal Republic after 1945

Stefan Wolff

Centuries of migration within and between empires resulted in an ever-growing number of ethnic German populations living in Central and Eastern Europe outside the traditional settlement areas of German-speakers. Mostly invited as settlers and colonists, they were welcomed by the then imperial rulers and local aristocracy, they enjoyed significant privileges, and made a considerable contribution to the advancement of underdeveloped stretches of land throughout the Russian, Austro-Hungarian, Ottoman and German empires. Interethnic tensions rarely occurred before the rise of nationalist ideologies in the nineteenth century.

By 1919, the break-up of the Ottoman and Austro-Hungarian empires and the territorial truncation of the German *Reich*, that is, the demise of three of the four empires dominating Central and Eastern Europe, had fundamentally changed this situation. New nation-states had been created, and with them new minorities. The minority protection system set up by the League of Nations after the First World War had never been fully embraced by either the host-states or their minorities, and certainly not by kin-states such as Hungary, Germany or Austria, which had lost territory and population as a consequence of their role in the war and as a result of the peace settlements of Versailles, St Germain and Trianon. Thus, doomed to fail from the outset, Poland's unilateral declaration in 1934 to opt out of the League's minority protection system was the final blow leading to the collapse of the League's system.

Ethnic minorities, perceived as a threat to a state's security and a nation's well-being and treated accordingly, were just as prone to fall for radical nationalist ideologies as the members of majority groups. Perceptions of mutual threat became a self-fulfilling prophecy with the advent of

Nazi ideology in Germany and its spread to German minorities in Central
and Eastern Europe. The dismemberment of Czechoslovakia in 1938/39,
the participation of ethnic Germans in war crimes committed by the SS
and the *Wehrmacht* and their collaboration with the German occupying
forces in many of their host-countries aggravated the situation further. This
is not to say that all Sudeten Germans welcomed the destruction of
Czechoslovakia, or that all ethnic Germans in other parts of Central and
Eastern Europe were SS volunteers, war criminals or collaborators. However, while many of them fought in the resistance movement against the
Nazis at home or in exile, a significant number condoned or actively participated in the German 'war effort', and it was this image of ethnic Germans as a fifth column and 'willing executioners' of Nazi policy in their
host-states that informed the attitudes of their non-German neighbours and
set the climate in which the mass expulsions of the post-1945 period could
take place.

Yet ethnic hatred on the ground was not the only factor in the process
of German mass migration. Already during the war, the Nazis had organised massive transfers of ethnic German populations from occupied or
allied countries and resettled them mostly in parts of occupied Poland. Ethnic German populations from many Eastern European countries were
evacuated (voluntarily or against their will) before the *Wehrmacht* with-
drew, while others jumped on the bandwagon of the retreating German
armies. Allied policy towards the problem was informed by a number of
considerations – the use of German labour for reparations, the territorial
compensation to Poland for its losses to the Soviet Union, and the future
prevention of a second Munich scenario. As a consequence of the first of
these items on the agenda, over 110,000 ethnic German men and women
were interned between January and March 1945 in Romania, Hungary and
Yugoslavia and sent to labour camps, primarily in the Ukraine. From February to April 1945, almost 80,000 more men were deported from Upper
Silesia and East Prussia. The major direction of the population movement,
however, was westwards. Territorial compensation for Poland and the
future prevention of another Sudeten crisis was to be accomplished
through 'orderly and humane' population transfers, but allied intentions
were rapidly overtaken by events on the ground when ethnic Germans in
the former Eastern territories of the German *Reich* and in the Sudetenland
of Czechoslovakia were uprooted in their hundreds of thousands and
expelled from their homes, often in a matter of hours. Thus, by 1950,
about fourteen million ethnic Germans had either fled their homeland or
had been expelled. Roughly two-thirds of them were resettled in what was
to become the Federal Republic of Germany.

Naturally, this created a number of problems for the Allies and the German authorities at local and *Länder* level. Not only had these refugees and
expellees to be provided with food, housing, and other living essentials,
they also needed to be integrated into the emerging democratic political

process and into civil society. There were numerous fears as to how this mass influx of people would affect the political and social stability not only of Germany, but also of the countries from where the refugees and expellees had come. Many of these fears proved groundless and after most of the initial restrictions on political and social organisations of expellees had been lifted, their contribution to the rebuilding of Germany has mostly been one that facilitated, rather than endangered, stability. In a similar vein, Schulze has argued in his case-study that the input of refugees and expellees was not only a political and social one, but also had a significant economic dimension. While the challenge of integration in general was a tough one, it was mastered impressively by postwar West Germany, which emerged from the integration process as a country of natives and expellees alike. In East Germany, conditions were much different, and so were the policies aimed at integrating refugees and expellees. While the administrative process of allocating housing and providing for basic necessities was completed faster than in the West, the overall living standard of the expellee population fell short of the declared goal of parity with the indigenous population, as Ther has shown. In neither of the two German states was the integration challenge mastered completely, as, primarily for ideological reasons, there was, and still is, no widespread public acknowledgement of the roots and traditions of the refugees and expellees as part of the postwar foundation of Germany. This ideological divide has been constantly revived, and partly reinforced, by the political agendas of some of the expellee organisations. Against the political realities of the Cold War and the post-Cold War era, representatives of Sudeten Germans and Upper Silesians in the Federal Republic have publicly made demands for a return of the former German Eastern territories and/or for the right to go back there and settle in their traditional settlement areas. Tonkin has shown in her study of the Sudeten Germans that these demands are not shared by the majority of refugees and expellees or their children and grandchildren.

The integration of the refugees and expellees who arrived in Germany during the first half-decade after the Second World War was not the only challenge the Federal Republic faced in relation to ethnic Germans in Central and Eastern Europe. From the end of the expulsions in 1950 on, a small number of ethnic Germans living in the countries of the Communist Bloc were allowed to emigrate to Germany year by year. Depending on the general state of political relationships between East and West, this number fluctuated between 18,000 and 65,000 annually. They came primarily from Poland and Romania, but also from Yugoslavia and a far smaller number from the former Soviet Union. The artificial restrictions put on emigration by the Communist Bloc countries made it relatively easy to integrate them into West German society. Many of them had relatives in the Federal Republic who helped with finding accommodation and work. Generous legal provisions supplied resources for language courses, occupational training, special education, and the purchase of property. German citizenship law automatically conferred to these *Aussiedler* the rights and privileges of a citizen of the Federal Republic. In general, it was recognised that they had suffered as a consequence of their German ethnicity, they were received and treated as victims of the Cold War; and the small numbers in which they arrived made it possible to afford them preferential treatment.

This situation changed drastically in the late 1980s and early 1990s when the collapse of communism in Central and Eastern Europe meant the end of all emigration restrictions, and *Aussiedler* figures soared to almost 400,000 in 1990. Although not comparable to the mass influx of ethnic Germans between 1945 and 1950, migration in these numbers posed a significant problem to unified Germany. Economically, Germany was heading into a recession after the unification boom in 1991 and 1992, making it more difficult for new arrivals to find work and suitable accommodation in a short period of time. Socially, integration of *Aussiedler*, especially of those from the Soviet Union, proved much more difficult because of the lack of language skills and the very different system of values and norms these population groups brought with them. Politically, rising xenophobia throughout the Federal Republic was directed at *Aussiedler* just as much as at asylum seekers, despite their legally being German citizens. From different angles, Heinrich, von Koppenfels and Senders explore these issues, concluding that the immigration situation for ethnic Germans has fundamentally changed over the past decade since the collapse of communism, but that the domestic response levelled at these new conditions by the German government has been rather inadequate.

These macro-level findings about the integration of ethnic Germans in the Federal Republic after 1945 are supported at the level of individuals' experiences. As a member of the expellee and refugee generation, the Sudeten German Walter Grill has stressed in his interview with David Rock that as bitter as the memories of the expulsion might be, it is now time to overcome them and to move forward to a common future. This coincides with Tonkin's account of the works of Gudrun Pausewang which also illustrate how the individual deals with loss and integration as experienced by so many of the expellees: the loss of their Sudeten German home has been a terrible experience, often relived upon returning there after 1989, but there are no bitter feelings against the people who live there today, be they Czech or German. Preece has emphasised in his account of Günther Grass that for the writer, who was expelled from Danzig/Gdansk as an adolescent, national identities are artificial constructs, and territorial claims are superfluous in the Central and Eastern European context where territories and the settlements on them were built and inhabited by more than one ethnic group. Mourning the past and present experience of loss for Grass, Grill and Pausewang means confronting them in their art, accept-

accepting them as a given, and looking to the future not for revenge, but for reconciliation.

The necessary steps towards such reconciliation between Germany and Czechoslovakia and Germany and Poland have been taken at the official levels. Germany has recognised the Oder–Neisse line as its border with Poland, and has concluded treaties with Czechoslovakia in 1992 and Poland in 1991 in which the signatories reaffirm their commitment to good neighbourly relations and peaceful cooperation and specifically include the rights of minorities in such a legal framework. Of equal significance was the German–Czech Declaration of 1997. In it, the German government expressed its sorrow for the crimes committed by Germans against Czechs during the time of National Socialism and acknowledged that these crimes contributed to preparing the climate in which the mass expulsions after 1945 became possible. The Czech government equally expressed sorrow for the policy of forced migration against the Sudeten Germans. Yet, both governments agreed that it was important to look towards the future and build their relationship on reconciliation and understanding.

Apart from these official efforts, it is increasingly also the work of individuals that contributes to this reconciliation process. Mounting an exhibition in Prague and Karlsbad, as Walter Grill did, is one such example, but there are countless others that often do not grasp media attention – private donations to help restore cultural memorials, investment of funds and expertise in economic ventures, preservation of traditions and customs. To some extent, reconciliation with the past is probably the one issue where the integration process of refugees, expellees and, to a lesser extent, of the *Aussiedler* as well, still has some way to go. For the forcibly resettled populations it is important to realise that their homeland as they knew it before 1945 does not exist anymore, that life has moved on for the Germans who were allowed to remain there as well as for the members of other ethnic groups who have settled there after 1945. Irredentist claims in whatever disguise and by whomsoever they are made do not encourage this process as they are more likely to open old wounds on both sides, and make it equally difficult for the broad spectrum of German political parties and actors in civil society to accept the expellees and refugees and their historical experience as part of contemporary German society. These issues can only be resolved by each individual himself or herself, yet individuals can only do this successfully if the political elites involved in the reconciliation process provide an adequate framework.

Reconciliation with the past experience of suffering concerns members of the original refugee and expellee organisations and their children and grandchildren as well as many of the later *Aussiedler* who came before or after 1989/1990. The difference between these two groups of ethnic Germans now living in the Federal Republic is primarily one of socialisation and experience. The chapters on Richard Wagner and Herta Müller highlight that difference. As David Rock has pointed out in his biographical account of Wagner, spending his childhood, youth, and a significant part of his professional career as a writer in socialist Romania has inevitably shaped him and his work as much as his origins in the German minority in the Banat. Even though this background is reflected in his writings, it is not his main theme. Wagner neither changed the linguistic medium in which he expressed himself when he emigrated to Germany nor his intent to produce a political literature. While his views may have become more 'Western', Wagner has remained a critical observer of society. Wagner had already taken this stance in Romania and in both geographic places it put him into the position of an outsider – among ethnic Germans, in Romanian society, and again in Germany. Not attaching great personal significance to the concept of *Heimat*, Wagner's recent prose works, as Graham Jackman has shown, reflect a continuing search for identity that might have begun with the arrival in the West, an identity that, rooted firmly in the Banat region of his birthplace, does not find a counterpart in the Federal Republic, where history starts in 1945 and is geographically confined to the space of its citizens' present existence rather than embracing their territorial origins as well – a deficiency already noted by Schulze in his study of expellees and refugees in Lower Saxony.

This lack of historical knowledge leads to a lack of appreciation of 'Germans abroad' when these latter come to the Federal Republic – an experience many of the later *Aussiedler* generations have had and one which has been the theme of several of Herta Müller's works. The critique of a society that, on the one hand, used to base its citizenship laws on descent, but then has increasingly denied its 'new' citizens the right to a German identity, is what Müller has focused on in a range of her books published after her arrival in West Germany in 1987. In a similar manner to Wagner, Müller writes about the unease of 'her' *Aussiedler* figures when coming to terms with German society and its expectations towards ethnic German immigrants, many of them rather unreasonable and growing out of ignorance of the history of German minorities in Central and Eastern Europe.

So, have refugees, expellees and *Aussiedler* found their home in the Federal Republic? This is a difficult question to answer for the entirety of the more than twelve million ethnic Germans who have come to Germany since 1945.The first generation of immigrants, those who were forced to leave their homelands in the east, certainly have been well integrated. They have built a home (*Zuhause*) for themselves, and for many of them, in particular for their children and grandchildren, Germany has also become their homeland (*Heimat*). For those expellees and refugees who have vivid memories of the time before the flight and expulsions, part of their homeland will always be where they spent some of their childhood, youth and adult life. While this may seem politically incorrect to some, and justifying a claim to a right to return to others, it is as indisputable a fact of today's German society as the significant contribution refugees and expellees have made to the reconstruction of postwar Germany. In a declaration (passed against the vote of some in the opposition parties) in May 1995, the German Bundestag acknowledged their contribution to the social, economic and political life in Germany after 1945 and specifically included in this those refugees and expellees who had lived in East Germany where their suffering was never publicly discussed and their history and particular identity denied.

For the generations of *Aussiedler* who came to the Federal Republic after 1950, and to united Germany after 1990, the story is a different one. As long as their numbers remained small, the integration process was relatively smooth. Existing family contacts and friends already in the Federal Republic also helped them to feel at home, as did knowledge of German language and culture. Thus, the integration of Romanian-Germans and ethnic Germans from Poland right until the early 1990s did not pose a major problem for German society, although for many of the immigrants, particularly those who arrived in the 1980s, coming to terms with their past and present experience and adjusting their individual identity has not been easy.

Finally, the arrival of hundreds of thousands of ethnic Germans from the successor states of the former Soviet Union made things more difficult. Most of them had come to Germany 'to live as Germans among Germans', something they had been denied for many decades in their host-countries. However, the German society they found upon their arrival was not very well prepared and now seems increasingly unwilling to make available the resources necessary for their integration. For many of the *Aussiedler*, and especially for the post-1990 ethnic German immigrants, the hope of 'coming home to Germany' has proven illusory.

Notes on Contributors

Walter Grill is a sculptor living in Bavaria, Germany.

Andreas Heinrich is a researcher at the Osteuropa Institut of the Free University of Berlin, Germany.

Graham Jackman is a Lecturer in the Department of German at the University of Reading, England, UK.

Amanda Klekowski von Koppenfels is a research officer at the International Organisation for Migration, based in Brussels.

Daniel Levy is Assistant Professor of Sociology at the State University of New York, Stony Brook, NY, USA.

Julian Preece is a Senior Lecturer in German at the University of Kent at Canterbury, England, UK.

David Rock is a Senior Lecturer in German at the University of Keele, England, UK.

Rainer Schulze is a Senior Lecturer in the Department of History at the University of Essex, England, UK.

Stefan Senders is a Visiting Assistant Professor in the Anthropology Department of the University of Michigan, MI, USA.

Philipp Ther is a researcher at the Center for Comparative History of Europe at the Free University of Berlin, Germany.

Kati Tonkin is an Associate Lecturer in German and European Studies at the University of Western Australia, Crawley, WA, Australia.

Richard Wagner is a poet and novelist living in Berlin, Germany.

John White is Professor of German at King's College London, England, UK.

Stefan Wolff is a Lecturer in the Department of European Studies at the University of Bath, England, UK.

INDEX

TURKISH CULTURE IN GERMAN SOCIETY TODAY

Edited by **David Horrocks** and **Eva Kolinsky**

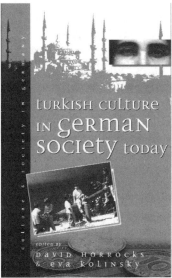

"... *a ground-breaking and well-researched study, a lucid documentation of the impact of Turkish migration to Germany, bringing together materials from a range of disciplines, including history, sociology, religious studies, and literature. The array of knowledge assembled in this volume is made accessible for the first time to an English speaking audience... provides detailed background and varied accounts of historical and socio-political changes in a rapidly changing German society struggling with it its self-perception and frictions arising from the coexistence of Turks and Germans... provides a well-founded academic analysis of data, trends, and traditions, yet still leaves room for the personal experiences and perspectives of Turks establishing their own identity and political voice in German society... a great source for graduate German courses investigating migrant culture and literature in contemporary German society.*"

—German Studies Review

"*offers and should be commended for an informative review of migrant literature in Germany, substantive statistics on the condition of migration to Germany, and a suggestive exchange with a migrant author in person—a rarity in the literature.*"

—H-Net Reviews (H-SAE)

"*..an instructive introduction into the history of Turkish migration*"

—Journal of Area Studies

For many decades Germany has had a sizeable Turkish minority that has lived in an uneasy co-existence with the Germans around them and as such has attracted considerable interest abroad where it tends to be seen as a measure of German tolerance. However, little is known about the actual situation of the Turks. This volume provides valuable information, presented in a most original manner in that it combines literary and cultural studies with social and political analysis. It focuses on the Turkish-born writer Emine Sevgi Özdamar, who writes in German and whose work, especially her highly acclaimed novel *Das ist eine Karawanserei*, is examined critically and situated in the context of German "migrant literature".

Volume 1. 1996. 160 pages, 20 tables, diagrams, bibliog., index
ISBN 1-57181-899-5 hardback **$49.95/£35.00/€57.50**
ISBN 1-57181-047-1 paperback **$19.95/£12.95/€21.25**

SINTI AND ROMA
Gypsies In German-Speaking Society and Literature

Edited by Susan Tebbutt

"... this collection...is most welcome... presents aspects of a fascinating and complex picture... this informative and thought-provoking project calls upon us, the readers, to re-examine our own moral and ethical positions."

—Monatshefte

"... a very welcome and...successful first account from a variety of perspectives of Sinti and Roma in German-speaking society... sensibly restricted to providing background information on the history and problems of Sinti and Roma as well as a more specific literary focus."

—Journal of European Area Studies

Volume 2. 1998. 160 pages, 2 tables, bibliog., index
ISBN 1-57181-912-5 hardback **$45.00/£30.00/€49.25**

VOICES IN TIMES OF CHANGE
The Role of Writers, Opposition Movements, and the Churches in the Transformation of East Germany

Edited by **David Rock**, Keele University

"..a useful contribution to the ongoing debate about the role of intellectuals in Germany."

—German Politics

Taking an interdisciplinary approach, this volume offers an overview of the role of writers, intellectuals, citizens, and the churches both before, but particularly after, 1989 in the GDR and the new Germany. Friedrich Schorlemmer provides the focal point, giving the book its coherence. Issues related to his role in the GDR church and citizens movement are examined, as well as his support for GDR writers both before and after unification, and his own writings on east and west German literature. After general surveys on the role of intellectuals, civil rights groups, opposition movements, and churches in the transformation of east Germany, the volume focuses on Friedrich Schorlemmer himself: a chapter on the significance of the role that he played is followed by interviews with him and an original essay by him, giving his personal view of the role of intellectuals, citizens, and writers in east Germany.

The volume is rounded off by a chapter on the reactions of lesser known writers, and, finally, on the responses of prominent GDR writers to unification and on the changing role of writers in society. Combining literary and cultural with social and political analysis, this volume provides a lively and multifaceted picture of the new Germany.

Volume 3. 2000. 160 pages, bibliog., index
ISBN 1-57181-959-2 hardback **$39.95/£25.00/€41.00**

CHALLENGING ETHNIC CITIZENSHIP
German and Israeli Perspectives on Immigration

Edited by **Daniel Levy** and **Yfaat Weiss**

In contrast to most other countries, both Germany and Israel have descent-based concepts of nationhood and have granted members of their nation (ethnic Germans and Jews) who wish to immigrate automatic access to their respective citizenship privileges. Therefore these two countries lend themselves well to comparative analysis of the integration processes of immigrant groups, who were formally part of the collective "self" but have become increasingly transformed into "others."

This volume brings together a group of leading scholars specializing in German and Israeli immigration from the perspectives of their various disciplines. This is reflected in the richness of the empirical and theoretical material offered, involving historical developments, demographic changes, sociological problems, anthropological insights, and political implications. Focusing on three dimensions of citizenship: sovereignty and control, the allocation of social and political rights, and questions of national identity, the essays bring to light the elements that are distinctive for each society but also point to similarities that owe as much to nationally specific characteristics as to evolving patterns of global migration.

Summer 2002, 288 pages, bibliog., index
ISBN 1-57181-291-1 hardback *ca.* **$75.00/£50.00/€82.00**
ISBN 1-57181-292-X paperback *ca.* **$25.00/£17.00/€28.00**

DISPUTED TERRITORIES
The Transnational Dynamics of Ethnic Conflict Settlement

Stefan Wolff

Ethnic conflicts have shaped the 20th century in significant ways. While the legacy of the last century is primarily one of many unresolved conflicts, the author contends that Western Europe has a track record in containing and settling ethnic conflicts which provides valuable lessons for conflict management elsewhere. The author identifies the factors at work in disputes over borders from Northern Ireland to Alsace, South Tyrol and elsewhere, demonstrating that they can also provide the seeds for their resolution.

Stefan Wolff was educated at the Universities of Leipzig and Cambridge, and the London School of Economics. He is currently Lecturer in the Department of European Studies at the University of Bath.

Summer 2002, 248 pages, bibliog., index
ISBN 1-57181-516-3 hardback **$69.95/£47.00/€77.25**
Studies in Ethnopolitics

PEACE AT LAST?
The Impact of the Good Friday Agreement on Northern Ireland

Edited by **Jörg Neuheiser** and **Stefan Wolff**

With a Foreword by **Lord Alderdice,** Speaker of the Northern Ireland Assembly

Spanning more than thirty years, and costing over 3000 lives, the conflict in Northern Ireland has been one of the most protracted ethnic conflicts in Western Europe. After several failed attempts to resolve the fundamental differences over national belonging between the two communities in Northern Ireland, the Good Friday Agreement of 1998 seemed to offer the long awaited chance of sustainable peace and reconciliation.

By looking at the various dimensions and dynamics of post-conflict peace-building in the political system, the economy, and society of this deeply divided community, the contributors to this volume offer a comprehensive analysis of Northern Irish politics and society in the wake of the Good Friday Agreement and conclude that this is probably the best chance for a stable and long-term peace that Northern Ireland has had but that the difficulties that still lie ahead must not be underestimated.

Summer 2002, *ca.* 256 pages, bibliog., index
ISBN 1-57181-518-X hardback **$69.95/£47.00/€77.25**
Studies in Ethnopolitics

PLURAL IDENTITIES — SINGULAR NARRATIVES
The Case of Northern Ireland

Máiréad Nic Craith

Northern Ireland is frequently characterized in terms of a "two traditions" paradigm, representing the conflict as being between two discrete cultures. Proceeding from an analysis of the historical and religious context, this study demonstrates the reductionist nature of the "two traditions" model, highlighting instead the complexity of ethnic identities and cultural traditions. It thus shows why attempts at reconciliation like the Good Friday Agreement of 1998, which seeks to promote the concept of a "parity of esteem" based on this identity model, are fraught with difficulties. Reflecting on the applicability of the concept of multiculturalism in the context of Northern Ireland, the author proposes a re-conceptualization of Northern Irish culture along lines that steer clear of binary oppositions.

Available, 256 pages, 13 ills, bibliog., index
ISBN 1-57181-772-7 hardback **$69.95/£47.00/€77.25**
ISBN 1-57181-314-4 paperback **$25.00/£17.00/€28.00**

www.berghahnbooks.com